M000317378

SOIL
FOR THE
SEED

Historical, pastoral and theological reflections on
educating to and in the faith

Jim Gallagher SDB

McCrimmons
Great Wakering, Essex, England

First published in the United Kingdom in 2001 by
MCCRIMMON PUBLISHING CO. LTD.
10-12 High Street, Great Wakering, Essex SS3 0EQ

email: mccrimmons@dial.pipex.com
www.mccrimmons.com

ISBN 0 85597 628 4

British Library Cataloguing in Publication Data.
A catalogue record for this book is available from the British Library.

Acknowledgements – For a complete list of acknowledgements see pages 324-327

Cover illustration by Richard Bradley
Cover design by Nick Snode. Layout Nick Snode and Alan Hencher
Body text typeset in Times New Roman, cover typeset in Baker Signet.
Printed and bound by Black Bear Press Ltd., Cambridge, United Kingdom

SOIL FOR THE SEED

DEDICATION

In memory of

Damian Lundy FSC

A very special friend and colleague.

In gratitude to

Patrick Purnell SJ

To many friends and former colleagues,
too numerous to mention.

Contents

Foreword 7

Preface

Let us cultivate the 'field of God' in hope 9

Part One

1   Becoming a Christian in the early
and medieval Church 23

2   The age of catechisms: the Reformation
and Post-Reformation 40

3   Critique of the catechisms 56

4   Attention to people, situations
and cultures 72

5   Vatican II and the General
Catechetical Directory 88

6   Tensions and controversies 107

7   Synod documents: evangelisation and
catechesis 123

8   Catechesis and the catechism of
the Catholic Church 144

Part Two

9   Faith, doctrine and life 167

10   Head faith, heart faith, hands faith 186

11   A variety of soil, a variety of approaches ... 207

12   Adults and the young, pilgrims
together on the road 224

13   The faith and young people today 246

14   Catholic schools: a pastoral and
educational ministry 265

15   Educating to and in the faith in our schools:
catechesis and religious education 285

16   On the road to Emmaus or Jerusalem? 309

Foreword

The debate about the relationship between Catechesis, Religious Education and Evangelisation has been raging steadily for many years. Newly published programmes for use in Catholic schools are always heralded by a refuelling of this same debate in some form or other.

Fr Jim Gallagher has observed and contributed to the debate over some years and this book is a distillation of his experience, practice and study. He approaches the subject by using new terms, perhaps thereby allowing us to reconceptualise the process of education and faith development and reach new understandings. He traces the growth of catechetical practice through history, marking the changes in context and ethos along with developments in theological understanding of the nature of faith. He speaks of "educating to faith" and "educating in faith", drawing attention to the difference made by the readiness of the listener to take the message to heart whether in the context of the family, the parish or the school. He addresses the potential and limitations of the school and asks serious questions about the appropriateness of the teacher and the classroom in the process.

This is a work of scholarship, but written in a language accessible to most teachers, catechists and parents. I believe that it will contribute greatly to a clearer understanding of what we are striving to achieve in our homes, parishes and schools.

Fr George Stokes
Director of Education, Diocese of Brentwood

Preface

Let us cultivate 'The field of God' in Hope

Having tested the ground, the Sower sends out his workers to proclaim the Gospel throughout the whole world and to that end shares with them the power of the Spirit. At the same time he shows them how to read the signs of the times and asks of them that special preparation which is necessary to carry out the sowing.[1]

Why this book?

A year or so ago it dawned on me, with some surprise and not a little shock, that I had been involved in the study and practice of catechesis and religious education for thirty years. Thirty years is a considerable period of time, yet it seems to have flown by. During those thirty years there have been remarkable developments in the theory and practice of catechesis and religious education. Since Vatican II there have been a number of key Church documents that deal with aspects of these pastoral tasks within the Church's mission. There are also a considerable number of inspiring and challenging writings from scholars and practioners in these fields. As a consequence of all this, it is now more readily recognised that the Christian community is the chief agent of catechesis and that it is not just the responsibility of one or two individuals within the parish or school. There are many more lay catechists who generously undertake the task of helping adults as well as children and the young grow and develop in Christian faith. It is acknowledged that this implies more than instruction in the doctrines of the Church, important as that is, but also a broader education in liturgical celebration, prayer and Christian living with all its personal and social implications. There is a deeper appreciation of the needs of people at the various stages of such faith

---

[1] *General Directory for Catechesis, (GDC)* Catholic Truth Society, 1997, nn.30-31

development as well as the need for suitable methods that involve people actively in their own faith development and engender greater confidence in their willingness to live and share their faith. To a large extent there is a better appreciation of the potential and limitations of families, even with committed parents, and of our Catholic schools in the process of educating the young to and in the faith. In parishes and schools there are a variety of programmes and resources designed to meet a diversity of need. There is also the challenge that comes from our awareness that many, especially among the young, are still generally untouched by our carefully planned and dedicated endeavours.

For the most part I, like many others, have found these past thirty years to be a demanding, daunting yet exciting time to work in these pastoral, educational tasks. I am aware that others have found a number of the changes and developments, especially in the provision of resources, to be disconcerting and confusing. Some have seen aspects the 'new catechetics' as generally unhelpful, if not unorthodox. At the very least, in their view, they have failed to educate adults and the young in the knowledge and practice of the Catholic faith. Over the years many of the developments in the theory and practice in evangelisation, catechesis and religious education have been recognised and given approval in various Church documents. The documents and a number of concerned Catholics also point out limitations and deficiencies. There has been and still is controversy among different groups in the Church. At times such controversy has been bitter and acrimonious. This is part of our lived history over the past thirty years. However, it is useful to bear in mind that similar debates and controversies have been frequent throughout the history of the Church. It is for this reason that in part one of this book I present some fairly general historical sketches and reflections.

After thirty years of being involved in the study and practice of evangelisation, catechesis and religious education in a variety of ways, I would like to share reflections on what I consider to be some important trends and issues in this particular aspect of the Church's pastoral mission. They are reflections that come from my reading and study and also from my own experience in these particular fields. I wish to share reflections firstly in the light of some key historical developments over the centuries, especially the 20th century, and, secondly, in the light of directives found in the documents of Vatican II and in more recent Church documents that deal with evangelisation, catechesis and religious education. Over the past thirty years I have been involved in these fields in a variety of roles. I was Head of R.E. in a Catholic secondary school and worked with various youth groups in retreat weekends and in Youth Easters. I then lectured in the Liverpool Institute of Higher Education, now Hope University College, in theology and religious education and facilitated courses for religious sisters who wished to take up work in parishes, especially in the field of catechesis. Later I took on the post of Co-ordinator of the National Project of Catechesis and Religious Education, *Living and Sharing Our Faith.* During my time as lecturer and co-ordinator of the National Project I visited many schools, facilitated many in-service days and addressed many teachers and governors. I also met and shared experiences with those involved in catechesis of both the young and adults at parish and diocesan levels. In this sharing I learnt a great deal from many people and I came to admire their dedication and energy. I also came to understand some of their deep-felt concerns, even anxieties, about the best way of undertaking their pastoral and educational mission. My study of the developments in the fields of catechesis and religious education as well as my sharing with such highly dedicated people are the sources of the reflections that I offer in this book. It is my hope that they may be of some help and give encouragement to parents, priests, teachers and catechists who labour long and hard in the task of educating the young and adults to and in the faith in today's complex, fast changing world.

Why the title of the book?

From the outset I have been clear about the theme that I wished to develop. I wished to consider key aspects of our task of educating adults and the young **to and in** the faith. However, I was for a long time less sure about a title. I wanted to reflect on the fact that we are involved in educating people of all ages to and in the faith or, as it as it is put in the Vatican II document on the pastoral office of bishops, 'summoning **to** faith and confirming **in** faith'[2]. In many Church documents catechesis is described as 'education in the faith'. Yet most of us are keenly aware that

---

[2] Vatican II, Decree on the Pastoral Office of Bishops, n.12 Abbot, Wm. (ed.) Geo. Chapman (1966)

not even all those who attend parish sacramental programmes or our Catholic schools are ready for 'education in the faith.' Strictly speaking that presupposes at least some basic, initial choice to follow Christ, to be a disciple, to take up the Christian faith and way of life as expressed and lived in the Church. Many have not reached that readiness for 'education in the faith'. Like it or not, this is now a common phenomenon among adults and the young. It is a concern and a challenge that is faced in homes, parishes and schools. The *General Directory for Catechesis* published in the wake of the Catechism in 1997 recognises the fact that there is a great variety of interest in and commitment to the Christian faith among people today. The Directory acknowledges that 'local Churches are obliged to address the entire panorama of these religious situations'.

The realisation that we are very often called to educate people to the faith, rather than too readily assuming that we can educate them in the faith, came home to me very powerfully during a General Chapter of my own religious congregation. In 1990 some two hundred delegates representing the 17,500 Salesians in provinces all over the world gathered in Rome. After elections, our main purpose was to reconsider how we could best fulfil our mission of evangelisation and catechesis especially of the young and poor in the contemporary world and Church. The Chapter lasted two months. The document that we produced at the end of our prolonged deliberations was entitled *Educating Young People to the Faith*. After considering and analysing various contexts and situations, the final Chapter text listed diverse categories of relationships among young people with regard to the faith and the Church. The text forcefully states that 'young people not in touch with the Church at all form the largest category'. Stated so baldly it shocks but nonetheless rings true. It is important that we acknowledge this fact. To fail to do so will lead inevitably to frustration and anxiety as we attempt to evaluate the 'success' or 'failure' of what is done in homes, parishes and schools. The Salesian chapter document also states that 'young people who are fully committed form a small minority, but their presence is a real sign of hope'. However, 'the large number of young people who remain far from the Church present a great challenge'.[3] This applies not only to young people but also to adults.

---

[3] 23rd General Chapter of the Salesians of Don Bosco, *Educating Young People to the Faith*, Editrice SDB, Rome, nn.76-77.

Reflecting on this situation, it is my view that we need to consider more carefully not only the seed of the Word which we wish to scatter, plant and harvest, but also the soil, the field which is people today, in which we scatter and seek to plant it. We may be over anxious to scatter and plant seed in soil not yet ready to receive it or in soil not suitable for that particular seed at that particular time. Frequently we may need to spend more time and exercise greater patience in tending and preparing the soil so that it may be more ready to receive the seed and bear some fruit. With a plan in mind of how we may best cultivate the field and the soil, we may actually overlook and fail to recognise some blossoming and flowering that is taking place in unusual ways and in expected places. Many a wild flower can blossom in what id deemed a desert. We may also have to be more prepared to live with what seems lack of 'success' or a partial harvest despite our best efforts. After all such was the experience of Jesus and the early disciples. I find this idea to a large extent affirmed in the treatment of the theme of the parable of the Sower that runs through the new *General Directory for Catechesis*. I found its reflections on this theme to be particularly helpful and hopeful. Hence the title of this book – Soil for the Seed.

The parable of the seed and the soil

Matthew gives the parable the title by which it is most commonly known: 'hear the parable of the sower' (Mt. 13,18). Mark and Luke give it no specific title. Most biblical commentators concur in pointing out that 'the parable of the sower' is the least appropriate title for the parable. Commentators suggest other titles: 'the Parable of the Sower, the Seed and the Soil', 'The Seed that Struggles to Grow', 'the Fourfold Field'. The sower is only mentioned right at the beginning of the parable. The focus is on the different types of soil in which the seed is scattered and on the different results that follow at harvest time. Most commentators also agree that while the parable was one told by Jesus, it has been allegorised and adapted so that it addresses specific situations encountered by various communities of the early Church. Jesus may have told the parable to the disciples who were disconcerted and somewhat disillusioned by the fact that Jesus himself had only partial success in his preaching and teaching.

Jesus has experienced his word falling on many kinds of ground, but in spite of the hardness and the poor showing, he assures his disciples that planting the word of God in the hearts of men is a worthwhile task. And a good harvest will come from it.[4]

Perhaps we do not reflect enough on this aspect of Jesus' life and preaching. He was frequently rejected. He was thrown out of towns and synagogues. He touched and cured many but not all appeared to be grateful. When invited by him not all took up the call to be his disciple. He gathered a small chosen band of disciples who struggled and failed from time to time to respond to his challenge and to follow his way.

In a retreat given to the priests of the archdiocese of Milan Cardinal Martini preached a meditation part of which he entitled 'Jesus the failed evangelist'. That certainly shocks. The cardinal says that he is amazed that Luke should begin his account of the public ministry of Jesus with a story of failure, his rejection by the people of Nazareth.

This is the first picture of Jesus that is presented to us: defeated, hunted, unheeded, unwelcome and it is indeed a mysterious scene if we consider that Jesus is the evangelist...Luke has put it here because it serves to illustrate a constant element of the Kingdom of God.[5]

In considering our own situation in the Church today, it can be helpful to reflect on this 'constant element of the Kingdom of God' and on the way Jesus' own teaching was received. It may temper somewhat over optimistic expectations and help us to evaluate more realistically our 'success' or 'failure' in our mission of preaching the Kingdom and of educating people to and in a living and active faith in the Kingdom of God as revealed in Jesus the Christ.

[4] D. McBride, The Gospel of Luke, Domincan Publ., 1991, p.105
[5] C. M. Martini, Ministers of the Gospel, St. Paul Publ., 1981, p.15

The three evangelists who give an account of the parable also use it as an allegorical interpretation of what was happening in communities in the early Church. As with Jesus and his disciples, the early Christians had a mixed reception to their preaching of the Good News of Jesus the Christ. In relating the parable the evangelists explored a variety of responses. Some in the early Church were frustrated by their apparent lack of success, by the slowness of many to respond, by the fickleness of the responses. Some who heard the Word never really took it to heart and so never became fully committed disciples. Others took up discipleship at first but turned away in time of persecution. Similarly, others were eventually lured away by concerns about wealth and success in the world of their time. There were also those who heard the Word, made it their own and lived as disciples. In recounting the parable the evangelists explore different reactions of people; they invite converts to re-examine their own response to the Word and the sincerity of their discipleship. The parable is also intended to encourage Christians dispirited by their lack of 'success' in preaching the Word. It is a call to patience in allowing the seed the necessary time to grow and it is a call to trust in God's care and love for all.

The sower knows that he has to wait; the process demands that he wait on the weather, the working of the soil, the slow thrust of life, before he can see the fruit of his labour...There is a time of work, of waiting, of hazard, of slow emergence.[6]

A constant theme of the General Directory for Catechesis

The need to attend to and care for the soil in preparation for the sowing of the seed and also during and after the planting of the seed is a constant theme throughout the 1997 General Directory. In this regard, the latest Directory seems to me to be more realistic than the previous Directory of 1971. In its introduction the 1997 Directory gives an inter-

[6] D. Mc Bride, op. cit., p.106

pretation of the contemporary world in relation to preaching the Gospel. In its opening section it clearly stresses the need to be aware of the situation in which we are called to plant the seed.

> *The purpose of this introduction is to foster in pastors and catechists a greater consciousness of the necessity to keep in mind the field in which the seed is sown, and to do so with the perspective of faith and mercy.[7]*

In a later section the text declares that sound, careful adaptation of the message to meet the needs of people in a variety of situations should be a fundamental feature of our preaching and teaching. Throughout the text we are reminded that the conditions of the soil into which the seed falls vary greatly. Any sower worthy of the name would look to the soil and consider how best it might be tended and prepared for the planting, and what sort of planting would best suit the particular variety of soil.

> *Such adaptation must be understood as a maternal action of the Church, who recognises people as the 'field of God' (1 Cor. 3,9) not to be condemned but to be cultivated in hope. She sets out to meet each person, taking into serious account diversity of circumstances and cultures and maintains the unity of so many in the one saving Word.[8]*

At the beginning of the 21st century we have guidelines and directives in many writings, official and otherwise, to help us in our mission. Among these we have two very recent and authoritative Church documents presented as reference texts that will assist and give direction to our endeavours to sow the seed of the Word and proclaim the Kingdom. The *Catechism of the Catholic Church* is a contemporary summary of the faith of the Church, of our Christian beliefs about God, our human lives and our world. In a sense we may see that as 'the seed'. In the parable, however, the seed is sometimes seen as the message and sometimes as the response to it. *The General Directory for Catechesis* published after the

---

[7] GDC n.14
[8] GDC n.169

Catechism in 1997 sets out some key principles that will guide our efforts in preparing and tending the soil, 'the field of God' that is today's children, young people and adults. As today's sowers these authoritative texts encourage and challenge us to preserve the seed and to look to the soil as we seek to take up the mission of sowing the Word after the example of Jesus and his faithful disciples over the past twenty centuries.

Historical, pastoral, theological reflections

In line with the recent Directory my basic intention is 'that of offering reflections and principles rather than immediate applications or pastoral directives'. I make no attempt to present practical schemes that might be of immediate and direct help to busy priests, parents, catechists and teachers in addressing particular groups for specific occasions. These can be found elsewhere. I wish to share some pastoral, theological reflections on the nature and purpose of our mission of evangelisation, catechesis and religious education in the complexities of today's world and Church. It is my hope that such reflections may not be too far removed from the practical realities involved in trying to educate both adults and the young to and in the faith. I would hope, rather, that what I have to share may provide some encouragement and inspiration, as well as challenge, to all of us involved in many different roles in this difficult and delicate mission. We all need to stand back from time to time to reflect on what we are doing and why we are doing it. We need time and space to up-date ourselves in recent thinking and to see ways in which this may apply to our particular situation. What I have to offer in the second part of this book are reflections on a number of key trends, as well as theological and pastoral issues which arise from these trends. For the most part I seek to do this with reference to the 1997 *General Directory for Catechesis* and other documents. In the first part I reflect, in what are 'sketches' not detailed studies, on some key developments over the course of the Church's history. I believe that it is useful and necessary to have some knowledge of historical developments if we are to appreciate some more recent trends and issues. Today's trends and issues have not come as a bolt out of the blue. They have roots in the past, in other people's endeavours to live and share their faith in their time and place. I am glad to see that some recent studies in catechesis and religious education have given

an outline of key developments over the centuries.[9] Frequently we may
see similarities between our situation and that of others in the past. This
may prove helpful and encouraging. It is also useful to realise that
throughout the history of the Church there have been times of crises and
great questioning which have been faced with courage and hope. I am
only too conscious of the fact that the history of such pastoral activity in
the Church is much more complex and very much richer than I can indicate in these pages. I paint the picture with broad sweeps of the brush.
The finer details that depict outstanding people, the work of religious
congregations and various associations and centres of study are missing.
I would hope to encourage others to take up this worthwhile task, possibly in dissertations and theses. In presenting these historical reflections I
take to heart the advice of Herman Lombaerts.

> *Trying to sum up the important and historical steps of the cat-
> echetical ministry leads inevitably to a caricature. In fact, such
> a rich multifaceted history cannot be reduced to a particular
> pattern. However, for the purpose of our reflection it can be
> helpful to use a simplified schema to place our concerns in a
> larger perspective.[10]*

Cultivate the field of God in hope

There is no doubt that many of us are anxious about what we judge as
our present 'success' or 'failure' rate in educating young people and
adults to and in the faith. Some are depressed, like the two disciples flee-
ing Jerusalem and taking the road to Emmaus. Some look for scapegoats.
In the Synod of European Bishops held in Rome in the autumn of 1999
many interventions spoke of the crisis of faith in Europe, a sense of the
absence of faith in God, the 'apostasy' of Europe. Some analyses of the
religious situation were sombre, even pessimistic. However, others spoke
against any sense of despair. At the conclusion of the synod the bishops

---

[9] See P.M. Devitt, That You May Believe, Domincan Publ., 1992; L. Kelly, Catechesis Revisited.
Darton Longman & Todd, 2000.
[10] H. Lombaerts, 'Religious Education Today and the Catechism', Sourcebook for Modern
Catechetics, vol 2, M. Warren (ed), St Mary's Press, Christian Brothers Publ., 1997, p.244

addressed a final message to the churches of Europe. It is a message of hope. They quote John Paul II's speech at the opening of the synod: 'do not give way to discouragement, to ways of thinking and living which have no future, for we place our hope in the Word of God'. The bishops go on to urge us to 'proclaim the gospel of hope, to celebrate the gospel of hope and to serve the gospel of hope'.[11] In his book *Clashing Symbols* the Irish Jesuit, Michael Paul Gallagher, speaks of the need for 'discernment' which for him is 'a specifically spiritual and Christian way of reading reality'. In this context he uses what I find a powerful and challenging phrase when he speaks of the need to 'recognise smoke signals of hope rising from what may at first sight seem like a burnt-out desert'[12]. These are themes to which I shall return in my reflections.

Meanwhile I conclude this preface with two exhortations. The first is from Paul VI in the closing paragraph of *Evangelisation in the Modern World* in which he urges us not to lack 'spiritual fervour' in the mission of evangelisation. Such lack of spiritual fervour, he says, is manifested 'in fatigue, disenchantment, compromise, lack of interest and above all in lack of joy and hope'

Let us preserve the delightful and comforting joy of evangelising, even when it is in tears that we sow. May it mean for us – as it did for John the Baptist, for Peter and Paul, for the other apostles and for a multitude of splendid evangelisers all through the Church's history – an interior enthusiasm that nobody and nothing can quench. [13].

The second is one from the recent Directory which I have already quoted in which we are urged to play our part in 'the maternal action' of the Church 'who recognises people as 'the field of God' not to be condemned but to be cultivated in hope'.

---

11 'Gospel of Hope', in Briefing vol. 29 n.11, 10th November 1999, pp.22-27.
12 M. P. Gallagher, Clashing Symbols, Darton Longman & Todd, 1997, p.124
13 Paul VI, Evangelisation in the Modern World (EMW), Catholic Truth Society, 1975, n.80

PART ONE

HISTORICAL SKETCHES
AND REFLECTIONS

Throughout the centuries the Church has produced an incomparable treasure of pedagogy in the faith: above all, the witnesses of saints and catechists; a variety of ways of life and original forms of religious communications such as the catechumenate, catechisms, itineraries of the Christian life; a precious patrimony of catechetical teaching of faith culture, of catechetical institutions and services. All of these aspects form part of the history of catechesis and, by right, enter into the memory of the community and the praxis of the catechist.

General Directory for Catechesis, n.141

Parents, pastors, and teachers who had not been following developments in the catechetical movement were often baffled by the new approach and the new religion books; usually most Catholics to this day are simply unaware that there was any catechetical movement behind all of this, and hence the bafflement about the new catechesis often persists to this day.

M.J. Wrenn

Chapter One

Becoming a Christian in the early and medieval Church

So you see how it is written that the Christ would suffer and on the third day rise from the dead, and that, in his name, repentance for the forgiveness of sins would be preached to all the nations, beginning from Jerusalem. (Luke 24:47)

The basic proclamation of God's Word is developed by the Church through catechesis. It is the education of those who are preparing to receive baptism or trying to fulfil its obligations... particular attention must be paid to the cultural and social context in which the faith of Christians is born and grows.[1]

The New Testament Church

No doubt we would like to know how the Church in the years after the death and resurrection of Jesus went about educating people to and in the faith. Unfortunately, little is known of the way the Church in the time of the apostles and early Fathers performed the task of initiating and forming new converts in the Christian faith. From the New Testament writings it is clear that the message of the Good News of the Kingdom which the disciples believed that they had experienced in the life-death-resurrection of Jesus, whom they called the Christ, was proclaimed first in Jerusalem then in many other cities and regions of the Roman Empire. Communities were established in which the wonderful event of Jesus and his message were recalled first in the oral tradition, then in the writings of Paul and others, latter in the written Gospels. The Gospels were in fact edited selections of the traditional material addressed to communities in specific situations.

---

[1] Bishops of England and Wales, Teaching the Faith the New Way, St Paul Publ., 1973 nn.30 & 31. This is a translation of the Italian Bishops' document Il rinovamento della catechesi, 1970

> *The very fact that Christians have four gospels and not one is a powerful symbol of how preaching the Good News was shaped from the beginning by the needs of different audiences or cultures. That the New Testament is written and comes down to us in Greek, and not in the language of Jesus himself, is an indication of a dramatic and painful decision by the early Church – to reach out beyond the Jewish circles to the huge culture of the Gentiles.*[2]

Almost from the beginning, distinct cultural groups existed within the Church. Among these we can count Palestinian Jews, Hellenistic Jews, Hellenistic Gentiles. Each of these groups came to Christianity from different experiences, with different cultural values, different ways of perceiving and understanding reality. Such differences were not entirely eradicated when new converts were received into the Christian community. The Christian faith was in radical opposition to many of the accepted ways of thinking and behaving of the time. It was in conflict with many aspects of Judaism and of Hellenistic culture. However, as they sought a fuller understanding of their new faith, as they tried to explain it, uphold and defend it, Christians were forced - some willingly, some reluctantly - to express it in categories of thought and language more suited to the Greco-Roman mentality. Some were very much against such an accommodation of Christian beliefs. They saw it as a contamination of the purity of the message of Jesus, the Christ. There were other Christians, generally known as Apologists, who undertook this dialogue and maintained that it was necessary if the Christian faith was to take root and develop in a world different from the Palestine of Jesus' day.

The Church has constantly struggled with the crucial and delicate issue of being faithful to the Good News as received from Jesus on the one hand, and of delivering the message in ways that are relevant and challenging to groups of people within different cultural contexts on the other. Throughout the history of the Church different opinions have been strongly expressed by various groups and individuals when faced with such questions. It is not a phenomenon that occurred only after Vatican II. We need only recall the account in the Acts in which Peter justifies to cer-

[2] M. P. Gallagher , Clashing Symbols, Darton Longman & Todd, 1997, p101.

tain Jewish Christians his visiting the uncircumcised and eating with them and accepting them into the community (11:1-18). Later in the Acts we read about the controversy in Antioch concerning the question of whether Gentile converts should first be circumcised. Converts from among the pharisees insisted on circumcision. We are told that this led to disagreement and a 'long argument'. It was arranged that Paul, Barnabas and others should go to Jerusalem to discuss the problem. A heated debate went on for a long time before the matter was solved (15:1-35). Delegates were sent to Antioch where they handed over the decision of the disciples gathered in Jerusalem:

It has been decided by the Holy Spirit and ourselves, not to saddle you with any burden beyond these essentials: you are to abstain from food sacrificed to idols, from blood, from the meat of strangled animals and from fornication. Avoid these, and you will do what is right. (Acts 15:29)

We are then told that the community 'read it and were delighted with the encouragement it gave them'. However, not all in the Christian community in Jerusalem were so delighted.

In the Church we have to face such questions from time to time and especially at times of rapid change in the society in which we find ourselves. There have been, and today there still are, frequent heated discussions and disagreements concerning the best way to address and meet diverse and changing needs and circumstances while being faithful to the tradition. Today we are in a period of rapid and profound change and development in the Church and society. There are still diverse opinions expressed about how best to set about the task of educating people, the young and adults, to and in the faith in our present situation. For some in the Church adaptation can amount to a process of watering down the faith, of turning from the divine revelation to mere human concerns. This is still a major concern and fear for some people in the Church today, one which Mgr Wrenn expresses very strongly:

> *It cannot be repeated too often that the faith is something that was 'delivered once and for all to the saints' (Jude 3) and has never in the Church's tradition been considered something to be adapted but rather something to be handed down intact.*[3]

Others argue that adaptation and inculturation are essential features of all evangelisation and catechesis: 'the best chapters of Church history constitute a long adventure of trying to make real, in new languages and cultures, the revelation of God's love in Jesus Christ'.[4] In the view of Kevin Nichols the 'adventure' is not without its dangers and risks and at times not without fault and error. Yet it is one that must be undertaken in different generations and cultures. This will be a constant source of tension in the historical development of catechetical theory and practice right through the twentieth century and into the twenty-first century.

> *To adapt is not to diminish or water-down. It is true the one involves the risk of the other. But it is an essential principle for the Church's mission generally, and also an incarnational one. Just as God became a particular man, so the Church must teach, as Jesus did, in the voice of its own time.*[5]

To return to the early Church, we know that many new converts were already well versed in philosophy and other disciplines. Some founded schools known as catechetical schools. These were similar to the philosophical schools of the time. Students at these would include those preparing for baptism (catechumens), those recently baptised (neophytes) and even unbelievers who were interested in discussing with the Christian teachers. The school of Alexandria was one of the best known of these schools and some of the teachers were out-standing Christian thinkers of the day: Clement, Origen, and Cyril. Such schools would cater for the more academic and well-to-do of Hellenistic culture. Instruction and formation for the vast majority would take place within Eucharistic liturgies and other meetings of the local community.

---

[3] M. J. Wrenn, Catechisms and Controversies, Ignatius Press, 1991, p.93
[4] M. P. Gallagher, op. cit., p.101
[5] K. Nichols, Cornerstone, St. Paul Publ., 1978, p.44

Such a general picture can be gleaned from the New Testament and early patristic writings. There is, however, no detailed description of how individuals, families and community groups were initiated into the Christian faith and community in the very early years. Dujanier maintains that it is not correct to deduce from this that little or no preparation for baptism was required. He argues against those who claim to conclude this from the New Testament itself. Some conclude this from incidents described in the Acts of the Apostles such as the conversion and baptism of the three thousand on Pentecost Day and the baptism of the Ethiopian by Philip as the travelled together. Dujarier, citing Augustine, insists that these descriptions do not signify that baptism was performed without any preparation. There is, in his view, evidence, even in these texts, of development, some personal journey of faith: there is an interest expressed, some discussion and reflection, some form of instruction and an assessment of the disposition of those seeking baptism. In an article in *The Tablet* David Konstant suggests that it is well to appreciate that these stories do not tell it all.[6]

It is easier to recognise some process or journey of conversion in the story of Philip and the Ethiopian whom he baptised on the road from Jerusalem to Gaza. We are told that the Ethiopian had been on pilgrimage to Jerusalem and was in fact reading the prophet Isaiah, a passage concerning the suffering servant. When Philip met up with him he asked him if he understood what he was reading. The Ethiopian replied that he needed a guide to help him understand. He invited Philip into his carriage to discuss it with him. We are then told that Philip 'starting with this text of scripture proceeded to explain the Good News of Jesus to him' and, on coming to some water, he acquiesced to his request for baptism. (Acts 8: 26-40). We can see some clear stages or steps of the journey of faith in the story. The Ethiopian already shows signs of a personal search in so far as he has been on pilgrimage to Jerusalem and is reading Isaiah. He invites Philip to help him understand and he listens to Philip's instruction. He then asks for baptism. These give some indication of a process of preparation for reception into the Christian community.

As Edwards points out, we have to be content with the fact that we do not know in any detail 'how the earliest Church performed its technically

---

6 M. Dujarier, A History of the Catechumenate, the First Six Centuries, Sadlier, 1979, pp.14-18; D. Konstant, 'Taking the Faith Seriously', The Tablet, 16th February, 1985, p.167.

educational tasks'. Yet, through the work of scholars, we can have some idea of 'the array of structures that existed to inculcate and reinforce a sense of Christian identity'. Interpretations differ concerning the method of initiating and forming adults. There is disagreement on the question of the baptism of infants and children in the early years of the Church. This is, of course, inevitable owing to the lack of clear evidence.

> *The new Testament has virtually nothing to say about the way children were educated in the faith, how non-believers were converted, how persons were prepared to receive Christian initiation, how the initiated continued and deepened their formation as Christians'.[7]*

Structured initiation: the catechumenate

Whatever their opinions of the early years of the Church's practice, most scholars concur in recognising evidence of a more structured process of initiation in the work, *Apostolic Tradition*, ascribed to Hippolytus, a Christian philosopher in Rome about A.D.215. They question authorship, dates and places but generally agree that

> *It almost certainly reflects the situation in some major church very early in the third century. Therefore the work is an important witness both to Christian usage at the time when both adults and children were being baptised, and to the rise and development of the catechumenate.[8]*

More people are now aware of this structured process because of the introduction of the *Rite of Christian Initiation of Adults (RCIA)* in many parishes. This is a re-discovery of the catechumenate adapted for today.

---

[7] O. C. Edwards, 'From Jesus to the Apologists', A Faithful Church, J. H. Westerhoff & O. C. Edwards (eds), Morehouse-Barlow, 1981, p.43
[8] R. M. Grant, 'Development of the Christian Catechumenate', Made Not Born, Murphy Center for liturgical research, University of Notre Dame Press, 1976, p.36

By the mid-twentieth century many of those involved in catechesis, especially in so-called missionary countries, were asking for the re-introduction of such a process to help ensure a proper and deeper preparation for baptism and entry into the Christian community. It was in response to request that the RCIA was introduced following the decision of the Bishops at Vatican II.

In the early Church the need for a more structured process or programme of initiation arose for several reasons. Firstly because there was growing number of people seeking baptism. Another reason was to ensure a fuller formation in the hope of preventing lapsing which was also on the increase owing to the fear of persecution or the failure to live up to the moral demands of Christianity. Yet another reason may well have been the need to try to prevent infiltration in times of persecution. From the *Apostolic Tradition* and other later works it is clear that those preparing for baptism, known as catechumens, were a distinct group in the Church. They were accepted as part of the community, like novices in religious congregations, and could take part in the first rites of the Eucharist. They were assigned a sponsor from among the community who assisted the catechumens and who gave witness before the community of the catechumen's suitability for baptism and membership of the Christian community. The judgement was made on the evidence of changed moral behaviour and general life-style, not so much on the candidate's knowledge of Christian beliefs. During this period, instruction in Christian beliefs was focused on the basic, central doctrines contained in the Creed and in the Our Father. More intense and systematic instruction came after baptism and some experience of the Christian community's way of life. This formation period could last for several years. At the end of this period the community would choose those deemed worthy. An intense period of preparation followed in the weeks leading up to the celebration of Easter. The candidate would receive and celebrate the sacraments of initiation – baptism, confirmation and eucharist – in the solemn Easter liturgy. Fuller instruction would take place after this initiation period.

By the fourth century this catechetical practice was further developed and definite stages in the conversion process were distinguished and named. The 'catechumenate' was the name given to the period in which those who enrolled as catechumens took part in the liturgy of the Word, discussed and prayed with the baptised. Once accepted by the community, they undertook an intense preparation, more like a spiritual retreat, during the lenten season. This was referred to as the time of 'purification' or 'enlightenment'. On certain Sundays the 'scrutinies' would take place. This took the form of a ritual examination of the candidate's suitability and readiness. On one of the Sundays they would be presented with the 'symbols of faith', the Creed and the Our Father. At the solemn celebration of Easter the candidates were baptised, confirmed and participated fully in the eucharist. After the celebration of the sacraments at Easter there followed the period known as the 'mystagogia' which led to a deeper understanding of the Christian mysteries and the implications of the sacraments that they had celebrated with the community. During this period the 'neophytes' were given special places and enjoyed special status in the community. Many of the bishops or leaders of local communities delivered outstanding catechetical homilies during the lenten preparation period and in the week after the solemn celebrations. Those of Cyril of Jerusalem, for example, give witness to the liturgical practice in the fourth century and to the theological understanding of the sacraments of initiation. Dujarier describes the initiation process of the catechumenate as 'less an institution than a way of doing things, a usage that spread rather rapidly and was subsequently recognised by the Church as the most suitable means to prepare converts for baptism'.[9]

The decline of the catechumenate

The conversion of Constantine in A.D.313 and the emancipation of the Church which followed had considerable effect on the practice of the catechumenate. With the end of persecution there was no need for Christians to take a courageous, defiant stand in the face of danger of imprisonment and death. It became socially acceptable to embrace the Christian faith and for some it was seen as the way to favour and promotion:

---

[9] Dujarier, op. cit., p.35; see also L. Kelly, Sacraments Revisited, Darton Longman & Todd, 1998, pp.37ff.

> As Christianity gradually became the preferred religion of the
> State, baptism came to serve another purpose quite different
> from entrance into the paschal mystery. It became a kind of
> credit card that one needed in order to get anywhere in
> Christendom.[10]

Since catechumens were recognised as Christians, some were content to join the ranks of catechumens and delay the reception of baptism. Many of those enrolled as children or in their youth by Christian parents might well be have been to some degree initiated and instructed in the Christian faith but not go forward for baptism. Augustine was an example of this practice. He was enrolled by his mother Monica but he was not baptised till after his conversion at the age of thirty-three.[11]

One reason for delaying baptism is probably to be found in the rather severe penitential practices of the Church at that time. Those who, after baptism, were publicly known to have committed serious moral faults were excluded from the community. Should they wish to reconcile themselves again with the community they joined the ranks of the 'penitents' who formed a distinct group along with the catechumens. At the beginning the public sins which merited such expulsion were apostasy, murder and adultery. However, others were later added and by the third and fourth centuries the list was substantially longer.[12] Those thus excluded could be reconciled with the community if they repented and gave proof of the seriousness of their intent by joining the ranks of the 'penitents' and by undertaking harsh public penances over a period of years. Like the catechumens, they were a distinct group and could only take part in the first part of the eucharist. There was only one opportunity for reconciliation. A second lapse meant total expulsion from the community. Examples of the penances imposed were the wearing of rough clothing, spending much time in prayer and fasting, and, in the case of the married, refraining from sexual intercourse. Since this last prohibition continued even after public reconciliation, several bishops and councils advised

[10] T. Guzie, 'Theological Challenge', Becoming a Catholic Christian, W. J. Reedy (ed), Sadlier, 1981, p.286
[11] Augustine, Confessions, Penguin Classics, 1961, p.31
[12] B. Carra de Vaux St. Cyr, 'The Sacrament of Penance, An Historical Outline', The Mystery of Sin and Forgiveness, M. Taylor (ed), St. Paul, Alba House, 1970, p.133; see also Kelly op. cit., p.100.

against permitting the young to undertake the penitential practices. Such penitential practices may well have deterred some from receiving baptism while remaining among the catechumens. It would appear from sources such as lenten homilies that many who were inscribed as catechumens failed to turn up at any of the sessions of instruction and formation. As a means of trying to overcome this laxity, attempts were made to revive the catechumenate by condensing it into the weeks of lent.

Other factors contributed to the decline of the catechumenate as a structured process of initiation into the Christian community. With the increase in infant baptism, adult baptisms were no longer the norm. As Bourgeois points out, this led to a modification in the ritual process:

> *When the baptised came to be usually children, there was an attempt at first to maintain the arrangement as it was. The parents were invited to take part themselves in the various liturgical stages provided by the catechumenate course. But they hardly ever did... Gradually the rite for baptism shortened the intervals between the various ceremonies undergone by adults. In the tenth to eleventh centuries infant baptism came to have a condensed form of the adult ritual.*[13]

For centuries, children were baptised with a form of the adult ritual. A rite of baptism specifically for children was introduced after Vatican II. It may be of some encouragement, though not a great deal of practical help, to frustrated priests and catechists to realise that the lack of enthusiasm among parents and others for sacramental programmes is not entirely new. It would appear to have been the case from very early days in the Church. In time, baptism came to be administered shortly after birth instead of being celebrated in the solemnities of Easter or Pentecost. Baptism therefore became more of a private ceremony and emphasis shifted from initiation into the Christian community to the cleansing from sin. Guzie and many other theologians maintain that Augustine popularised the concept of 'original sin' in reaction to Pelagius who denied that baptism was necessary for the forgiveness of sins. According to

---

[13] H. Bourgeois, On Becoming Christian, St Paul Publ., 1984, p.44.

Guzie it was because of Augustine that 'the western Church has given a curious priority to the mystery of evil'. This, he says, has had a lasting effect on the pastoral approach to infant baptism. Vatican II, he suggests, has brought about a shift of perspective.[14]

Gradually, for a variety of reasons, the three sacramental rites of baptism, confirmation and eucharist became three distinct rites celebrated at different times. This led to an inversion of the previous initiation process. Catechesis no longer preceded baptism. The separation gradually brought about a change in the significance attributed to confirmation. There has been a shift of focus from a stage in initiation to an understanding of confirmation as a sacrament of commitment and maturity. Centuries later the Reformers used the confirmation rite as a public examination of young Christians in the knowledge of Christian doctrine, as a way of giving public witness to their faith. Once the young had witnessed before the community in this way they could then participate fully in communion. Mitchel remarks that the Reformation period was marked by a revival of catechetical instruction associated with confirmation rather than baptism.[15] Today some Catholics speak of confirmation as a sacrament in search of a meaning. Some now question the understanding of confirmation as a sacrament of commitment and maturity because it seems far removed from the understanding and practice of the early Church in the catechumenate. When confirmation is celebrated in the teen years, many refer to it somewhat cynically not as the sacrament of commitment and maturity but as the sacrament of 'Goodbye' to the Church, at least till some may ask for the sacrament of marriage. There is still a lot of discussion in the Church about the theological significance of confirmation and about questions concerning the age at which it should be celebrated. There is a variety of practice in different dioceses in England and Wales. The 1997 *General Directory for Catechesis* acknowledges this situation.

---

[14] T. Guzie, reactions to a paper read at a symposium on 'Catechetics of Children and Youth', Catechesis: Realities and Vision, B. Marthaler & M. Sawicki (eds), U.S. Catholic Conference, 1977, p.106.

[15] L. L. Mitchel 'Christian Initiation: the Reformation Period', Murphy Center, op. cit., pp.85-87

> *Very often at this time the pre-adolescent, in receiving the sacrament of Confirmation, formally concludes the process of Christian initiation but from that moment virtually abandons completely the practice of the faith. This is a matter of serious concern which requires specific pastoral care.[16]*

Frohnes highlights another factor that had considerable effect in bringing about a change in theological understanding of baptism and in catechetical practice: the mass conversion and baptism of the Saxon tribes, decided and collectively brought about by the baptism of the ruler – *cuius regio, eius religio*. This 'compulsory nature of the too hurried and mostly improvised mass baptisms' caused the social, community aspect of baptism to be overlooked. Baptism was no longer seen as incorporation into the community. The lack of preparation as well as the lack of free, deliberate choice or acceptance on the part of many who were baptised ensured a faith that had shallow roots, was little understood and scarcely practised unless under certain compulsion. Naturally; lapsing was frequent.[17]

Catechetical activity in the Middle Ages

The catechumenate reached its high point by the fourth century, was already in decline by the end of the fifth, and between the sixth and fifteenth centuries was totally eclipsed. Some in the Church seem to imply that no worthwhile catechetical activity took place after the demise of the catechumenate. This is hardly a fair judgement. Even if the stages and rites of the catechumenate were no longer practised and celebrated, it is not true to say that no fruitful catechetical activity took place in the Middle Ages. Jungmann holds the view that there was in fact a wealth of catechetical practices but no important works of theory.[18] In the introduction to their translation of The Catechism of the Council of Trent, McHugh and Callon maintain that 'there was no general neglect of proper instruction even during these centuries' but rather 'faith was so fruitful

---

16 General Directory for Catechesis, Catholic Truth Society, 1997, n181; see Kelly op. cit., p.52.
17 H. Frohnes, 'Mission in the Light of Critical Historical Analysis, Concilium, 114, 4, 1978, p.10
18 J. A. Jungman, Handing on the Faith, Burns & Oates, 1959, p.18.

as to give its very name to those ages'.[19] That is no doubt a somewhat rosy and romanticised view. Kavanagh warns against romanticising the era while acknowledging its accomplishments.[20]

It does seem that for the most part there was no regular, formal post-baptism catechesis for children. Parents and godparents were urged to take upon themselves this responsibility. Schools were already in existence and were generally attached to cathedrals, parishes and monasteries. The setting up of elementary schools, especially in the cities, was on the increase. McHugh and Callon refer to these schools and conclude that through them basic catechetical instruction was provided for a good number of the young, both rich and poor. [21] Jungmann is more tempered in his opinion and merely states that some religious training was made possible for a small section of the youth. Most catechetical work was done by the clergy in the liturgy throughout the year and was addressed mainly to the adult congregation. The Sunday homily at Mass was especially important as the occasion when the priest would explain Christian beliefs and urge the people to live moral and upright lives. Local synods frequently exhorted the clergy to be diligent in performing this duty. Basic instruction was to be given at least several times in the year with special importance attached to the traditional formulas found in the Creed and Our Father.

It is significant testimony to the Church's obedience to the catechetical task in the early Middle Ages that catechetical texts like the Creed and the Lord's prayer are almost invariably among the oldest surviving samples of writing in the newer European languages.[22]

Lent was still looked upon as a period of preparation for Easter even when baptism was no longer solemnly celebrated as its climax. By the thirteenth century the faithful were urged to confess their sins at least

---

[19] J. A. Mc Hugh & C. J. Callon, Catechism of the the Council of Trent for Parish Priests, Herder, 1934, p.XIII.
[20] A Kavanagh, The Shape of Baptism, Puebla Publ., 1978, p.117.
[21] Mc Hugh & Callon, op. cit., p.13
[22] M. Mc Gratch, 'Basic Christian Education from the Decline of the Catechumenate to the Rise of Catechisms', Westerhoff & Edwards, op. cit., p.92.

once a year and to receive communion in the Easter period. Lent was seen as a time to remind congregations of this duty and to assist them to prepare for these sacraments. By this time the severe penitential practices of the early centuries had been replaced by the practice of more frequent, private confession made to a priest. The Celtic monks introduced this practice in the seventh century and it gradually spread, largely by the missionary endeavours of many of these monks. The performance of harsh public penances was no longer required. Over time the stress has shifted from the performance of penances to the personal sorrow for sins confessed and for which milder, more moderate penances would be given. Booklets known as 'penitentials' were published to assist penitents prepare for the sacrament. These were mainly reflections on the commandments together with some prayers and devotional helps. Jungmann saw these as the forerunners to the catechism.

Apart from the penitentials there were other works of a catechetical nature published during this period. McGrath gives examples of 'a literature too vast to be surveyed in a short space'. He maintains that it is possible to conclude that 'Churchmen laboured long and hard in pursuit of this duty to instruct the folk in the basic truths of the faith'. Bourgeois considers that certain features of the catechumenate can be found in the new penitential practices of the Church

> *Now personalised and at scattered intervals, the sacrament of penance took on the function of the ancient catechumenate: discovery of God's forgiveness, learning a minimum of religious knowledge (the person going to confession had to recite the Creed and the Our Father). In other words, sacramental penance, once termed a kind of 'second baptism', became one of the main practical forms of baptismal remembrance.[23]*

From the very fact that the Reformation took place it is obvious that all was not well in the Church. There were many abuses: misuse of power, political ambition, immorality among the clergy, nepotism, the buying and selling of canonical offices and religious favours. Janelle acknowledges such abuses but maintains that despite them much of value went on in the Church and in the way Christians were formed.

---

[23] Bourgeois, op. cit., p.47.

> *However deplorable the abuses...their influence upon the faithful were far less than might have been expected. They persevered in the straight path despite faulty institutions. This appears clearly from a study of the religious literature, the piety and mysticism, the parish life, and the very architecture and decorative art of the period. The impression arrived at is not that of spiritual impoverishment, but, on the contrary, almost one of a renaissance.[24]*

Janelle and others highlight several religious features of this period which are clearly linked with and had an effect on catechesis understood broadly as education to and in the Christian faith. There was, beside the works already mentioned, a plentiful literature on religious subjects: the life of the saints, devotional practices, spirituality. *The Imitation of Christ* is a well-known example. Religious art was extremely rich: cathedrals and churches with their stained glass windows, tapestries, carvings and frescoes. All of these told biblical stories, depicted scenes in the life of Christ and so spelt out a message. These were, as Jungmann expressed it, 'books for the unlettered'. Nicholas Lash expressed the same point in an article in *The Tablet* in which he outlines his vision for top-level adult education in the Church in England and Wales today.

> *When most people could not read, church windows and buildings – the context of the liturgy that is always the fundamental form of Christian education – were their library.[25]*

Religious drama flourished: the mystery plays were performed in villages, towns and cities. New religious orders such as the Franciscans and the Dominicans undertook the task of preaching to the ordinary folk.

At this time family life, religious life and life in society were all of a piece. The year was centred round the liturgical seasons of Christmas, Easter and Pentecost, feasts of Mary and the saints. All this made for a fairly strong religious formation. However, in the view of Jungmann and

---

[24] P. Janelle, The Catholic Reformation, Colliers, Macmillan, 1977, p.17.
[25] N.Lash, 'The Laboratory We Need', The Tablet, 15th April, 2000, p.514

others 'this era contented itself too easily with religious usage and paid too little attention to the religious formation of the mind'.[26] There was without a doubt a less attractive side to all of this. There was an overemphasis on the externals of religion, at times verging on the superstitious and magical, too much reliance on fulfilling religious duties, the keeping of countless religious costumes in the hope of gaining 'merit' for heaven and protection on earth. It was against such practices, among other issues, and the theology underpinning them, that Luther would eventually lead his revolt in the hope of reforming rather than dividing the Church. Yet, over all, it cannot be said that these were fallow years from the point of view of catechetical activity. Sloyan's sweeping judgement that 'one should not hesitate to characterise the intervening centuries between then (i.e. the break up of the catechumenate) and the pre-reformation period as a catechetical vacuum' is surely open to question.[27] Haugaard rather argues that 'catechesis, whether effective or not, was woven into the warp and woof of the entire complex mesh of their community life'.[28]

Conclusion

One of the frequent complaints made by those engaged in catechesis and religious education in parishes and schools today is that such a faith or religious background cannot be assumed among those taking part in programmes or lessons. Often children arrive in primary school unable to make the sign of the cross or recite the common Catholic prayers. Parents who wish their children to be baptised and receive first communion appear to have minimal comprehension of the religious significance of these events. Many adults and children have minimal or no experience of liturgy and the celebrations of the major liturgical seasons, nor do they have an appreciation of the richness and beauty of religious ritual or symbol. We have to acknowledge the fact, unpalatable as it may be for us, that very many baptised Catholics are, for the most part, untouched by the

---

[26] Jungmann, op. cit., p.19.
[27] G. S. Sloyan, 'The Relation of the Catechism to the Work of Religious Formation', Modern Catechetics, G.S. Sloyan (ed), Collier, Macmillan, 1964, p.95.
[28] W. H. Haugaard, 'The Continental Reformation of the Sixteenth Century', Westerhoff & Edwards, op. cit., p.118

Church and have little knowledge of Catholic beliefs and practices. In our consumer society the Church is seen as one stall in a large market place and to many it is not a very attractive one. There are, of course, occasions when parents wish 'the goods' delivered at the time of baptism and first communion. We should not conclude from this, however, that people are in no way religious or in no way hungry for the spiritual, though they may, from our point of view, have different ways of showing and expressing it. Like those in the early and mediaeval Church we have to face our particular situation and seek new ways of educating to and in the faith, of taking up the call for 'new evangelisation' for which John Paul II makes frequent appeals. Like them, too, we shall have our successes and failures, we shall have different opinions on how to tackle the problem and, like them, we shall debate and argue. These historical sketches and reflections will bear this out and I can only hope that they may be of some help.

Chapter Two

The Age of the Catechisms: The Reformation and Post-Reformation

'Catechism' had come to denote, with varying shades of emphasis, both the process of nurture in the faith and particular written instruments designed to communicate that faith.[1]

The production of those manuals set the pattern of catechising in the Roman Church for the next four hundred years.[2]

W hen considering the Reformation and Post-Reformation periods from the point of view of educating to and in the faith, the most obvious and distinguishing characteristic is the publication and use of the printed manuals known as catechisms. In writing about significant emphases in catechesis during the Reformation period, Haugaard stresses the central role of the many different catechisms.

The sixteenth century was the golden age of the catechism, for, in spite of some precedents in earlier centuries, the written catechism, as we know it, was born among the Lutherans and Reformed, taken up by their associates in England, adopted by the Jesuits for counter-Reformation use, and employed much more sparingly by the Anabaptists.[3]

The term 'catechism', at least at the beginning of the Reformation period, was used to denote both a process of Christian education and formation, mainly through instruction, and the content of such instruction which was to be found in the printed manuals, the catechisms.

---

[1] Haugaard, op. cit., p.124
[2] M. C. Bryce, 'Evaluation of Catechesis from the Catholic Reformation to the Present', Westerhoff & Edwards, op. cit., p.204
[3] Haugaard op. cit., p.118

Form and styles of catechisms

These manuals came in a variety of forms and styles. Some were rather lengthy expositions of Christian doctrine for the use of clergy and others who were to some degree more versed in theology. The Catechism of the Council of Trent, for example, was intended for clergy especially 'should they be not very familiar with the more abstruse questions of theology'.[4] Some were in the form of small pamphlets intended for the use of lay Christians of different ages. A good number were meant as resources for the instruction of children and the young. It is often thought that these catechisms, because they were born out of the break up of the Church, were essentially polemic and defensive in character. The motives for writing catechisms were certainly polemic: to defend, preserve and propagate Christian truth, as each denomination perceived it, against the errors and falsehoods which were being spread by others who claimed to be the Christian Church. The texts, however, were not overly polemic nor did they concentrate on controversial issues. These would be discussed and argued in the universities, the theological schools and in more learned tomes. Crichton disagrees with those who hold the opinion that all Catholic catechisms of this time were counter-blasts against the protestant controversies. Stevick also holds that anti-Catholic and anti-Protestant polemics were minimal in the catechisms.[5]

The basic texts of the catechisms were more in line with the traditional presentation of the truths of faith expressed in the Creed, Our Father and the Commandments. These were the key features of Christian beliefs and practice which were presented during the catechumenate and later to the faithful in the Middle Ages in liturgical homilies and in the sacramental celebration of penance or confession. The ordering of the traditional material varied in different catechisms and brought out particular theological positions. Luther, for example, began with the Commandments before the Creed and Our Father. The ordering of the material in this way was in keeping with his conception of the Law as God's judgement on our human, innate inadequacy and helplessness. It was through the Law that

---

4 Mc Hugh & Callon, op. cit., p.5.
5 J. B. Crichton, 'Religious Education in England and Wales in the Penal Days (1559-1780), Shaping the Christian Message, G. S. Sloyan (ed), Macmillan, 1958, p.73; D. B. Stevick, 'Christian Initiation: Post-Reformation to the Present Era', Murphy Center, op. cit., p.102.

we were aware of our sinfulness and of the fact that our salvation was to be found in trusting in God's mercy which was articulated in the Creed and Our Father.

Catechisms of Luther and the Reformers

Luther was among the first to popularise the catechism. He made good use of the printed word to further his aim of overcoming ignorance and error among Christians. In 1520 he published his *Brief Form of the Ten Commandments, the Creed and the Lord's Prayer.* He published some texts in the form of 'tabulae', wall charters, for use in schools, homes and churches. In 1529 he published his *Small Catechism* and the larger *German Catechism* in which he urged the heads of families to instruct and examine their children and servants in the articles of faith. Luther's work proved immensely popular and many copies and translations were soon made. Other Reformers followed suit: Brucer – *The Larger Catechism* (1534), *The Shorter Catechism* (1537); Calvin – *Instruction in Faith* (1537); The Anglican *Book of Common Prayer* (1549); the Heidelberg Catechism (1563). The text of the Catechism of the Council of Trent refers to 'those who intended to corrupt the minds of the faithful and pour into their ears their poisoned doctrine'. It goes on to remark that they adopted the strategy of not only writing 'voluminous works' but also composed 'innumerable smaller books which, veiling their errors under the semblance of piety, deceived with incredible facility the unsuspecting minds of simple folk'.[6] It was in reaction to this widespread use of catechisms by the Reformers that Catholics began to produce their own catechisms.

The catechism of the Council of Trent

In response to the religious and political upheavals of the time, many in the Church wished to call a general council. That proved no easy matter. Eventually, largely due to the reforming efforts of Paul III, a council was summoned and met in Trent in 1545. Trent was chosen because of its location close to Germany, the birthplace of the Reformation, while, at the same time, it was within the domain of the Emperor- a fact that would

---

6 Mc Hugh & Callon, op. cit., p.14.

ensure the safety of the cardinals and bishops who would attend. The council's purpose was twofold. On the one hand, it set out to preserve Christian orthodoxy in doctrinal matters against the erroneous teachings of the Reformers. On the other hand, it had a pastoral and organisational purpose: to strengthen ecclesiastical discipline and to ensure that bishops and clergy performed their ministerial tasks for the benefit of the people. The work of the council was spread over eighteen years. The Fathers of the Council met on three occasions with lengthy intervals in between. As early as 1546 the bishops discussed the need to produce a catechism for children and uninstructed adults who were 'in need of milk rather than solid food'. This text would be written in Latin and the vernacular and would deal with the primary duties of the Christian life. This was given general approval. The question of a catechism, however, was considered of less weight than more central issues of doctrinal controversy and ecclesiastical discipline. It was, therefore, left in abeyance for some time.

A catechism for parish priests

The matter of the catechism was taken up again towards the end of the Council in 1562. By this stage the bishops had changed their original plan of writing a catechism for children and the uninstructed. They decided instead to produce a larger work destined for the use of the clergy in the work of preaching and instruction. The work on this catechism was not completed by the end of the Council in December 1563, at which time it was handed over to a committee appointed by the Council under the leadership of Cardinal Charles Boromeo. The members of the committee were told to avoid giving the opinions of particular theological schools or of individual theological thinkers. They should present the doctrine of the Universal Church in the light of the directives and teaching of Trent. Three years later the text was published under the title *Catechismus ex Decretis Concilii Tridentini ad Parachos*, more commonly referred to as *The Roman Catechism*. It is written in expository prose, not in the question and answer format of many catechisms. In the introduction to their translation McHugh and Callon speak of it as 'a handbook of dogmatic and moral theology, a confessor's guide, a book of exposition for the preacher, and a choice directory of the spiritual life for pastors and flock alike'.[7] The Roman Catechism set out to provide 'reliable matter' for priests who were 'less acquainted with theological opinions'. It made no claim to present Christian doctrine in its entirety since, it says, it is not possible to present in one volume all the dogmas of Christianity explained in detail. The catechism presents only things to assist pastors in discharging their duty of instruction should they not be very familiar with the more abstruse questions of theology. It states its purpose in this way:

> *To issue, for the instruction of the faithful in the very rudiments of the faith, a form and a method to be followed in all churches by those to whom are lawfully entrusted the duties of pastor and teacher.*[8]

Aims and methods

The goals of religious instruction are enumerated in the catechism:

- to know Christ, who is eternal life
- to keep his commandments
- to walk as he walked in the way of justice, godliness, faith, patience, mildness
- to fulfil the law of love
- to excite the faithful to a love of the infinite goodness of God towards us.

Great stress is put on the proper manner of communicating and imparting religious instruction. The text gives a clear injunction that may come as a surprise to many Catholics today and may sound more like relatively recent catechetical theory.

> *But as in imparting instruction of any sort the manner of communicating it is of the highest importance, so in conveying religious instruction to the people, the method should be deemed of the greatest moment. Age, capacity, manners and condition must be borne in mind... The priest must not imagine that those committed to his care are all on the same level, so that he can follow one fixed and unvarying method of instruction to lead all in the same way to knowledge and true piety...in*

---

[7] ibid. p.XXXVII
[8] ibid p.4

> *announcing the mysteries of faith and the precepts of life, the instruction is to be accommodated to the capacity and intelligence of the hearers.9*

The Roman Catechism was not intended for use with children, young people or with particular adult groups within the Church. It was a sourcebook to help clergy in the task of instructing different groups by setting out Catholic doctrine. The division of the material in the text was the traditional one: 'our predecessors in the faith have very wisely reduced all doctrine of salvation to these four heads: the Apostles' Creed, the Sacraments, the Ten Commandments and the Lord's prayer'.10 It has to be remembered that the Catechism of the Council of Trent addressed the particular needs and problems faced by Catholics in the upheaval of the sixteenth century Reformation.

The understanding of faith in the catechism

The emphasis of the Roman Catechism is quite definitely doctrinal, it is more of a theological sourcebook. The treatment of Scripture is scant. The indiscriminate reading of Scripture was seen to be dangerous since authentic interpretation was the duty of the lawfully appointed pastors and teachers, the bishops. Parts of Scripture were used but more as proof texts for official doctrinal positions. This is one of the weaknesses of the catechism but one that is understandable in the controversial theological climate of the time. Tom Groome is of the opinion that Trent's catechism 'was widely employed and shaped, probably more than any other document, the popular understanding of Roman Catholicism down to our own generation'. He considers that what it says about faith 'had greater significance for the day-to-day life of the faithful than the council decrees'.11 The catechism recognises the fact that faith has a variety of meanings in Scripture but goes on to state:

---

9 ibid. pp.7-8
10 ibid. p.9
11 T. Groome, Christian Religious Education, Harper & Row, 1980, p.78

> *We speak here only of that faith by which we yield our entire assent to whatever has been divinely revealed... We yield our unhesitating assent to whatever the authority of our Holy Mother the Church teaches us to have been revealed by God.*[12]

Groome and others see this as one of the main sources which strengthened the popular understanding of faith as synonymous with belief and belief as intellectual assent to officially stated doctrines. Other dimensions of faith – faith as trusting and faith as doing – were not specifically dealt with or developed.

> *In popular Catholic consciousness faith came to mean giving intellectual assent to the teaching of the official magisterium. Dulles summaries this well: 'From the counter-reformation until the present generation, Catholics have generally looked upon faith as a submission of mind to the teaching of the Church.*[13]

Herman Lombaerts says that what the Council of Trent attempted to achieve shows that the Church 'was working on fundamental questions and struggling with basic issues of a changing society'. It faced the specific problems of the sixteenth century.

> *Taking into account the historical context, the effects of the Council of Trent and the redaction of the catechisms in the sixteenth century cannot be valued enough. They reflect the honest self-questioning of the Church to look at the historical situation and to make a sound diagnosis. It also shows the difficulty of standing back and seeing the value of new (and different) approaches.*[14]

Many of the tensions that are still felt in catechesis and religious education are concerned with the understanding of faith and the significance of

---

[12] Mc Hugh & Callon, op. cit., p.59.
[13] Groome op. cit., p.59; see A Dulles, The Survival of Dogma, Doubleday, Image Books, 1971, p.153
[14] H. Lombaerts, 'Religious Education Today and the Catechism', Warren (ed.) op. cit.

each of the key dimensions of faith, not just the cognitive dimension, as well as the proper balance in the interplay of content and methods.

The catechisms of Canisius, Bellarmine and others

While the Council of Trent continued its debates, Peter Canisius (1521-1597) wrote a catechism that became a model for many that followed later. Canisius' catechism was published in three editions, each intended for a different group. The 'Maior', *Summa Doctrinae Christianae* (1550), was addressed to undergraduate students. It was more a compendium of theology and presumed in the reader a reasonable understanding of theology. It was set out in question and answer form. The answers varied in length. The intention was to encourage reflection; it was not intended for memorisation. The 'Minus' (1556), with fifty-nine questions, was written for children. The answers were brief and could be memorised. It included a series of prayers for different occasions. The 'Minor' (1558), probably the best known, was aimed at adolescents. It contained questions, answers, illustrations and prayers. Each edition was written first in Latin and then translated into German. Chadwick describes the work of Canisius:

> *It was written in a style to be understood, it was lucid and attractive and supported by biblical texts, it was not armed to the teeth against assailants. It was an uncontroversial state-ment of the Catholic faith, and won praise even among Protestant divines.[15]*

Robert Bellarmine (1542-1621), an Italian Jesuit, wrote his catechism, apparently unaware of the work of Canisius, on the orders of Pope Clement VIII for use in the Papal States. The work of Bellarmine was based on a series of lectures that he gave to a group of Jesuit Brothers. These proved so popular that many lay people asked to be able to attend.

---

[15] O. Chadwick, The Reformation, Penguin Books, 1964, p.264.

The first catechism appeared in 1597, *Dottrina Breve da Impararsi a Mente*. This was produced in the format of teacher's questions and pupils' responses in clear, precise language. In 1598 his teachers' manual was published, *Dichiarazione Piu Copiosa della Dottrina Cristiana*. This reversed the format: pupils' questions were followed by the teacher's more lengthy replies. Bellarmine's work, like that of Canisius, became a model on which other catechisms would be based. Sloyan points out that it should be borne in mind that Bellarmine's work was originally addressed to adults and those dedicated in religious life. This was, of course, a very different audience from the young people in schools and parishes in Europe and indeed in other parts of the world, with whom the catechism was later used. Alberich speaks of the imposition of the Bellarmine catechism in Asia which 'made a significant contribution to crystalising foreignness of Christians in that continent'.

> *This ahistoric catechism spread rapidly throughout Asia and contributed towards the creation of both psychological and social ghettoes of Christian communities in the continent. From then onwards catechisms tended to be literal translations of texts which had been created for other cultural milieux.*[16]

While the catechisms of Canisius and Bellarmine can be considered the classics, many other catechisms were produced. It is in fact possible to speak of a proliferation of catechisms. It was felt that there was widespread religious ignorance among the people not only in countries such as India and Asia but in the towns and villages of Europe. It was deemed necessary that the faithful be preserved from the heresy of the reformers. Within the Church itself there were a number of theological schools. Catechisms were produced which were based on the approaches of these schools. Another reason for the multiplication of catechisms was the fact that bishops wished to exercise their right and duty as the first and chief teacher of the faith in their own diocese. Towards the end of the eighteenth century there were a number of attempts to bring some unity into this 'war of catechisms'. Maria Teresa of Austria in 1777 approved a sin-

---

[16] E. Alberich, 'Is the Universal Catechism an Obstacle or a Catalyst in the Process of Inculturation', Concilium, 204, 4, 1998, p.89

gle catechism to be used in her empire. In 1806 Napoleon imposed his 'imperial' catechism throughout his dominion. The desire for more unity in the matter of catechisms grew in the time of industrialisation when massive immigration to the large cities took place. From time to time, bishops of a particular country or region made efforts to produce a single text. There were many in the Church who favoured the multiplicity of catechisms and many others who thought it was harmful to the unity of the Church to have so many different catechisms. The bishops at Vatican I would give considerable time to this debate.[17]

Catholic catechisms in England

In England, as on the continent, catechisms played a major role in religious instruction, especially of Catholic children. During the years of persecution, Catholic traditions were kept alive through the ministry of priests who arrived secretly from seminaries and colleges on the continent. They celebrated Mass and preached mainly in large country houses belonging to Catholic gentry. The sons of such families were often sent abroad to seminaries and colleges for their education. As early as 1567 Laurence Vaux (1519-1585) of Manchester published his *Christian Doctrine necessarie for children and ignorante people.* This was based on the work of Canisius. After receiving a summons to appear before the ecclesiastical commission of Elizabeth I, Vaux fled to Louvain where he founded a school for children of English exiles. It was during that period that he wrote his catechism. He returned in 1580, was arrested and died in prison five years later. About 1649 there appeared what has come to be known as the *Douai Catechism* written by Henry Tuberville (1591-1678) which was based on the catechism of Bellarmine.

Bishop Challoner's catechism, *Abridgement of Christian Doctrine*, is perhaps the best known of English catechisms. It was published in 1772. Pickering traces the sources of this work of Challoner and maintains that there is proof that Challoner himself was the author, though others, such as Crichton, are less sure.[18] Challoner was an outstanding catechist who,

17 Guida al Catechismo della Chiesa publ., Elle Di Ci, Leuman, Turin 1993, pp.29-33.
18 B. Pickering, 'Bishop Challoner and Teaching the Faith', The Clergy Review, 65, 1, 1980, pp.8-15; J. D. Crichton, 'Challoner's Catechism', The Clergy Review, 63, 4, 1978, pp.140-146.

in his numerous works, displayed a remarkable breadth of interest, and met the many needs of Catholics. His books include the translation of the Bible (1750), *Memoirs of Missionary Priests* (1771-71), the translation of Augustine's Confessions (1773), *Meditations for Every Day of the Year* (1775) and the well known *Garden of the Soul* (1740), a much used prayer book and manual of instruction. As Bishop of the London District he founded two schools for Catholics at a time when they did not find it easy or economic to send their children abroad.

Challoner's catechism is the source of the so-called Penny Catechism, *A Catechism of Christian Doctrine*. Crichton in an article on Challoner's catechism discusses four revisions that were made to Challoner's work during the nineteenth century. He draws attention to the difference, especially in language and tone, which the work of the redactors made to the original Abridgement. Challoner's tone is easy and his language is frequently colloquial while the texts of the redactors are highly theological, considerably more polemic and difficult for children. Some examples given by Crichton should make this clear. When dealing with the first article of the Creed, in response to the question 'Who is God?' Challoner's answer reads; 'He is the Maker of heaven and earth'. The Penny Catechism answers 'God is the supreme Spirit who alone exists of himself, and is infinite in all perfection'. In reply to the question about Jesus Christ 'Why is He true God?' Challoner's text reads 'Because he is the true and only Son of God the Father born before all the ages and perfectly equal to him'. The work of the redactor reads 'Because he has the nature of God, being of the self same substance with God the Father'. The later texts are expressed in more abstruse theological and philosophical concepts. They introduce the abstract notions of the trinitarian and christological controversies of the fifth century – 'nature' and 'substance'. This may well be the language of Chalcedon but it is far removed from the normal language of nineteenth and twentieth century children, and adults for that matter. Chrichton makes another useful comparison: the *Abridgement* has 236 doctrinal questions, the Penny Catechism has 332. Allowing for the fact that the first Vatican Council had defined papal infallibility, the Penny Catechism, in Crichton's view, provides 'a mini-treatise on the papacy'.

The Penny Catechism for children in schools

The Penny Catechism, *A Catechism of Christian Doctrine*, was used in schools for many years and is still published with some minor variations. At the beginning of the twentieth century it was the chief, often the only, text for religious instruction in Roman Catholic schools.

> *The printed catechism was supreme and the only teaching method was learning by heart. The more gifted teacher made some attempt at explanation but the system was vitiated by the imposition of difficult and abstract answers on small children... What was peculiar to the English situation was that at that time Catholics were a very small minority in the country, very conscious of the influence of Protestantism everywhere in public life. This gave a certain rigidity of outlook in the field of catechetics, and the need for fixed and very clear statements of doctrine was felt to be all-important in the face of vague yet dissolvent heretical teaching that permeated the atmosphere.[19]*

The sense of being a persecuted minority, as well as the increasing number of Irish Catholics who were coming to British cities and towns in search of work, gave to British Catholicism a defensive attitude that had its effect on the work of catechesis. The newly established Catholic hierarchy saw the faith of the poor and the simple being endangered not only by the Protestant heresy but, possibly even more, by the general religious indifference of the time. They therefore put great stress on the need to educate poor Catholics and the necessity of building schools for that purpose. In the first synod of Westminster, 1852, the bishops declared:

> *The first necessity, therefore, is a sufficient provision of education, adequate for the wants of the poor. It must become universal... Do not rest until you see this want supplied; prefer the establishment of good schools to every other work. Indeed, wherever there may seem to be an opening for a new mission, we should prefer the erection of a school, so arranged to serve temporarily for a chapel, to that of a church without one... It is the good school that secures the virtuous and edifying congregation.[20]*

---

[19] Jungmann op. cit., p.51.
[20] E. Guy, The Synods In English, St. Gregory Press, 1886, p.268.

Today, some Catholics, particularly clergy, question the value of Catholic schools in the process of educating pupils to and in the faith. They often ask whether we are getting our money's worth when large numbers fail to practice by attending church on Sundays. They would hardly say that the school 'secures the virtuous and edifying congregation'. The issue concerning our Catholic schools as part of the pastoral task of the Church is a challenging one. I shall reflect on it in more detail in part two.

At the turn of the century, school began to have a special importance as attendance became compulsory and families were deemed less able to form children in the Christian faith and instruct them in doctrine. The rise of many religious congregations dedicated to education of the young led to the founding of Catholic schools for children of the rich and the poor. School was the place for catechesis, catechisms the instrument and method for catechesis. There were, of course, many individuals who were outstanding catechists and educators who met the religious needs of both adults and the young in a richer, broader way than is implied in mere catechism learning. Throughout Europe and elsewhere many catechisms were published by many different individuals and dioceses addressing a variety of groups within the Church

Vatican I and the call for a universal catechism

The first Vatican Council took place in the year 1869-70. Its work was never completed due to the outbreak of the Franco-Prussian war. It may come as a surprise to many Catholics to know that the bishops spent more time debating the question of a universal catechism than they did on the question of papal infallibility. Ten of its eighty-nine sessions were given to discussion of the schema entitled *The Compilation and Adoption of a Single Short Catechism.* Pius IX submitted this schema suggesting that a Latin manual be edited that would be based on the work of Bellarmine. He intended such a work to be universally adopted in the desire to eliminate the great variety of catechisms.

Some bishops lamented the vast number of catechisms with their variety and diversity. They complained that Catholics could not understand one another because they were taught from different catechisms. This, they said, was an inconvenience in an age of easy travel and frequent migration. During the debates some bishops argued against the call for such a universal catechism. They argued on the basis of diverse pastoral needs among different people and regions. It took away the right of the diocesan bishop to develop his own catechism to meet such needs. Other bishops maintained that many Catholics would be unhappy and confused if they lost the catechisms they already knew. It was also argued that a universal catechism would not allow for adaptation to cultural settings, to the age and capacity of those being instructed. In the view of some bishops it was educationally unsound to imagine that a single universal text could be written for children of different ages. Alberich quotes the statement of Cardinal Rauscher, the archbishop of Vienna, when he lamented the use of a universal catechism for all parts of the world:

> *The attentive chorus of our enemies could shout out, 'Here they are giving the very same catechism to Germans and to Indians; oh, what sublime ignorance of the art of teaching.*[21]

During one of the debates an archbishop from Hungary forcefully declared that 'to catechise the people is one of the great duties and rights of a bishop; if a catechism is dictated to us, our sermons will be dictated next'.[22] According to Donnellan 'the issue became a divisive one and, as the debate wore on, the problem centred more on the relationship of bishops to the Holy See than on the improvement of religious education'. A minority of bishops agreed that there was need for greater doctrinal unity but they were nonetheless against a uniform catechetical text because of the diversity of culture, situations and age. The majority were of the opinion that a universal catechism was needed to overcome the increasing ignorance and indifference among the people, because of the danger of nationalism in the Church and because of the great numbers of migrants who were on the move in Europe in search of work. Other bishops went along with the majority but wished to introduce some amend-

---

[21] E. Alberich, op. cit., p.89.
[22] M. Donnellan, 'Bishops and Uniformity in Religious Education: Vatican I to Vatican II', Sourcebook for Modern Catechetics, M. Warren (ed), St Mary's Press, Christian Brothers Winona, 1983, p.234.

ments. They thought that there should be a catechism for the whole Church but they suggested that the writing of the text should be left to bishops who were members of Council, not the Pope. At the very least there should be consultation among the bishops. This could be done through an international commission. They did not want the catechism to be obligatory and upheld the right and duty of the local bishop.

After prolonged discussion the schema was amended and a new draft introduced. The catechism would be written for the instruction of children and was to be learnt by heart. It would be modelled on the work of Bellarmine. There would be a central core text that should be accepted everywhere in the Church. Bishops could produce an appendix separate from the core text in which they could give explanations suited to local needs. The amended schema was accepted by the bishops on May 4th 1870. The votes were 491 for; 56 against; 44 approved with reservations. Because of the outbreak of the Franco-Prussian war the decree was never promulgated. Some attempts were made in the years following Vatican I to implement the decree on the catechism without success. The question was again raised in preparation for Vatican II. The bishops at that time decided not to undertake a catechism for the universal Church. They published instead *The General Directory of Catechesis*. More than a century later *The Catechism of the Catholic Church* was published, though it must be borne in mind that it is a very different document to the one envisaged by the bishops at Vatican I. That story, however, is part of the developments of the twentieth century.

Conclusion

Reviewing the history of catechetical activity from the Reformation up to more or less the present, Bryce enumerates three characteristics which dominated and ultimately defined the task of catechesis:

> *First, catechesis became identified with a printed manual; secondly, catechesis was directed principally to children and youth; and finally, in relation to the first two, formal catechesis came to be associated with schooling – to the point that it was almost synonymous with textbooks and classrooms.*[23]

Such a situation lasted well into the twentieth century and continues to some extent in many places as we enter the new century. It is clearly very different from what went on in the period of the catechumenate and in the Middle Ages. However, new developments began to take place during the first half of the century, especially in the years before Vatican II. A number of these were endorsed by the Council and are accepted in the theory and practice of catechesis today. They are frequently the source of controversy and heated debate. Already early in the twentieth century many were beginning to be critical of the catechism as a method of educating the young to and in the faith. Later, others questioned whether it provided an adequate summary of the Christian faith with its emphasis on a scholastic theology and on the cognitive dimension of the faith. Not many would agree with the sentiments expressed by Cardinal Cicognani in the early 1950s, when he was Apostolic Delegate to the United States: 'No human book can compare with the catechism in certitude or in power. It transforms tender children into sure theologians'.[24] Few would see the aim of catechetical instruction to be that of turning tender children into sure theologians. Some would begin to question whether the theology of the catechisms was an adequate summary of the Good News of Jesus Christ and the Kingdom.

---

[23] M. C. Bryce, op. cit., p.204
[24] Quoted by Donnellan op. cit., p.242, note 4.

Chapter Three

Critique of the Catechisms

There arose around 1900 the Catechetical Movement. What the movement had aimed at was an improved method of catechesis, through which the subject matter of catechesis should not only be imprinted on the child's memory but also be grasped by the understanding.[1]

There was a time when religious education consisted mainly in learning doctrine. Then we saw a move to Salvation History. We saw God's dealing with man as a continuing dialogue stretching over the centuries and most evident in the history of the Jews, the life of Jesus and the continuing life of the Christian Church.[2]

The twentieth century has a rich history in the development of both catechetical theory and practice. The century began with a call for a universal catechism specifically addressed to the young that would ensure unity and orthodoxy in religious instruction. In the first half of the century many, influenced by educational theories, were expressing criticism of catechisms. Liturgical, patristic and biblical renewal as well as a renewed theology of Revelation and Church had a profound effect on those involved in the work of catechesis and religious education. Much of this had an impact on the thinking of many bishops attending the second Vatican Council. The bishops chose to promulgate a Directory offering guidelines to national bishops' conferences rather than a catechism for the universal Church. The catechumenate was reintroduced as a structured process of education to and in the faith for adults. Great emphasis was placed on the catechesis of adults. The community was seen as the agent of catechesis in which the school was one important yet limited partner along with the home and the parish. During the seventies official documents were urging the recognition of cultural pluralism and the need for unity in diversity in catechesis and religious education. In the eighties many Catholics were expressing concern that the movement in this direc-

---

[1] Jungmann op. cit., p.33
[2] D. Lance in the introduction to J. R. Rymer, 11-16: Old Testament, DLT, 1969

tion may have gone too far. In the nineties *The Catechism of the Catholic Church* was published as 'a point of reference' for catechetical materials produced in various regions. In the opinion of many of those who attended the International Catechetical Congress in Rome in 1971 the developments were seen as 'positive and providential'. At the same time the Congress recognised 'very serious questions and some immense needs which originate from the profound changes in the people, society and the Church of our day'. Throughout the century there was constant discussion, reflection, questioning, debate and frequent controversy. In the words of Duckworth it was a 'stimulating and exhausting experience'.[3]

The influence of educational theory

At the beginning of the twentieth century catechesis was still very much identified with teaching children Catholic doctrine in school by means of catechisms. In England and Wales the main catechism in use was the Penny Catechism, *A Catechism of Christian Doctrine*. The founding of two catechetical reviews towards the end of the nineteenth century marked the beginning of a fairly widespread criticism of the general content and methods used in teaching from the catechisms and of a more concerted effort at bringing about change. The review *Katechetische Blatter* was founded in Munich in 1875 and *Christlich Pedagogische* in Vienna in 1887. The term 'catechetics' was introduced to describe an aspect of pastoral theology that was concerned not only with doctrinal instruction but also with the formation of the person, the whole Christian. Catechetics refers to the study and theory of catechesis. The influence of educational theories made an impact on catechetics. Emphasis was now placed on how children learn and come to understand concepts rather than on the mere imparting of information and learning by heart. In catechetics this became known as the 'Munich method' since the approach was endorsed at a congress held in Munich in 1928. The method was basically an adapted version of the learning steps advocated by J. F. Herbart (1776-1841). According to this theory, learning takes place first through the perception of the senses, then through intellectual understanding and finally through practical application. The means of

---

[3] R. Duckworth, 'Ten years of Religious Education in England', Lumen Vitae, 30, 3-4, 1975, p.375

learning were in fact the senses, the intellect and the will. Based on this theory, phases or steps in Christian instruction were identified:

- a presentation – an appeal to the imagination by means of a story or visual aid;

- an explanation of some part of Christian doctrine or moral teaching in a way that children come to some understanding of its meaning;

- a practical application to everyday life by suggesting something the children could do.

In this approach the catechism text was no longer the starting point of the lesson. The text came after arousing interest and the explanation of some aspect of doctrine. There is evidence of the influence of Montessori and others in this way of teaching: children learn by doing, not simply in sitting and listening.

Drinkwater: a pioneer in catechetical matters

The chief exponent of this approach and method in England was Canon Drinkwater (1886-1982). On the occasion of his ninetieth birthday Kevin Nichols edited in his honour a series of essays written by leading catechetical scholars. In his introduction he had this to say of Drinkwater:

> *In the days when the catechetical movement was young and raw, ill understood and slightly suspect, he set going new modes of thinking and new initiatives in practice which were to prove important and influential, which were to stand the test of time. He became one of the few English Catholics whose life, thought and work was to have influence throughout Europe and throughout the world.*[4]

As with so many other people who made substantial contributions to the progress of catechetics, it is not possible to do adequate justice to the work of Drinkwater in these pages. He was ordained priest in 1910 and

---

[4] K. Nichols, Voice of the Hidden Waterfall, K. Nichols (ed), St. Paul Publ., 1980, introduction.

began working in a parish in the archdiocese of Birmingham. That same year Pius X issued the decree *Quam Singulari*. This set as the age for the first reception of communion and the sacrament of penance, confession, 'the age of reason' which was thought to be about the age of seven. The Pope encouraged more frequent reception of these sacraments and declared that full and complete knowledge of Christian doctrine was not required before children could receive them. Fuller instruction should come later and should be given gradually and in a manner suited to the abilities of the children. In the opinion of Drinkwater this was the true beginning of catechetical reform since, in his view, the decree gave official recognition to the psychological realities of childhood and he urged all involved to take them seriously. Drinkwater based his own theory and practice on the Pope's statement that children should learn gradually and in a way suited to their capacities. He was influenced by educationalists such as Montessori, though his expertise was rooted in his experience as a priest in a parish and as chaplain to the forces in the 1914-18 war. While working with the troops he became aware of how little of the doctrinal texts of the catechism the soldiers remembered but he was impressed by the fact that they showed interest in and remembered the practices and the devotions, the practical side of religion. This experience was enriched by his reading and reflection.[5]

The Sower review

After the war he returned to parish work and in 1919 he began to publish the catechetical journal *The Sower*. In this journal he expressed his views and made known the thinking and practice of others in the field. Drinkwater was not against the notion of a catechism which he accepted as a traditional summary of Christian doctrine. However, he recognised knowledge of such doctrines to be only one feature in understanding and living the Christian faith. His main contention was that the language of the Penny Catechism was abstract, more suited to the theology courses in seminaries and, therefore, too difficult for children to understand. He was strongly against what he termed the 'parrot system': 'by which I mean the rote-learning of scientific language before the mind is ready to receive

5 F. H. Drinkwater, *Educational Essays*, Burns & Oates, 1951, pp.90-100

it'.[6] There was a place for learning some things by heart – poetry, for example. However, catechism texts, unlike most poetry and prayers that are in the language of life, were in exact, technical, theological language that cannot be understood without prior experience and explanation. To fail to take note of this was, in his words, 'to drill masses of children in verbal repetition'. He was appointed religious inspector for schools in the archdiocese of Birmingham in 1922. In his article 'What the Sower Stands for' (1933) he was somewhat scathing of the work of the religious inspectors and thought that they should be abolished. Their main task appeared to be to examine the pupils' knowledge of the catechism in a way that greatly influenced the teachers in their approach to religious instruction. It is interesting to note that in those days this part of the curriculum was often referred to as R.K, religious knowledge as well as R.I, religious instruction. More recently we speak of R.E., religious education, or R.S., religious studies. The change in name speaks of a change of emphasis in content, method and the aims and purpose of the teaching activity. Speaking of the diocesan religious inspectors Drinkwater claimed that 'whether religion appears primarily as a subject to be learned or a life to be lived depends on the bishop and his visiting representative even more than the teacher'.[7] For the most part these clerical inspectors appointed by the bishop were concerned almost entirely with the pupils' knowledge of the text of the catechism. For many children and teachers these visits were a rather frightening ordeal. I have vague memories of such visits during my primary school years and I recall that some pupils who were not brilliant at memorising the words were told to stay away on the day of the inspection. We considered them the lucky ones.

Drinkwater's practice

In line with the teaching of *Quam Singulari* and contemporary educational theory, Drinkwater set out a scheme that would ensure that the catechism was learnt gradually. In this scheme he suggests that very little, if any, catechism should be taught in primary schools. Teachers should be encouraged to adopt methods and approaches more suited to

---

[6] Ibid. p.73
[7] ibid. p.77.

the needs of younger children, especially involving them in activities. The catechism could be learnt in the secondary school at a time when the pupils would be more ready to learn and understand the truths of the faith. In this way he thought that the catechism would be approached with greater interest since it would be new and novel for the pupils who would come to it for the first time in secondary school. He introduced this as an optional scheme for the schools in Birmingham. Such a suggestion was considered revolutionary by many and few seem to have taken it up. He also advocated the use of a variety of methods. He stressed the importance of celebrating liturgy with children and the value of telling Bible stories. He encouraged the use of drama. Another feature of his approach was the making of homemade catechisms which the children could compile and in which they could include their own stories, reflections, illustrations and captions.[8] Drinkwater considered religion not simply as a subject to be taught. It was also a commitment with implications for life and, consequently, the best method of teaching was through the practice of religion in corporate and private acts of worship and prayer, as well as in the display of religious articles around the school. What he stood for can best be summed up in his own words:

You see how it is: love, interest, self-discipline, trust, creative teaching, happy activities, free speech, the desire to spread the faith. The things to be avoided were boredom, fear, suspicion, compulsion, legalism, the parrot-system and bigotry.[9]

The contribution of Drinkwater to the catechetical journey in the twentieth century was creative and courageous. Through *The Sower* he had considerable influence, possibly less in England than in other European countries. An international survey of religious instruction (1937) praised Drinkwater and The Sower scheme by highlighting its 'freshness, optimism, gradual movement, its refusal to offer to teachers or to pupils the predigested or the ready made'. It would not be entirely accurate to suggest that teaching method was his only concern. Underpinning the general unease of Drinkwater and others was also the reaction against the

[8] F. H. Drinkwater, 'Homemade Catechisms', Lumen Vitae, 5, 2-3, 1950, pp.417-425.
[9] Drinkwater, Educational Essays, p.74

over-defensive, authoritarian spirit of the Catholic counter-reformation, and the rather narrow intellectualism that was a direct influence of the enlightenment and rationalism. They were sensitive to the currents of change already beginning to take place in theology, education and other disciplines. More radical questioning would come later.

Jungmann and the kerygmatic movement

J.A. Jungmann (1889-1975), an Austrian Jesuit, was the undisputed leader of the next phase of catechetical development. It is normally referred to as the 'kerygmatic stage' because it stressed the Good News of the Christian message (the Kerygma) over and against the narrow doctrinal approach of the catechisms. Jungmann was very much in touch with new movements and currents of change that were taking place in the Church. Erdozain is of the opinion that the kerygmatic renewal was the most influential in the history of catechetics in the twentieth century. He points out that it did not simply fall from the sky but had its roots in other movements that advanced biblical, patristic, liturgical studies and in a renewed theology of Church.[10] Catechists who had developed the Munich method had, to some extent, paved the way for this deeper challenge to the catechism. Developments in the human sciences such as education, psychology and sociology gradually made an impact on catechetical thinking. There were also developments in theological thinking. As early as the mid-nineteenth century, the German scholars of Tubingen university were developing the theological concept of the Church as community. This attempted to balance the rigidly legalistic and hierarchical understanding of Church as a perfect society, a sort of bank in which the divine truths of Revelation were deposited and then distributed through the ministry of the clergy. Pacana considers the approach of the Tubingen school to be one of the enriching factors or influences in the process of catechetical change.[11] Erdozain maintains that the writings of these scholars – Sailer, Noehler, Hirscher among others – 'remain as witnesses to an attempt to supersede a composite scholasticism'. He cites a passage of Hirscher written in 1823:

---

[10] L. Erdozain, 'The Evolution of Catechetics: A survey of Six International Study Weeks in Catechetics', Warren op. cit., p.87.
[11] H. C. Pacana, 'Development of the Theology of Revelation', Teaching All Nations, 7, 3, 1969, p.261.

> *We live in troubled times, but it is the Gospel, not the works of scholasticism, which has been promised unerring validity from on high. It is by clinging to the Gospel that we shall triumph.*[12]

In 1879 Leo XIII wrote his encyclical *Aeterni Patris* which declared the philosophical method and system of Thomas Aquinas, the scholastic method, to be the best suited for examining and safeguarding Christian truths. Scholasticism was more or less canonised as the Christian philosophy. However, the renewed interest in and research of the works of the Fathers of the early Church as well as the study of Christian archaeology led to the rediscovery of the liturgical and catechetical practices of the early Church. This gave a boost to the liturgical movement which was also helped and developed by the monks of Solemnes. One of the main influences for change was without a doubt the advance made in Catholic biblical scholarship. L'Ecole Biblique was founded in Jerusalem in 1890 and began publishing the *Revue Biblique* in 1892. Under the leadership of Lagrange the school espoused the historical-critical method. Over the decades this caused many controversies. In 1943 Pius XII wrote his encyclical *Divino Afflante Spiritu* which dealt with questions concerning the study of Scripture. In the view of Schmid this encyclical was the 'liberation encyclical' that 'opened the road to modern Catholic biblical scholarship and gave it a powerful impetus'.[13]

The works of Jungmann

Jungmann was very much influenced by these developments. He wrote a doctorate thesis on the catechetical and kerygmatic formulation of the doctrine of grace in the first three centuries. He was well versed in patristic studies and in the history of the early Church. He later lectured in pastoral theology and liturgy in the university of Innsbruck. He himself speaks of these influences on his thinking.

---

[12] Erdozain op. cit., p.87; see also S. O'Riordan, 'The Present State of Pastoral Theology', The Furrow, 36, 4, 1985, p.210

[13] J. Scmid, 'Biblical Exegesis', Encyclopedia of Theology, K. Rahner (ed), Burns & Oates, 1975, p.123.

A new attitude sprang from the development which gave birth to the liturgical movement. There was an increasing apprecia-tion of history and tradition...the writings of the Fathers and the liturgical sacramental life of the early Church were discov-ered. A first fruit was the gradual return to a fuller under-standing of the Church... A new inspiration besides liturgy was Sacred Scripture.[14]

All these strands came together in his catechetical works. A landmark in catechetical renewal was his book *Good News and Our Presentation of the Faith* published in 1936. The German original was eventually with-drawn on the urging of the Holy Office because, in the historical climate of the time, it seemed to question papal directives concerning the scholas-tic method and approach as the best safeguard of Catholic doctrine and appeared uncomfortably close to certain features of modernism. In 1962 an abridged version was published in English under the title *The Good News Yesterday and Today*.[15] Influenced by his studies and the develop-ments already mentioned Jungmann challenged not so much the method but the content of the catechism. He saw the catechism as an arid sum-mary of Christian doctrine that failed to give a dynamic presentation of the core of the Christian message found in the Gospels. In the opinion of Jungmann the task of catechists is to proclaim the message, the Good News, the grandiose plan of God encompassing the salvation of human beings and centred on Jesus Christ. For him, catechesis was a pastoral task rather than a task of imparting instruction. Many Christians, he thought, knew the doctrines but failed to see the overall message of God's love incarnated in Jesus Christ.

But what is lacking among the faithful is a sense of unity, see-ing it all as a whole, an understanding of the wonderful mes-sage of divine grace. All they retain of Christian doctrine is a string of dogmas and moral precepts, threats and promises, customs and rites, tasks and duties imposed on unfortunate Catholics.[16]

[14] Jungmann, op. cit. p.396
[15] J. A. Jungmann, The Good News Yesterday and Today, Sadlier, 1962
[16] J. A. Jungmann, 'Theology and Kerygmatic Teaching', Lumen Vitae, 5, 2-3, 1950, p.258.

In his view, many Catholics had little or no understanding of the redemptive significance of these doctrines. The Christian message should, therefore, be presented whole and to this end he put stress on four sources or languages of the Good News, namely the Bible, systematic teaching, liturgical celebrations and the witness of Christian living. This fourfold presentation of the Christian faith became one of the central tenets of the kerygmatic movement. The international study weeks held in Eichsatt (1960) and Bangkok (1962) would endorse the general approach of Jungmann and especially the four sources of presenting the faith.

Hofinger and kerygmatic texts

If Jungmann was the founder of the kerygmatic movement, Hofinger can be considered its apostle. Hofinger was also an Austrian Jesuit and studied under Jungmann. Later he taught in the East Asian Pastoral Centre in Manila. He was Director of the centre between 1957 and 1965. During that time he lectured in many places around the world, including Britain and the United States, where he addressed large gatherings of clergy, teachers and catechists in courses and summer schools. Ruth Duckworth was of the opinion that these experiences were an important feature of the catechetical movement in England. Through these and the 'shock waves' they caused, the kerygmatic movement was launched here. Barker makes the same point when he speaks of the influence of Hofinger's lectures in the United States. According to Barker these unleashed 'a plethora of manuals and text books based on the kerygmatic approach'.[17] National catechisms and other texts were published in the kerygmatic mould. Chief among these catechisms were the German catechism translated into English in 1957, and the Australian Catechism of the nineteen-sixties. The method or approach came to be called the 'Salvation History' approach. The approach modeled itself on Scripture which was considered God's method of revealing himself, first in the history of Israel, most clearly in the event of Jesus Christ, and finally, in the history of the Christian Church.

[17] Duckworth op. cit., p.378; K. Barker, *Religious Education, Catechesis and Freedom*, Religious Education Press, 1981, p.52,

Derek Lance's *Eleven to Sixteen* was perhaps the best known English attempt to translate such an approach into lesson plans for teachers. Lance describes his approach:

> *There was a time when Religious Education consisted mainly of learning doctrine. Then we saw a move to Salvation History. We saw God's dealings with man as a continuing dialogue stretching over the centuries and most evident in the history of the Jews, the life of Jesus and the continuing life of the Christian Church.*[18]

The aim of this approach, according to Lance, was to enable the pupils 'to look at themselves and their real lives and to examine these in depth so that they may come to see God present there, alive, active, saving now.' The four languages of presenting the Christian message are to be found in these texts: Scripture, doctrine, liturgical celebrations and witness in a Christian lifestyle. In practice weaknesses and limitations in this approach soon became evident. Unlike Lance, a history graduate and an outstanding teacher with a solid grasp of the theological principles underpinning the approach, many of those involved in teaching religion in classrooms were ill equipped to cope with the change in content and approach. Many verged on a sort of fundamentalism at a time when biblical scholarship was making great advances in the Church. Many failed to make the historical approach relevant to twentieth century children. Pupils could easily get the impression that God revealed himself to people a very long time ago without coming to the understanding that Lance advocated of God present, alive and saving in their real lives. Babin expressed it in this way:

> *Speak of grace to some students today and they yawn... Announce Christ the Saviour, Christ the Truth who speaks to the world, and we wonder if we should continue to teach.*[19]

---

18 D. Lance, op. cit.,see also his Till Christ Be Formed (1965) and Eleven to Sixteen, (1960), DLT.
19 A. Babin, Options, Burns & Oates, 1967, p.13

Pupils often found stories of Abraham, Isaac and Jacob as dull as any catechism text. Many teachers used the Bible as a textbook without making necessary adaptations to the needs and capacities of the pupils. Already in the early sixties Goldman and Loukes, influenced by the cognitive development theories of Piaget, were pointing out the difficulties and dangers in teaching the Bible in this way.[20] Gabriel Moran, an American Catholic religious educationalist, whose work I shall consider later, criticised the kerygmatic approach and maintained that in many ways it did not differ greatly from the more doctrinal stress of previous years. As he saw it, it was still very much a matter of 'a rigid construction of words and ideas imposed upon people from outside their lives...a report from the past to be accepted by men of the present'.[21] This was not the intention of Jungmann although it was present in the practice of a good number of teachers who sought to follow his approach. Warren maintains that a careful reading of Jungmann's work shows that 'he consistently worked from a conviction that the Word of God is meant as a word finding its response in human beings'. There was, Warren says, an experiential, anthropological focus in his writings even if it was not as evolved as the later concern for human experience in the catechetical movement.[22]

International catechetical study weeks

Hofinger initiated six international catechetical study weeks which had considerable influence in spreading the new thinking in the Church. These meetings also influenced the direction of catechetics by providing the opportunity for catechists from different countries to voice their opinions and concerns and to be aware of and question those of others working in the field. These study weeks took place between 1959 and 1968, that is in the years just before Vatican II and the years immediately after the Council. The concern was the presentation of the Christian message in today's world. The focus was, therefore, wider than a concern for children in the context of school. They were specifically considering

---

[20] R. Goldman, Religious Thinking from Childhood to Adolescence (1964), Readiness for Religion (1965), Routledge and Kegan Paul; H. Loukes, Teenage Religion (1961), New Ground in Religious Education (1965), SCM.
[21] G. Moran, God Still Speaks, Burns & Oates, 1967, p.43
[22] Warren op. cit., p.26

catechesis in the context of the missionary activity of the Church. These meetings influenced a number of the bishops and experts who attended the second Vatican Council and they are the source of many present-day trends in catechetics. The first was held in Nijmegan in 1959 and discussed the theme 'Liturgy and the Missions'. The second took place in Eichstatt in 1960 and dealt with the topic 'Catechetics and the Missions'. Many see this study week as a landmark, the high point of the kerygmatic stage because the four languages of presenting the faith were generally accepted and widely used in the Church. We can detect other new features in the understanding of the purpose and methods of catechesis.

> *The catechist does what Christ did and commissioned the Church to do: he or she proclaims the Good News of salvation and helps people to accept it and become disciples who will give witness to it. Catechesis then does more than teach the doctrines of the Church; it wins men and women and children for Christ and after baptism unites them further to Him. All principles and methods of catechising flow from the missionary command of Christ.[23]*

The conclusions of Eichstatt states that the message proclaims that 'God is not merely an idea or a remote and silent being but a living personal God'. The whole of catechesis must be centred on Christ. Catechesis makes Christians aware of their responsibility for the world and the improvement of human life. The Bible is the basis of the Church's proclamation and, thus, also of catechesis. The catechism with its systematic presentation of the faith 'gives the learner spiritual insight into the relationship between the faith and the Christian life and enables him or her to cope with the questions of the day as an articulate Christian'. It calls for adaptation to the life and thought of peoples and an appreciation of their laudable views and customs.

> *Catechists seek to recognise the special character, manner of thought, outlook, customs and culture of their catechumens, Beginning at the point from which the catechumen can follow, the catechist instructs according to the psychology of age groups, sex, and special circumstances.[24]*

[23] ibid. p.43
[24] ibid. p.38

Many of these themes would be further developed in later conferences and in the work of others engaged in catechesis and religious education. The East Asian study week was held in Bangkok in 1962, the Pan-African week in Katigondo in 1964. In these weeks a certain unease with regard to the kerygmatic approach was beginning to be expressed by some. Concerns were expressed about the need to adapt and accommodate the message to different cultural settings and human needs and aspirations. The fifth and sixth meetings in Manila in 1967 and in Medellin in 1968 would continue this critique and lead into the next phase of the catechetical movement – the anthropological or experiential stage. This development will be discussed in the next chapter.

Assessing the kerygmatic movement

In assessing the kerygmatic movement, Rummery considers that, in hindsight, it can be seen that many of the changes brought about by the second Vatican Council 'were possible mainly because of the deepening began by the kerygmatic movement and the questions to which it led'.[25] He enumerates some long-term influences of the movement. The first was the new attitude to the use of the vernacular bible. This he sees as being especially significant in fostering ecumenism. Secondly, he mentions the broadening of understanding of catechesis no longer conceived simply as 'instruction prior to the reception of first sacraments and an explanation and memorisation of basic doctrine over the years of schooling'. Catechists came 'to a wider appreciation of the relevance of religious belief and practice in life and of the importance of the support of a believing community in liturgical celebration and social action'. There was no longer an almost exclusive stress on post-Reformation polemics. Finally, he considers that the German, Australian and other national catechisms made possible the transition from the post-Trent model to one more suited to the contemporary situation.

While appreciating these and other aspects of the kerygmatic movement, some were nonetheless critical of some features of the movement. Among these is the criticism highlighted by O'Hare when he speaks of a danger-

---

[25] R. M. Rummery, Catechesis and Religious Education in a Pluralist Society, E. J. Dwyer, 1975, p.16

ous dichotomy between proclamation of the Good News (kerygma) and theology (doctrine). He expresses a concern that catechists of this school, while arguing against an arid intellectualism, might in fact take up an anti-intellectual stance. This might be implied from some of the passages in which Jungmann distinguishes the kerygma from Christian doctrine. O'Hare suggests that there is the danger that having been 'disabused of religious education which is dogmatic, excessively verbal and rationalistic', it might be 'replaced by religious education which is incipiently anti-intellectual and sentimental'.[26]

Wrenn, who is highly critical of many aspects of the 'new catechetics', expresses appreciation for the work of Jungmann and Hofinger. He sees the fundamental principles of the kerygmatic approach as 'a definite contribution to the teaching of religion'. He acknowledges that some of these principles 'were warmly embraced and adopted by the magisterium of the Church'. Nonetheless, he expresses strong regret that one of the principal motivations for Jungmann's approach seemed to be the 'apparent conviction that all the catechesis that had come before him was lamentably deficient'. Wrenn, who is very much in favour of a strongly doctrinal emphasis, laments this critical attitude to the Church's customary catechesis and what he sees as a 'disdain' for the orthodox interpretation of certain doctrines and proper teaching methods. He praises the trail blazed by the Eichstatt study week but he is of the opinion that the study weeks that followed did not continue on that trail and so had unfortunate, not to say disastrous, consequences for the theory and practice of catechesis and religious education. The remaining four study weeks, according to Wrenn, introduced 'a troublesome new element': the notion of 'adapting' the faith that would lead to a stress on the human rather the divine, on social justice over doctrine. The result was, in his view, that catechesis and religious education got 'sidetracked into things that, however important in themselves, are not in fact the primary aim of catechesis'.[27] This view appears to overlook the fact that Eichstatt did more than endorse the kerygmatic principle of the four languages of presenting the Christian message and that reports of the study week had already introduced some of this thinking which would be further developed later.

---

[26] P. O'Hare, Religious Education: Neo-Orthodox Influence and Empirical Corrective', Religious Education, 76, 6, p.633. Scholar Press, Atlanta.
[27] M. J. Wrenn, op. cit., pp.91-94.

Conclusion

In the first half of the twentieth century catechists began to put emphasis not only on what should be taught, instruction in the doctrines of the Church, but also on how children and adults learn, on educational processes and methods. While the catechism was recognised as a summary of Christian doctrine, questions were raised about how it should be used in classrooms with children of different ages. The catechism provided the content; the teacher and catechist had to provide suitable methods which would encourage learning and understanding in the light of educational theory. Jungmann and others returned to the question of what should be taught, the proclamation of the Good News of Jesus Christ. In this they found the catechism to be inadequate with its stress on the cognitive, on the learning of doctrines, often without appreciation of their significance within God's wonderful plan of salvation. Many catechists and teachers were enthused by the teachings of Jungmann, Hofinger and the directives of the first catechetical study weeks. However, by the late fifties questions were being asked not only about the content and presentation of the Christian message but also about the readiness of people in different situations and cultures to receive it, accept it and make it their own. At the same time others were expressing criticism and concern along the lines set out by Wrenn. All of this is part of the next stage or phase in the story of the theory and practice of catechesis and religious education in the Catholic Church.

Chapter Four

Attention to People, Situations and Cultures

The Work of renewal in religious education among Roman Catholics has been under way since the turn of the century. It is part of the response to a felt need among many leaders for a more effective catechesis and in part a result of socio-economic and theological developments which conspired to bring about radical changes in the Church.[1]

Just as the proclamation of the Word was the dominant characteristic of the second phase of the modern catechetical movement, the interpretation of experience is the distinguishing feature of the third phase.[2]

The next stage of the catechetical journey is generally described as the 'anthropological' stage, 'anthropos' being the Greek word for human being. Those who belonged to this school of thinking stressed that the catechetical focus should not only be on the Word proclaimed, the core of the Christian message, but also on the persons being addressed in specific and diverse situations. Elements of this approach were already present in the writings of Jungmann and others. These would be further developed especially under the influence of those working in the so-called missionary countries where, for the most part, those who were being addressed were not Christians. Others would claim that many parts of Europe should be considered missionary territory since many of the baptised had not undergone any real conversion or were greatly affected by the secularised society in which they lived. It was important, they argued, that consideration be given to the legitimate needs and aspirations of people and that catechists seek to understand the environment in which the people lived. Attention should be given not only to the seed to be planted, but also to the soil in which it was to be planted. Work had to be done

---

[1] B. Marthaler, 'The Modern Catechetical Movement in Roman Catholicism: Issues and Personalities', Warren op. cit., p.275   [2] ibid. p.282

in preparing the soil to receive the seed if it were to grow and blossom. The *General Directory of Catechesis*, published in 1997 in the aftermath of the *Catechism of the Catholic Church*, takes up this point. As I have already mentioned in the preface, the Directory states in the introduction that its purpose 'is to foster in pastors and catechists a greater consciousness of the necessity to keep in mind the field in which the seed is sown'.[3] The 1997 Directory acknowledges this is a necessary but difficult and delicate task.

> *Regarding the differences between cultures in the service of the faith, it is difficult to know how to transmit the Gospel within the cultural horizons of the peoples to whom it is proclaimed, in such a way that it can be really received as Good News for the lives of people and of society.*

Using the analogy of the parable of the Sower the Directory continues:

> *Having tested the ground, the Sower sends out his workers to proclaim the Gospel through all the world and to that end shares with them the power of his Spirit. At the same time he shows them how to read the signs of the times and asks of them that special preparation which is necessary to carry out the sowing.*[4]

The attempts to undertake this special preparation which is necessary in the context of the demands of the varied and rapidly changing situations in the Church and society is one of the major concerns in catechesis and religious education today. At the same time, it is one of the main areas of tension and of controversy that is still very much with us at the end of the century and the beginning of the new. It has been a fairly constant feature of this pastoral ministry throughout the history of the Church.

---

3 GDC, n.14
4 ibid. n.31

The French catechetical school

Many French and German catechetical scholars upheld the tenets of the kerygmatic approach. Within this general thrust the German school tended to lay great stress on the historical, biblical and liturgical dimensions. The French, on the other hand, maintained strongly that the religious lesson should not simply be a lesson in biblical history. Influenced by the empirical research of Piaget and others, the French attached great importance to the need for catechists to take account of the psychological development of the person and the social conditioning effect of the environment on the person. The French catechist Canon Colomb wrote a three volume catechism, *Catechisme progressif*, in which he presented the subject matter according to the age and capacity of the child, not according to the logic of a theological system.[5] Based on his opinion concerning the capacity for understanding concepts of the younger child, Colomb suggested that certain Christian doctrines which he considered difficult for them – original sin, the divinity of Christ among others – should not be included in the texts for this age group. They should be introduced at a later age. This view was opposed by many and in 1957 the French Episcopal Commission on religious teaching issued a statement which asked that corrections be made in the texts and that these doctrines be introduced at an early age and taught more explicitly and with fuller explanations later. According to the statement of the commission, very young children should be taught 'in a global way at least' these fundamental truths. The commission also stated that the term *Catechisme progressif* should not be used. They did not condemn outright the approach of Colomb but sought to 'assist in avoiding certain dangers'.[6] Barker describes Colomb as 'a pathfinder for anthropological catechesis'.[7] Colomb introduced the notion of the 'double fidelity': fidelity to the Word of God and fidelity to people and their situations. Catechists had to look to both these essential features of proclaiming the Good News. The phrase 'double fidelity' and what it stands for will be taken up by others and will feature in later official Church documents. While

5 J. Colomb. Catechisme progressif, Emmanuelle Vitte, 1950, published in three volumes with a teacher's book.
6 See G. Dulcuve, 'The Catechetical Movement in France', Lumen Vitae, 12, 4, 1957, pp.671-702
7 K. Barker, Religious Education, Catechesis and Freedom, Religious Education Press, Alabama, 1981, p.57

Colomb and others were drawing attention to the issue of psychological development, others of the French school were concentrating on the social factors which influence persons, including the way they appreciate, understand and try to live the Christian faith. Many looked upon France in the technological age of the postwar years as a de-christianised country. Christian faith could no longer be presumed even in those who had been baptised. Many were nominally Christian, if Christian at all. Their Christian faith lacked maturity. There was no commitment in life or practice. France, in the opinion of some, could be considered mission territory every bit as much as some countries of Asia or Africa. In 1950 Godin and Daniel wrote their book entitled *La France, pays de mission?*

In 1946 Lumen Vitae, an international institute of pastoral catechetics opened in Brussels. The institute published a catechetical periodical with the same name *Lumen Vitae*. The institute and the periodical had a profound influence on the theory and practice of catechesis. Till recently the periodical was also published in English. Pierre-Andre Liege lectured in the institute and wrote many articles for the periodical. Liege thought that the Gospel was falling on deaf ears and argued that it was necessary to analyse why this was so. He identified two sets of obstacles: first, what he called poor or bad dispositions arising from apathy, boredom and prejudice, and second, inhuman social and cultural conditions. In his opinion, if catechists were to be effective, it was necessary to tackle and overcome these obstacles. It was not enough, he thought, to plant the seed of God's word, the soil in which it was to be planted had to be cared for and prepared. In this context he coined the term 'pre-evangelisation'. By this he meant that catechists must make contact with people in these social, cultural situations, come to understand their attitudes and questions from within the situation. Nebreda described 'pre-evangelisation' as 'preparing people so that the kerygma may have meaning in this milieu and for that individual'.[8] The kerygma could not be proclaimed cold, an initial period of acclimatisation and preparation was needed and to achieve this catechists had to be sensitive to the conditions in which people found themselves. This was a necessary initial stage in the catechetical process. In his

---

[8] A. Nebreda, Kerygma in Crisis?, Loyola University Press, 1965, p.46

writings Liege links yet distinguishes evangelisation and catechesis: 'two essential functions of the ministry of the Word'. He urges that care must be taken not to confuse opposition with distinction: 'there are not two kinds of faith nor two successive stages of faith – the stage of conversion, the stage of doctrinal belief – but two dialectical elements of Christian faith, one living reality.'[9] Much of this thinking will be developed and find a place in catechetical documents after Vatican II.

Nebreda, a student of Liege and later Director of the East Asian Institute after Hofinger, developed the concept of 'pre-evangelisation' and the anthropocentric or experiential direction that it took. In 1965 he wrote the book *Kerygma in Crisis?* In which he argued that before proclaiming the Gospel message it was necessary to establish true dialogue with people who were 'shut in by cultural prejudices, sociological ties and psychological patterns'.[10] In outlining the programme of studies in the Manila institute he spoke of the need for pre-evangelisation which starts by 'taking man as he is and where he is, makes human dialogue possible and awakens a sense of God'. As a consequence of this view, he considered it an urgent task of catechists to undertake 'serious research into the socio-psychological networks of the respective culture or group or individual'. The declared aim of the Manila institute under his leadership was 'to render missionaries, lay and religious, capable of setting up an intelligent dialogue with the Asiatic community today'.[11] Speaking of the catechesis of young people in the Christian countries of Europe and North America, he talked of 'pre-catechesis': catechists should take account of the world of pluralism – ideological and religious; the power of the media; and reaction to poor teaching already received. In this context he also spoke of the 'double fidelity'.

More international study weeks

Missionaries in many of the developing countries began to claim that it was not enough simply to proclaim the Gospel message to people. Like the catechists of the French school, they considered that some basic preparatory work had to be done. Many missionaries became con-

---

[9] P.A. Liege, 'The Ministry of the Word', Warren (ed), op. cit., p.321
[10] Nebreda, op. cit., p.46
[11] A Nebreda, 'Studies Program of the East Asian Pastoral Institute', Lumen Vitae, 21,4,1966, p.573

scious of the fact that after many years of missionary effort there were often only external signs of Christianity such as church buildings, schools, hospitals, but very little real, deep Christian faith. Often, it seemed, missionaries brought the Christian faith wedded to and expressed in the cultural and national customs of the European countries from which the missionaries came. There was need for the missionaries to appreciate, respect and understand the cultures of Asia and Africa if they ever hoped to set up dialogue and speak of the Christian message in a way that might make sense to the people of different cultural outlooks.

Bangkok

During the discussions at the Bangkok study week (1962) catechists began to speak more forcefully of the need for adaptation and called for the use of 'analogies, images and forms of expression familiar to peoples of given regions and cultures'. Bangkok took up the theme of pre-evangelisation. Reporting on the study week Nebreda stated:

> *The guiding principle of pre-evangelisation is anthropological because we must start with the individual as he or she is. The way must be prepared in order that a person be able to understand the message not as a mere presentation of words which make sense to us but as a challenge by words which make sense to him or her. This follows from the very essence of the message, which demands that we speak to not at a person'.*[12]

Catechists at Bangkok identified three distinct stages in the catechetical process with those not yet of the Christian faith: pre-evangelisation, evangelisation (these two phases were the pre-catechumenate), then followed catechesis proper in the catechumenate phase. The aims of pre-evangelisation were to arouse interest, to prepare the ground for dialogue, to bridge the gap for the kerygma, and to arouse hope and the sense of God. The means of achieving this were patience, love, understanding and respect for people as they are. On the part of the catechist personal contact and Christian witness should be their priorities. In the evangelisation phase those taking part were faced with the challenge of the Christian message, of God's Revelation in Christ. They were gradually introduced

---

[12] A. Nebreda, 'East Asian Study Week on Mission Catechetics: 1962', Warren op. cit., p.52

to the core of that message. The aim of this phase was to arouse an internal spiritual change in a person whereby he or she could accept Christ as Lord. Catechists could recognise conversion by such signs as repentance, prayer, an eagerness to meet Christ, a Christian life-style. In the catechesis proper fuller instruction would be given by means of 'a detailed development of God's message, always focused on the core'. A clear distinction was made between the catechism to be used by the catechumen and the guide for catechists. The guide would contain suggestions, principles and directives for all three stages. The catechism would not be used during the pre-evangelisation period: 'since the process followed during this period would depend essentially on persons and circumstances – taking people as they are – a catechism cannot have the content of a pre-evangelisation'.[13] The catechism given to the catechumen 'should begin with a recapitulation of the kerygma'. Some of the features and language of the ancient catechumenate can be seen in texts of the Bangkok study week.

In his survey of the six international study weeks Erdozain speaks of the foundations of pre-evangelisation. He poses the question 'what is one to think of this new orientation?' and asks whether it is fear of failure or a concession to psychological trends. Certainly, he says, 'it is not some pastoral strategy designed to attract approbation from one's contemporaries'.

The reasons go much deeper. It is an admonition to remain faithful: a) to the very manner in which the Master and the first apostles presented the Christian message, b) to the Church's tradition as evidenced in the history of catechetics, and c) to the very nature of the Christian message.

He sees evidence of this approach in the fact that there are four Gospels 'regarded as four interpretations and theological elaborations of the message with an eye to the public for which they were intended'. He also finds signs of it in the preaching of Paul, especially in his address before the Areopagus in Athens.[14]

---

[13] ibid. p.48
[14] Erdozain, op. cit., p.94

Katigondo

The Pan-African study week held in Katigondo, Uganda, in 1964 continued this direction in the process of educating people to and in the faith. It called for 'a faith so deep that it will overflow into every sphere of personal and social life' and 'seek out whatever is of value in African traditional belief and endeavour to give it a Christian fulfilment'. To this end great stress was put on the formation of adult catechumens and adult Christians.[15] Participants warned against the wrong use of the scholastic method while maintaining that its qualities of clarity and precision should be retained. Theology in seminaries should be taught in a way that will prepare priests to proclaim the Good News of Christ 'in a living and concrete manner and in harmony with the thinking and feeling of the peoples of Africa'. The fourth final resolution of the study week states: 'let them (priests) be made well aware of the problems of our day, be brought up-to-date on the progress made in pedagogy and psychology, and learn how to draw profit from this for their ministry'. They insisted that there was 'the absolute need for Scripture in the vernacular'. To this end they encouraged working with Protestant authorities in order to publish the Old and New Testaments 'in versions adequate, both exegetically and linguistically.'[16] The Constitution on the Liturgy promulgated by Vatican II had been published by the time of the gathering in Katigondo. There was considerable discussion on the necessity of adapting liturgical rites and symbols to the African culture.

Manila

When catechists next gathered for a study week in Manila (1967) the Vatican Council had just finished and the anthropological, experiential thrust was more radical. The council had, in the view of many, encouraged this approach. A more politically orientated theology was urging solidarity with the poor and underprivileged. There was a renewed commitment to safeguarding human values and dignity. The Church, it was said, should take up a more active struggle for real and deep reform in developing countries as distinct from a somewhat paternalistic dispensing of social services. This, it was claimed, left unjust situations unchanged and unchallenged: 'through commitment to human values,

---

[15] R. Ledogan, Katigondo, Presenting the Christian Message to Africa, Geoff Chapman, 1965, p.126
[16] 'Final Resolutions: Pan-African catechetical Study Week: 1964', Warren op. cit., pp.54-56.

especially the struggle for social reform, Christians must bear witness to their spirit of loving service'. A remarkable feature of this study week was the emphasis put on respect and appreciation for other religions: 'it is particularly necessary to have a theology of the plurality of religions and of the mission of the Church in this context'. In the context of Asia and Africa in particular, this was and is understandable and largely accepted. However, it is now becoming an issue not only in Asia and Africa but also in many parts of Europe, including our British towns and cities. A good deal of heated discussion goes on about the actual or possible presence of pupils of other faiths in our Catholic schools. There is also debate about the study of other faiths in the religious curriculum in Catholic schools. A consultation paper has recently been prepared and distributed by the Bishops' Conference on this subject, *Catholic Schools and Other Faiths (1997)*. I shall touch on this in the second part of this book. Participants at Manila also expressed regret that the Church 'appeared glaringly foreign in her way of life, her liturgy, architecture, and even her mentality' to many of the people in the so-called missionary and developing countries of the world.[17]

Such radical thinking seemed to verge on the dangerous to many in the Church. Again Wrenn expresses some of this thinking in his forthright criticisms. In the work of Katigondo and Manila he sees signs of 'the telltale corrosive criticisms of the Church as she actually is'. He expresses his opinion, which no doubt articulates the thinking of a good number within the Church:

> *The struggle for social justice would soon far outweigh in importance any such thing as a doctrine of faith in the minds of many catechetical theorists. Social justice, as such, is not the point of catechesis but rather the whole content of the faith is. By the time the sixth of the international catechetical study weeks came about in Medellin the thrust to change the world by means of the new catechesis rather than (so much more modestly) merely being content to focus on trying to hand on the faith effectively was long since in full swing.[18]*

---

17 'Implications of Vatican II for the Mission in Asia', a report of discussion groups, Warren op. cit., pp.57-64
18 Wrenn op. cit., p.94

Others would question and wish to discuss further the understanding of 'the faith' which underpins such criticism and condemnation. In the anthropological, existential approach, as in the others, there are those enthusiasts who only partially understand the theological and educational thinking behind it and apply it in some impoverished, even dangerous fashion. As always, some so-called disciples of the more outstanding teachers do fail to integrate it into a more balanced and effective catechesis or religious education. There are, nonetheless, important lessons that we can learn from aspects of this approach as we realise more clearly today that much of our work in catechesis and religious education is a matter of educating many people **to** the faith, not yet **in** the faith. The 1997 Directory will take up some of these key themes.

Medellin

This more radical trend was further confirmed in the conclusions of the study week held in Medellin, Columbia (1968). Within the context of theology in Latin America a political stress became very clear. 'Political' not in the sense of allegiance to any particular political party or ideology, but in the broad sense of awareness of the general context in which human life unfolds and develops and of the influences brought to bear on human beings in their socio-economic situations. It is intended as a reminder that the Gospel confronts not only the individual but also social structures and institutions. Catechists gathered at Medellin were conscious of the great changes taking place in Latin America and of the effect that these had on the life of the people. Those present urged that pluralism within catechetical work should be seen as necessary and they declared 'a universal catechism of a monolithic type to be impossible'. Consideration of human situation is seen an essential aspect of understanding the process of Revelation.

Contemporary catechesis, in agreement with a more adequate theology of Revelation, recognises in historical situations and in authentic human aspirations the first sign to which we must be attentive in order to discover the plan of God for men and women today. Such situations are an indispensable part of the content of catechesis.[19]

---

[19] 'General Conclusions of the Medellin International Study Week: 1968', Warren op. cit., p.68

The 'sign' of human experience, the historical situation, is a source along with the sources set out in the kerygmatic approach – Scripture, Church teaching, liturgy and the witness of a Christian life. Many would question whether human experience can be designated as 'the first sign'. Still, in the opinion of those taking part in the discussions at Medellin, without appreciation of the sign that is 'historical situations and human aspirations', the other sources can be rendered meaningless to people today. This opens up the question of how Revelation and Christian faith are theologically understood which is still a major issue in the theory and practice of catechesis.

Moran and the experiential approach in schools

By the late sixties and early seventies the anthropological, experiential approach in catechetics began to influence the way teachers taught religion in Catholic schools. Both in the United States and in Britain it was mainly the early works of Gabriel Moran – *Theology of Revelation* and *God Still Speaks* in particular – that encouraged this development. Moran was critical of the kerygmatic understanding of 'salvation history' claiming that it could easily give the impression that there was a 'sacred history' that stood apart from and was irrelevant to the present history of Christians. It was his opinion that 'catechesis is concerned with the understanding of God's revelation now taking place in the student's life'.[20]

Teaching of religion begins with the student's own history within his community. The student will not adequately understand that history until he sees it as part of God's cosmic dealing with the people of Israel, the humanity of Jesus Christ, the Christian community, and all mankind. Nevertheless, he cannot be attentive to the history of the world, without first discovering the people and events in his own history. It is here that God is dimly but truly confronting him, holding out the communion of knowledge that we call revelation.[21]

20 G. Moran, God Still Speaks, Burns & Oates, 1967, p.97
21 G. Moran, Vision and Tactics, Burns & Oates, 1968, p.46

He considered absurd and dangerous the reaction of some in the kerygmatic school against catechesis that was 'too intellectual and too concerned with knowledge and understanding'. This could lead to the undervaluing of the intellectual and rational dimension that is an essential feature of all catechesis. He asserted that 'the one way in which religion was almost never taught has been by appealing to children's intelligence'. He declared himself in favour of a total Christian formation but he doubted that schools could bring this about. They could make 'a small but valuable contribution'.[22] He maintained that education could not be equated with schooling. It was a lifelong process of growth and development. The religious education of adults was of prime importance. He was critical of the term 'pre-evangelisation' and maintained that it was simplistic to apply the term in the same way to missionary work in Asia, Africa or elsewhere, and to the work of teachers in Catholic schools in North America. There were 'vast differences'.

> *In many respects the problems are exactly the opposite, that is, we suffer not from a lack of acquaintance with and scarcity of relationships with Christianity, but from an over-saturation (without any accompanying assimilation) of Christian ideas and words. It is not that our students have never heard of Christian revelation; many are sick to death of hearing about it.*[23]

Perhaps nearly forty years on, we may wonder if it is still true that pupils are sick to death of hearing about Christianity. We may rather wonder whether, in their family lives and in the multi-media world in which they live, many pupils in our schools or young people in catechetical programmes have heard or experienced much of Christianity. Pope John Paul II is keenly aware of this situation and it is because of this that he frequently calls for 'new evangelisation'. In chapter eleven I shall examine how the 1997 Directory reflects on this situation and offers some general pastoral guidelines.

In Moran's conception of revelation most people 'have begun to discover the God of Jesus Christ in the love of a human being, in the joyful face

---

[22] ibid. p.44
[23] Moran, God Still Speaks, p.143

of a believer, and in the secret longings of their own heart'. Scripture and Christian teaching – 'the verbal deliverance of the message' – help clarify and 'bring into explicit and reflexive consciousness the knowledge of the Christian God'.[24] As a consequence of this view, Moran considered dialogue and discussion to be the heart of the religious lesson. In his later works Moran shows evidence of a more radical break with the kerygmatic understanding of revelation and catechesis. Mary Boys sees in the works of Moran an analogy with the development of thinking in the international study weeks. She identifies a shift from the kerygmatic to an anthropocentric catechesis which acknowledges and respects the central place of human experience and which goes on to develop a clear political dimension which looks beyond the experience of the individual to the wider needs of society.[25] In these later works he became increasingly critical of catechesis which was, he thought, too Church-centred and an intramural activity. Marthaler voices the generally held opinion that Moran had 'unrivalled influence on catechesis in the United States'. His influence was also significant in Britain.

Developments in education

Educational and cultural developments besides, the developments in theology helped bring about the move from kerygmatic to the experiential in catechesis. That does not imply that the kerygmatic approach was completely abandoned. Describing the influences that brought about these changes, Duckworth puts as the strongest among them the changing ways in which education is understood. For her, 'there is no longer a neat corpus of knowledge, the possession of which makes a person at home in the world'. Duckworth, along with Exeler and others, perceived a certain affinity between the new attitudes in education generally and in the ways of understanding catechesis ('education in faith') and religious education. Faith, she says, since it is concerned with some kind of knowledge of God, 'must be a continual quest' and, therefore, 'methods of education which foster a spirit of inquiry are eminently proper'. Faith for Duckworth is no longer understood 'as a static something, given at bap-

---

24 ibid. p.145
25 M. Boys, Biblical Interpretation in Religious Education, Religious Education Press, 1980, p.153

tism, sustained by authority, threatened by inquiry, undermined by doubt, characterised by clarity, productive of certainty'. Faith is rather conceived 'as a free and personal act, fostered by community, growing through ceaseless inquiry, seeming to need the tension of doubt for its development, walking in uncertainty, open to infinity'.[26] There are features here of the present debate about the nature and purpose of religious education as an area of the curriculum in our Catholic schools.

Influenced by the writings of Moran in the United States, of Babin and Van Caster in Europe, by the research of Goldman and the appeal of Loukes for 'more reality in school', many Catholic teachers eagerly took up the existential approach in their religious lessons. Duckworth, in lectures to students of Corpus Christi College, suggested three stages in this approach:

1. sharing experience by helping the pupils, by means of a variety of methods, to explore and understand their experience;
2. deepening and widening the experience by stimulating reflection and enabling pupils to correlate their experience with the experience of others through discussion, literature and the media so that the universality as well as the uniqueness is recognised;
3. seeing and appreciating such experience in the context of the total Christian experience – the witness of the teacher, the history of Israel, the event of Jesus Christ, the Christian tradition and the traditions of other faiths.[27]

Duckworth herself acknowledged, however, that many teachers did not fully understand what they were about and 'were justly criticised for floundering in activities which were really an escape from the increasingly arduous and ungrateful task of teaching religion'. It has to be admitted that many lessons were little more than endless, aimless, supposedly topical discussions. In some cases there was the search for 'relevance' which, in fact, often trivialised both human experience and Christian doctrines. At is best, this approach should lead not to the search for some sort of trendy relevance but for the deeper significance of human life in the light of our Christian beliefs. In *Cornerstone*, Kevin Nichols refers to this

[26] Duckworth op. cit., pp.382-385.
[27] R. Duckworth, unpublished notes given to student of Corpus Christi College, October 1968.

approach and he points out that it was often labelled 'humanistic'. He maintains that 'some of its expressions do seem to add up to humanism with a vague aura of divinity'.[28] Such criticisms are still made by some in the Church concerning more recent catechetical and religious education resources and of the way they are taught. Wrenn makes the point in a strong, rather black and white judgement.

> *Basically, what occurred in catechesis was a shift from God to man; from supernatural faith to more human concerns; from proclaiming the Good News of salvation in Jesus Christ and everything that follows from that to espousing a purely human kind of effort featuring a struggling humanity trying to save itself by political means from opposition and injustice.[29]*

Conclusion

As with all the developments in catechetics and religious education over the years we must study the implications carefully and attempt to recognise and appreciate what was of value at that particular time and what may be of value today, while recognising also the limitations and weaknesses inherent any such developments. In this way we can learn from what has gone before and we can build on the best of the past as we continue the journey into the new century. It is clear, however, that many Catholics consider the experiential dimension of the 'new catechetics' to be dangerous, even erroneous, little concerned with Christian tradition expressed in Scripture and the teaching of the Church. Others maintain that in putting stress on the experiential dimension they are being faithful to the tradition which has from the beginning sought to bring the Good News to people of different times and situations. Legitimate adaptation is necessary if the tradition is to continue and develop rather than turn itself into a museum piece. It is recognised that it is a risky enterprise, but one that cannot be avoided if God is to be experienced as still speaking to peo-

---

[28] K. Nichols, Cornerstone, St. Paul Publ., 1978, p.66
[29] Wrenn, op. cit., p.96

ple today. Controversy seems inevitable and may well indeed be healthy for the Church, even if painful for those involved. Debate and argument will continue throughout the century. The 1997 *General Directory of Catechesis* asks us to look to the field in which the seed is sown. It reminds us that the Sower sends us out to proclaim the Gospel, but, at the same time, asks us to read the signs of the times and undertake the preparation which is necessary to carry out the sowing. Van Caster speaks of revelation as 'an interpersonal relationship: it is God who speaks to us'. This calls for that 'double fidelity':

> *Fidelity to God's word also concerns the word insofar as it is addressed to man. It comprises, therefore, fidelity to man insofar as he is a partner in the dialogue with God. The first law of catechesis is to help man receive God's word in faith.[30]*

It seems clear that attention to people, their situations and cultures, must be a feature of sound catechesis and religious education although how that is done is open to discussion and debate.

[30] M. Van Caster, The Structure of Catechetics, Herder & Herder, 1965, p.110

Chapter Five

Vatican II and The General Catechetical Directory

Our duty is to dedicate ourselves with an earnest will and without fear to that work which our era demands of us, thus pursuing the path which the Church has followed for 20 centuries.[1]

In the last quarter of the twentieth century Roman Catholics have a broader and more positive view of the task of catechesis than they had in the period immediately before and after the Council of Trent.[2]

In the 1960's the Roman Catholic Church witnessed a veritable whirlwind of change. Ideas and opinions that had previously been propounded by theologians and experts in various fields were now on the Council agenda being carefully deliberated by the world's bishops and their theological experts or consultants and reported and discussed in the media. The essentially pastoral orientation of the second Vatican Council was in marked contrast to that of most previous councils. Councils were normally summoned to face some particular problem and address a specific issue. They were more concerned with important and often controversial points of doctrine or aspects of religious discipline. John XXIII called the council for the purpose of sensitising the Church to the world of the twentieth century. He termed it 'aggiornamento', updating. During and after the council a great deal of pent-up energy was released with many Catholics truly sensing the excitement of renewal, while others felt threatened and disorientated by what they saw as the forced entry of the world into the sacred fortress of the Church. During this period the catechetical movement took great strides mainly due to the spirit of research and renewal unleashed in preparation for, and in the aftermath of, the council and by the international study weeks. This period also witnessed a good deal of controversy, at times bitter and acrimonious, between different groups within the Church in England

---

[1] Pope John XXIII at the opening of the Vatican Council quoted by John Paul II, *Catechism of the Catholic Church*, p.2
[2] M. C. Boyce, 'Evaluation of Catechesis from the Reformation to the Present', Westerhoff & Edwards op. cit., p.232

and Wales and in other countries. It was particularly marked in the late sixties and early seventies.

The spirit of the Council

The second Vatican Council (1962-65) did not issue a specific document on catechesis although certain features of the catechetical task within the Church are dealt with in several of the documents of the council. Many catechists maintain that it was the spirit and general approach of the council rather than any specific text that had the most effect on the theory and practice of catechesis. Nebreda, for example, considers that the *Pastoral Constitution on the Church in the Modern World* canonised the anthropological, experiential approach and provided an outstanding example of how to set about it. The constitution is openly pastoral and undertakes to dialogue with all human beings; it seeks to illuminate the mystery of human life in the light of Christ and to co-operate with all people of goodwill in seeking solutions to the great problems and issues of the contemporary world. The tone and terms of the opening lines of the constitution in a sense summarise the purpose and approach of the constitution.

The joys and hopes, the grief and anguish of the people of our time, especially those who are poor or afflicted, are the joys and hopes, grief and anguish of the followers of Christ as well. Nothing that is genuinely human fails to find an echo in their hearts. For theirs is a community of people united in Christ and guided by the Holy Spirit in their pilgrimage towards the Father's kingdom, bearers of a message of salvation for all humanity. That is why they cherish a feeling of deep solidarity with the human race and its history.[3]

The Church is viewed not as standing aloof, apart from the human condition, defending Truth and dispensing Grace, but, rather, as universal sacrament: sign and instrument of union with God and unity among people. It is described as pilgrim and servant. This mentality, many claimed, should be the hallmark of the catechist and all catechetical activity.

[3] Vatican II, **Constitution on the Church in the Modern World,** n.1, A Flannery, **Vatican Council II,** Dominican Publications, 1996.

The option for a directory rather than a catechism

In the preparatory stages of the council many bishops and others sent in proposals concerning catechesis as they did for many other areas which the council would consider. Some suggested that the council should take up and complete the work of Vatican I on a catechism for children. There were various suggestions for some kind of universal catechism, each with a different emphasis or with a different readership in mind. Bishop Lacointe of Beauvais put forward the argument that a single catechism for the whole Church was not possible or at least not proper. Literal uniformity was not what was required. In his view it would be better to produce directives or guidelines which would assist in the catechesis of different groups in the Church. Between 1961 and 1962 several preparatory commissions drew up draft schemas which dealt with aspects of catechesis. The commission for the Eastern Churches expressed concern about the growing diversity throughout the world and called for a more uniform teaching and learning of Christian doctrine. They favoured a compendium or single catechism for the universal Church. They also wished that due respect be paid to the oriental rites. Another commission that was dealing with questions of discipline for the clergy and laity was asked to draw up plans for a new catechism that would include liturgy, Church history and social teaching. This commission concluded that a single catechism for the universal Church was not feasible because conditions differ so greatly from country to country, from individual to individual. While reaching that conclusion, the commission nonetheless was opposed to the proliferation of catechisms with each diocese writing its own. They accepted Lacointe's idea of a catechetical directory that would establish general rules and norms which would have to be observed in compiling individual catechisms. Application of these directives and norms would be left to the episcopal conferences. A third commission which was dealing with the matter of the sacraments asked that, just as catechetical courses were required for the reception of the sacraments of baptism and confirmation, there should also be catechesis for those preparing for marriage which should include examination about Christian doctrine.

It was left to the central commission to co-ordinate the work of all the preparatory commissions. It was decided that various aspects of catechesis would be incorporated into a new schema *'On the Care of Souls'*. The first part dealt with the pastoral office of bishops and the second considered specific pastoral issues, including catechesis. The second part of the new schema brought together and reworked the points mentioned in the suggestions from the previous commissions. Again a catechetical directory was preferred to a universal catechism. In a footnote the commission set out for the first time an outline of what the directory should contain. The schema was re-edited several times. While this work was going on, another schema was being prepared and discussed – *'The Bishops and Diocesan Government'*. In the spring of 1964 a completely new schema was written *'The Pastoral Office of Bishops'* which came about by bringing together much of what was contained in the schemas on diocesan government and the care of souls. The decree was finally approved and promulgated on October 28th 1965. It is a wide ranging document which deals with many aspects of the rights and duties of bishops in their relationship with the universal Church and with their own particular churches or dioceses. It also speaks of the ways bishops co-operate for the common good of several churches by means of synods, councils and regional episcopal conferences.

Decree on the bishops' pastoral office

There are several sections of the decree on the Pastoral Office of Bishops that touch on catechetical matters. The decree states that announcing the gospel of Christ is among the chief duties of bishops: 'they should, in the power of the Spirit, summon people to faith or confirm them in a faith already living'.[4] It is important to note that here we have mention of two distinct yet complementary dimensions of the ministries of evangelisation and catechesis: *summoning **to** faith* and *confirming **in** faith*. This is, in my view, a distinction that is generally overlooked in preparing and evaluating various parish or school programmes, whether for the young or for adults. The 'summoning to faith' is frequently seen as applying only to the so-called missionary territories. Often it is too readily assumed that we are engaged in the task of confirming in faith, whereas we may be more realistically involved in summoning people, especially adolescents and young adults, to faith. If we fail to appreciate this fact, we may be frustrated with the outcome of our efforts or be harshly and crudely judged by those who see the task as one of simply confirming 'in faith

---

4 Vatican II, Decree on the Pastoral Office of Bishops, n.12, Abott op. cit.

already living'. The recent *General Directory for Catechesis* (1997) speaks of this and distinguishes basic situations or religious needs that may be present in any group of people with whom we may be involved in our work of catechesis and religious education. Frequently within the same group there may well be some people who are more in need of 'missionary activity'. They are people who have as yet no Christian faith or have 'lost a living sense of faith' as well as a more developed, on-going catechesis for those who 'are fervent in their faith and in Christian living'.[5] There is some resonance here with the distinct stages of pre-evangelisation, evangelisation and catechesis proper which were made by earlier catechetical writers. The Vatican II document reminds bishops that they have the task of overseeing the whole, integral process of educating to and in the faith from initial conversion through the lifelong, gradual process of maturing in the faith. As the prime teachers or educators to and in the faith the bishops are reminded that:

> *Bishops should present Christ's teaching in a manner relevant to the needs of the times, providing a response to those difficulties and problems which people find especially distressing and burdensome. They should safeguard this doctrine, teaching the faithful themselves to defend and spread it.*[6]

Again the twofold duty is underlined: adapting to the needs and situations of people, being sensitive to the problems which most trouble and burden them, and also guarding the purity and integrity of the tradition. It is the duty of the bishop, through those appointed by him, to see that both elements of the task are safeguarded, neither aspect of the task can be ignored or overlooked; they are essential elements of the one task.

In the next section of the document the aims of catechetical training are stated: 'to make people's faith become living, conscious and active, through the light of instruction'. Instruction in doctrine is not an end in itself, it should enable people to lead lives enlightened and enriched by the Christian beliefs and vision of the meaning and purpose of human life. Such training 'should be very carefully imparted, not only to children or adolescents but also to young people and even adults'. Methods used

5 GDC, n.58
6 Pastoral Office of Bishop, n. B, Flannery op. cit.

should be 'suited not only to the matter in hand but also to the character, the ability, the age and the lifestyle of their audience'. Instruction should be based on 'holy scripture, tradition, the liturgy, and on the teaching authority, and life of the Church'.[7] There are echoes here of the four sources or languages of faith as outlined by the kerygmatic school. Bishops are reminded that catechists should be properly trained for their task. They should be acquainted with the doctrine of the Church and have a theoretical and practical knowledge of the laws of psychology and of educational methods. This is a clear statement that both content and method are important and must be integrated in the work of catechesis and religious education. Here, too, it is not a question of either or; they belong together and cannot be separated in any sound education to and in the faith. The final section of the decree prescribes the revision of the Code of Canon Law and the drawing up of various directories concerning the pastoral care of special groups of people in the Church. Among these is a catechetical directory:

> *A special directory should also be compiled concerning the pastoral care of special groups of the faithful according to the various circumstances of the different countries and regions, and also a directory for the catechetical instruction of the Christian people in which the fundamental principles of this instruction and its organisation will be dealt with and the preparation of books relating to it.[8]*

It would take another six years before the Directory was finally approved and published. The delay was in large part due to the process of consultation involving national episcopal conferences.

Documents on missionary activity and education

Certain features of the task of catechesis are touched on in other documents of the council. The Decree on the Missionary Activity of the Church is described by Warren as 'a brilliant treatise on evangelisation'.[9] Dialogue and sharing in cultural and social life are seen to be a necessary part of evangelisation. The decree calls for radical adaptation to various

---

[7] ibid. n.14   [8] ibid. n.44
[9] M. Warren, 'Evangelisation: a Catechetical Concern', Warren (ed), op cit., p.334

cultures: 'the lay faithful belong at one and the same time both to the People of God and to civil society'. Catechesis should prepare them to take up their duties as citizens: they must give expression to their Christian values 'in their own society and culture and in a manner that is in keeping with the traditions of their own land'. They must be familiar with this culture. They must purify and guard it, they must develop it in accordance with present day conditions 'so that the faith of Christ and the life of the Church will not be something foreign to the society in which they live, but will begin to transform and permeate it'.[10] The struggle for human betterment and liberation is an essential aspect of evangelisation: 'they should share in efforts of those people who, in fighting against famine, ignorance and disease, are striving to bring about better living conditions and bring about peace in the world.[11] Work for social justice is a task of Christians and catechesis should educate to this dimension of the faith. The need for true conversion is stressed. Conversion is described as the beginning of a spiritual journey, as a progressive change of outlook and way of life. These should be gradually developed during the time of the catechumenate. The catechumenate is to be introduced. It is viewed as a process 'which is not merely an exposition of dogmatic truths and norms of morality, but a period of formation in the entire Christian life, an apprenticeship of suitable duration, during which the disciples will be joined to Christ as their teacher'.[12] Throughout the decree great stress is placed on the work of lay people in the Church including the work of evangelisation and catechesis. Adequate training for lay people should be provided. The process of Christian initiation through the catechumenate should be taken care of not only by priests but also by the entire community, especially of the sponsors. The task of catechesis is no longer seen as the prerogative of priests and appointed lay teachers, the Christian community is the agent of educating to and in the faith. Different members within the community have different roles and responsibilities – parents, teachers, catechists, priests and bishops. The document's acceptance of lay people in this work is very different from what is said in the 1917 Code of Canon Law where it is seen very much as the preserve of the clergy who only on occasions should permit lay people to instruct children and others.

---

[10] Vatican II, Decree on the Church's Missionary Activity, n.21, Flannery, op. cit.
[11] ibid. n.12
[12] ibid. n.14

The *Declaration on Christian Education* speaks of catechetical training as one of the foremost means by which the Church discharges her educative function. Such training should give clarity and vigour to faith, nourish a life lived in the spirit of Christ and encourage active participation in liturgy and apostolic action. Later Church documents will speak more openly of the distinction and link between catechesis and religious education in the school context. This is the result of discussions that took place in various countries in the years after the council. The council document speaks only of 'catechetical instruction'. Later Vatican documents and studies by others will speak of 'religious instruction' as distinct from, yet complementary to, catechesis. The value of Catholic schools is upheld. The text speaks of several distinct purposes of a Catholic school: creating within the school community an 'atmosphere animated by a spirit of liberty and charity based on the Gospel'. Such an atmosphere will enable pupils to develop as Christians; bringing to all human culture the light of faith. It expresses esteem for schools in the missionary countries 'which contain large numbers of students who are not Catholic'. the council document exhorts the Catholic community to spare no sacrifice in helping Catholic schools to become effective. It urges Catholics to show special concern for the needs of the poor, of those who are deprived of the assistance and affection of a family or of those who do not have the gift of the faith.[13] This is all very much part of the way Catholic schools can and should be part of the Church's mission of evangelisation in the widest sense. It seems to me that this 'missionary' dimension ('summoning to faith') should not be overlooked when planning and judging the catechetical and religious education activity in our schools. I shall discuss these points concerning schools in relation to catechesis and religious education more fully when considering key principles and issues later in part two.

The General Catechetical Directory

The implementation of the council's decision to produce a directory was left to the Congregation for the Clergy. Over the next six years there were several phases of consultation with different groups in the Church. In 1966 a working committee was set up consisting of specialists in the field residing in Rome and lecturing in Roman universities and as

---

[13] Vatican II, Decree on Christian Education, nn.8 & 9

well as lecturers in faculties in other parts of the world. It was their task to draw up a rough draft for consultation. In 1967 a commission of theologians was set up with the task of outlining the principle doctrines which would make up the content of catechesis. Also in 1967 the first synod of bishops after the council took place in Rome. Again some bishops requested a catechism and again there were a variety of emphases and aims among the proposals. Cardinal Seper recalled the desire of the council as set out in the decree on the bishops' pastoral office. Cardinal Villot, prefect of the Congregation for the Clergy, gave a report on work done on the Directory to the bishops at the synod. This was to begin a period of broad consultation with the national and regional bishops' conferences. The cardinal asked for a written memorandum of what should be included in the Directory. To help in this he enumerated a list of twelve questions for their consideration. In May 1968 an international commission of eight experts met in Rome to plan the directory in the light of suggestions and recommendations received. In October of 1968 the work was submitted to a plenary session. Some further suggestions were made and the text was re-edited. In April 1969 a draft text was sent to the bishops' conferences for their reactions. Twenty-seven responded of which twenty-three were generally in favour although some extensive changes were made as a result of the responses of the conferences. The modified text was sent to a special theological commission and was also sent to the Congregation for the Doctrine of Faith. A joint commission of six drew up the final text. Before its publication an appendix was added giving directives for the age of first confession and communion for children. This caused heated debate. *The General Catechetical Directory* was published on Easter Sunday 1971.

It is important to bear in mind that the Directory is an authoritative document requested by the council and that the final text is the result of wide consultation. This is one of its main strengths. However, inherent in this very strength there is, in the view of some, a certain limitation. While it takes into consideration many differing views, the end result is a consensus document. According to Boys it is 'a political statement directed towards building consensus' rather than enunciating 'visionary or creative proposals'.[14] That is hardly what the bishops asked for in the

---

14 M. Boys, 'The Standpoint of Religious Education', Religious Education, 76, 2, 1981, p.132

council. They sought general principles which would guide them in their different situations. The text of the Directory states that it 'is intended for countries which differ greatly in their conditions and pastoral needs', consequently it recognises that 'only common and average conditions can be considered'[15]. The text specifies that each local hierarchy must undertake an analysis of its own religious situation as well as the sociological, cultural and economic conditions which affect the work of evangelisation and catechesis. In the light of what has been said in previous chapters, this must surely be acknowledged as a very considerable step forward in so far as it gives official recognition to the diversity in which we seek a sound unity in catechetical endeavours rather than a bland uniformity. It seems to me that such is the value and limitation of texts that are the result of wide consultation. While they may not be as visionary or creative as some individuals would like, they do delineate an overarching vision which for many in the Church can be challenging. Nonetheless, the limitations of consensus documents are all too clear in this and other directories and synod documents. They tend to overlook or blur differences of opinion. It is the task of experts in the field to take up and tackle these issues in greater depth. In the following section of this chapter I shall focus on the first five parts of the directory which 'provide the basic principles of pastoral theology' which should underpin any sound theory and practice of catechesis and, to some extent, of religious education in Catholic schools.

The call for renewal in the theory and practice of catechesis

In the first part the Directory calls for renewal in a time of sweeping and rapid changes. It begins by stressing the need for catechists to be aware of the main features of change which have repercussion on the way the Christian faith can be presented, understood and lived. The document suggests that in a world of rapid change, growing secularisation and religious indifference, it is not enough simply to harp back to the traditional faith which has little effective influence on people's actual lives. In the opinion of many in the Church it is 'bound too much with ancient and obsolete for-

15 GCD, n.5

mulations and too much tied to Western culture'[16]. A consequence of these developments is the fact that 'the faith of many Christians is strained to a critical point' and 'great numbers are drifting little by little into religious indifference or are in danger of keeping faith without the dynamism that is necessary'[17]. It is in order to address such a 'a period of crisis' that the Directory calls for renewal of catechesis, a renewal which must be more radical than 'eliminating ignorance of doctrine which must be taught' or simply providing 'more frequent catechetical instruction'. Such a remedy is 'altogether unequal to the needs' and people who hold such a simplistic view are partly the cause of the crisis. Catechetical renewal 'has to do with continuing education in faith, not only of children but also for adults'. Another major obstacle to the necessary renewal is to be found in people 'who are inclined to reduce the Gospel message to the consequences it has in men's temporal existence'. The work for peace and justice is a clear demand of the Christian faith however, due witness must be given 'to Jesus Christ…whose mystery must be proclaimed openly and in its entirety to those being evangelised, and must be examined by them'.[18] The text tries to hold the essential dimensions of doctrinal understanding and Christian social action in a healthy balance and is highly critical of either aspect being seen as the absolute, almost the exclusive dimension of education to and in the faith. It denounces either extreme position.

Catechesis a form of the ministry of the Word, an act of a living tradition

In the second part of the Directory catechesis is discussed in the context of the ministry of the Word and Revelation. The source of much of this section is the *Dogmatic Constitution on Divine Revelation* of Vatican II. Revelation is described as 'the act by which God communicates himself in a personal way'. God appears as 'one who wishes to communicate himself, carrying out a plan which proceeds from love' consequently, 'catechesis ought to take its beginning from the gift of divine love'.[19] This plan of God is made known in the events of the history of salvation and by the inspired words which accompany these events and make them clear.

---

[16] ibid. n.8,   [17] ibid. n.13,   [18] ibid. n.9,   [19] ibid. n.10,

> *The ministry of the Word should proclaim these deeds and words in such a way that the loftiest mysteries contained in them are further explained and communicated by it. In this way the ministry of the Word not only recalls the revelation of God's wonders which was made in time and brought to perfection in Christ, but at the same time, in the light of this revelation, interprets human life in our age, the signs of the times, and the things of the world, for the plan of God works in these for the salvation of all.[20]*

Through the ages 'the Church in her teaching, life and worship, perpetuates and hands on to all generations all that she herself is and all that she believes'. This is tradition, 'a living tradition since through it God continues his conversation'. Catechesis is a form of the ministry of the Word that 'gives voice to this living tradition'. It does so under the guidance of the Church's magisterium and in this way, the ministry of the Word is 'not a mere repetition of ancient doctrine, but rather it is a faithful reproduction of it, with adaptation to new problems and with a growing understanding of it'.[21] Once again we have the principle of the twofold fidelity: the Word kept alive and safeguarded in the Church's tradition and presented to people of each age 'in a manner corresponding to the difficulties and problems by which people are most burdened and troubled'. This was clearly seen as one of the main tasks of bishops in the Vatican II decree on their pastoral office. It is a point that is almost laboured in this and other documents as well as in the writings of leading catechists. It is again unambiguously stated as the aim and purpose of catechesis.

> *Catechesis strives to teach this Word of God with complete fidelity. The function of catechesis, however, cannot be restricted to repetition of traditional formulas; in fact, it demands that these formulas be understood, and be faithfully expressed in language adapted to the intelligence of the hearers, using even new methods when necessary. The language will be different for different age levels, social conditions, human cultures, and forms of civil life.[22]*

---

[20] ibid. n.11, [21] ibid. n.13, [22] ibid. n.34

Catechesis and the life-long development of faith

The ministry of the Word can take a variety of forms which include evangelisation and catechesis. Evangelisation 'has as its purpose the arousing of the beginnings of faith' and catechesis develops initial faith to become 'living, conscious and active'. Catechesis presupposes 'some adherence to Christ's Gospel as presented by the Church'. The text acknowledges that it is often directed at those who 'though they belong to the Church, have in fact never given true personal adherence to the message of Revelation'. This means that 'evangelisation can precede or accompany the work of catechesis'. In this context Sloyan and others speak of 'evangelising catechesis'. Once more this gives recognition to the fact that in most groups there will be a variety of levels of interest, understanding, practice and commitment. Catechesis takes various forms according to the age, condition and needs of those taking part. The Directory puts great stress on the need for the catechesis of adults.

> *Catechesis for adults, since it deals with persons who are capable of an adherence that is fully responsible, must be considered the chief form of catechesis. All other forms, which are indeed always necessary, are in some way oriented to it.[23]*

This is a shift in emphasis from the more traditional practice of catechesis as addressed to children and the young in schools. We are reminded that 'the life of faith passes through various stages'. Consequently the life of faith admits of various degrees of acceptance, understanding and commitment.

> *The acceptance of this faith and its explanation and application to life are different according to whether there is a question of the very young, children, adolescents, young adults, or adults. Catechesis has the function of lending aid for the beginning and the progress of this life of faith throughout the course of a person's life.[24]*

[23] ibid. n.20
[24] ibid. n.30

Often some rather crude judgements are made about the knowledge, understanding and practice of the faith of children and the young because the expectations behind the judgements are more suited to the faith of an older age. Often when parents, clergy and others complain that our young people do not know the faith, I ask what question they put to them. Frequently the question does not take account of a child's or young person's way of understanding and expressing what they know. Too often a set formulation is expected. The child or young person may well have knowledge at least of certain aspects of a doctrine which the questioner may fail to appreciate because it is in the language of the child or young person. It is vital that all who are involved in catechesis and religious education and those who pass judgement on their success or failure should have an appreciation of the stages of a person's development and the implications of this for the understanding of doctrine.

Catechesis according to age levels

The fifth part of the Directory takes up this discussion and develops at some length general principles of a catechesis adapted to various age levels. It touches on the importance and key characteristics of each stage from infancy to old age. Some of this will be considered later. However, it is worth mentioning here that much space is given to the needs and characteristics of the pre-adolescent, the adolescent, the young adult and adults. Adolescents, we are reminded, are searching for the meaning of life and although they are no longer content with the religious forms of their childhood, they are searching for significance in their lives. In the light of this, the text spells out a suitable approach and some of the tasks of educating them to and in the faith.

The method that seems most desirable is that of treating fundamental problems and problems of most concern to this age with the serious, scholarly apparatus of the theological and human sciences, using at the same time a suitable group discussion method...

> *The principal task of catechesis in adolescence will be to fur-*
> *ther a genuinely Christian understanding of life. It must shed*
> *the light of the Christian message on the realities which have*
> *greater impact on the adolescent, such as the meaning of bod-*
> *ily existence, love and the family, the standards to be followed*
> *in life, work, leisure, justice and peace, and so on.*[25]

The importance and value of the group for the adolescent is stressed. These features should be included in catechetical and religious education resources. Some Catholics criticise school and parish resources because they include such material in their content and because they encourage group discussion methods. The criticism is hardly valid unless, of course, such methods are used without any reference to the Christian understanding of these aspects of life in a way suited to the capacity of the pupils.

The Directory affirms the need of catechesis for adults. Among the reasons for this, it mentions the fact that they have responsibilities in their family, social and political life; they have greater experience of life; they pass through periods of crises. They need to shed the light of Christian faith on their various tasks and responsibilities as well as on their hopes and fears in the times of crises so that their faith can 'be constantly illumined, developed and fortified'[26]. The text speaks of the need to recognise the importance of old age, especially as the number of the elderly is increasing. It points out that 'the aged can contribute no small benefit to the community both by their work, which is not always justly appreciated, and by the witness that flows form their experience'[27]. Special forms of catechesis for adults are mentioned: the catechumenate, catechesis for the principal events of life such as marriage, baptism of children, first communion and confirmation; times of illness; at times of change in the circumstances of life. The occasions of preparing children for the sacraments can also be an opportunity for adult catechesis that addresses some of the needs and questions of parents at the stage they are at in personal and faith development. These occasions should offer more than instruction about what and how the children will celebrate. Parents may be more motivated on such occasions and

[25] ibid. nn.83 & 84
[26] ibid. n.92
[27] ibid. n.95

be more open to reflection on their lives in the light of our faith tradition. Of course, in any group, as the texts have acknowledged, there will be a variety of commitment, questions and needs. It is certainly not an easy task.

Catechesis and the Christian message

The third part of the Directory speaks of the criteria according to which the Christian message is to be presented and gives an overview of the more outstanding elements of the message. It begins by making the distinction between two aspects of faith: faith as the personal adherence, under grace, to God's revelation of himself and his loving plan, and, on the other hand, faith as the content of revelation and of the Christian message. Theology makes this distinction by using useful Latin tags: 'fides qua' – the faith by which a person believes, 'fides quae' – the faith which a person believes. The first refers to how a person comes to believe, to the personal journey to and in faith. The second refers to what is believed, the faith of the Church, the Christian message. The subject of this third part is the content of the faith and is, therefore, concerned with the 'fides quae', the Christian truths. This holds true of the *Catechism of the Catholic Church*. It is offered as a compendium of the truths of the Christian faith, it addresses 'fides quae'. What I discussed in the previous section of this chapter under catechesis and the life long development of faith is more concerned with the 'fides qua', the way in which people can be helped to come to faith, to make it their own.

The Directory links catechesis with the prophetic ministry of the Church. The aim is to make the content of the message intelligible to people in all ages, in order that they may be converted to God through Christ, and that they may interpret their whole life in the light of faith. The goal of catechesis is to present the entire Christian message. However, this can only be done gradually and at the pace of those who are being catechised, that is, 'in a way appropriate to the various cultural and spiritual conditions of those being taught'[28]. The text states that 'it is not possible to deduce an order which must be followed in the expression of the content'. At times it is right to begin with discussion of God, at times it is right and proper to begin with reflection on human realities.

---

[28] ibid. nn37 & 38

> *Thus the General Catechetical Directory does not attempt to draw up a doctrinal synthesis, nor to predetermine the best way to order the contents of catechesis. Given the Directory's emphatic insistence on adaptation to each socioeconomic and psychological condition, it is difficult to see how the authors of part three could have taken any other tack.[29]*

Methods and the role of experience in catechesis

In a brief fourth part the Directory says something about methods in catechesis. It is acknowledged that throughout the twentieth century 'catechists have thoroughly investigated questions raised by the psychological, educational and pedagogical sciences'. Studies have been undertaken with regard to suitable methods, the role of active participation, the place of experience, imagination, memory, and differentiation in learning according to age, social conditions, and degree of psychological maturity. The work of the catechist is considered 'of greater importance than the selection of texts and other tools'. The Directory sets necessary boundaries around the role of the catechist, and, we might add, of the R.E. teacher.

> *They are responsible for choosing and creating suitable conditions which are necessary for the Christian message to be sought, accepted and more profoundly investigated. This is the point to which the action of catechists extends – and there it stops. For adherence on the part of those to be taught is the fruit of grace and freedom, and does not ultimately depend on the action of the catechist.[30]*

Priests, catechists, teachers and parents may be helped by this declaration in the Directory. Faith ('fides qua') is a free response to grace by the person. We cannot simply give faith to others, nor can we demand faith of them. Our task is to create the atmosphere, the conditions which will

[29] B. L. Marthaler, Catechesis in Context, Our Sunday Visitor Inc., 1973, p.XXXV
[30] GCD. n.71

allow them to decide for themselves. We can walk with them at their pace on the journey. We are called to accompany and support them and while doing so, we are urged 'to have the greatest possible regard for the freedom and creativity of those to be taught'.

The text sees great value in the inductive method that encourages active participation of those being taught and touches on the realities of daily life, 'concrete things', in the explanation of more abstract concepts. At the same time it upholds the usefulness of formulas which are appropriate for a correct explanation of the faith and which 'make it possible for a uniform way of speaking to be used among the faithful'[31]. Again, it is stressed that formulas should be preferred which express faithfully the truth of the faith and are at the same time adapted to the capacity of the listeners. As I have said already, this point is almost laboured in this and other documents. However, I think it useful to keep repeating them it in order to underline the point made constantly in these official documents.

The place of human experience in the process of educating to and in the faith is considered. A number of important reasons for addressing people's life experiences are given. In the experience of life we are faced with 'concerns and questions, hopes and anxieties, reflections and judgements'; we look for meaning and significance in all this. Catechesis, therefore 'should be concerned with making people attentive to their more significant experiences, both personal and social' and it has 'the duty of placing under the light of the Gospel the questions which arise from those experiences'. In this way experience can help people respond to the gift of God. Reflection on experience can help make the Christian message more understandable. This was the approach of Jesus who illustrated the nature of the Kingdom with parables drawn from the experience of the people. In catechesis experience must be enlightened by the light of revelation and should help those who take part 'to explore, interpret and judge their own experiences and also ascribe a Christian meaning to their own existence'. The Directory accepts that this is a difficult task but it is one that must not be overlooked.[32]

---

[31] ibid. n.73
[32] ibid. n.74

Conclusion

It is fairly obvious that *The General Catechetical Directory* of 1971 did not come out of the blue. Many groups and individuals were directly involved in producing the text. The teaching of Vatican II is one of its chief sources. Some of the thinking of catechetical writers of the past can be traced in the final text. The educational approach of Drinkwater and of many in the French school is there. There are features of the kerygmatic and anthropological movements. A good deal of the thinking expressed in the six international study weeks is present in the Directory. The understanding of catechesis is very much broader than it was at the turn of the twentieth century. There is a radical shift of emphasis from the three Cs – the catechism to children in classrooms. Catechesis as part of the ministry of the Word has a place in pastoral theology and is concerned with the education to and in faith of people of all ages, from a variety of cultures and with a great diversity of experiences and needs. I see three essential aspects of the task of catechesis which flow from such an understanding. Firstly, catechists should recall, make available and more readily understandable the Christian tradition – scripture, the teaching of the Church, liturgy and a life of service in building the Kingdom of justice, love and peace. Secondly, they should be aware of and attentive to the stages of personal development and contemporary aspirations, questions and issues. And thirdly, catechists must seek to enable Christians to integrate faith and life, the tradition and contemporary experience. This is a noble yet daunting task. Holding the various aspects in a healthy balance is a delicate task and one about which there will be still more disagreements and controversy.

Chapter Six
Tensions and Controversies

The situation of catechesis in the Church since the late 1960s has been marked by more or less continually recurring disputes about what was being taught in religion classes and how it was being taught.[1]

We would encourage mutual charity, honest dialogue, and a sincere search for understanding and reconciliation among the varying views within the Catholic community. It must be made clear that, in any age, the truths of the faith always remain the same...the manner in which they are expressed necessarily varies according to cultural, social and linguistic conditions.[2]

As I pointed out in the previous chapter, the whirlwind of change brought about by the second Vatican Council caused different reactions among Catholics. Some were enthusiastic, others were less so, some were even worried and depressed by some of the changes or at least by the way they were introduced. By the late sixties there was, to say the least, a certain amount of turmoil in the Church. In England and Wales such turmoil was felt in a particular way in the fields of catechesis and religious education, as well as in liturgical matters. I pick out three events that, in my view, bring to the fore these tensions which were often expressed in heated controversies. Others could be considered but these three had special significance in the discussions and debates about the process of educating both the young and adults to and in the faith in the last decades of the twentieth century.

The Roman International Congress

In 1971, the year of the publication of the *General Catechetical Directory*, the Congregation for the Clergy called a large gathering of some one thousand three hundred delegates for a catechetical congress in

---

[1] Wrenn op. cit., p.99
[2] 'Final and Approved Report of the English Language Group', International Congress, Rome 1971, Warren op. cit., p.82

Rome from 20th to 25th September. Four key addresses were delivered as well as short communications that outlined the main aspects of the state of catechesis in various countries. Thirteen pages of conclusions were drawn up. In the general conclusions it was noted that there had been considerable development in catechesis in the course of the century and that it 'is a very positive and providential phenomenon in the life of the Church'. At the same time it was acknowledged that catechetical activity presents very serious questions 'which originate from the profound changes in the people, society and the Church of our day'[3]. There is evidence in the discussions, in the conclusions of different language groups and in the reactions to the Congress of tensions and disagreements about the best way to tackle these very serious questions in a time of profound change. In England and Wales these tensions and disagreements were forcefully expressed in two events which I shall consider in this chapter, namely, in the republication of the Penny Catechism in 1971 and in the story of Corpus Christi College (1965-75).

General conclusions of the Roman Congress

In the preamble to its conclusions the International Congress underlined the significance of such a large gathering of bishops, priests, lay people and religious: 'the fact that participants from numerous countries have shown the same concern is a sign of the importance placed on catechetical work'. Many of the suggestions put forward had already been raised and discussed in the international study weeks and in the writings of scholars. Without wishing to repeat these unnecessarily I shall simply mention them briefly and I shall touch on some of the key issues in the general conclusions and in those of the language groups. I shall highlight some of the points raised concerning the theology of revelation in which it is possible to detect clear differences of opinion, not to put it more strongly.

In the general conclusions from all groups it is stressed that 'attention must be given to the age and the interests of the recipients'. Active educational methods are encouraged. There are various responsibilities in the work of catechesis which are to be fulfilled by priests, religious and lay

[3] ibid.p.72

people. The need for adaptation to the various situations in which people find themselves is central to the task.

> *One of the riches of catechetical work these last decades is the discovery of the multiple aspects of the human situation: the individual dimension, the family situation, the cultural and social situations. Men and women cannot be considered apart from these multiple aspects in which they exist.*[4]

This is seen not only as a 'pedagogical technique' but also as 'a fundamental demand of the Word itself, because the Incarnation concerns the real person, to communicate to him or her the life of the Son of God'. Considering the situation of 'the young churches' in Africa, Asia and elsewhere, it speaks of the proclamation of the message as 'a word of liberation' since 'salvation brought by Jesus Christ has the power to transform the world even in its social and political aspects'. Education and formation are not confined to schooling but extend to the whole of life. Catechesis must include an ecumenical dimension: 'it will educate at times to a profound sense of particular identity while at the same time maintaining an openness without reticence or sectarianism'.

With regard to the understanding of revelation, the text says that it involves 'the self-communication of God as Person to persons'. It is set in the context of an 'interpersonal relationship' and is seen as 'more than the communication of truths in formulas adapted to cultural situations'. Perhaps surprisingly, the text declares that 'God's revealing activity is not limited to Christian communities'. Consequently 'there is a need to discern God's presence and interpret his activity expressed in all legitimate movements'. Those attending the Congress called for further study which would help clarify 'the relationship between catechesis and theology, and between revelation and experience'. The Congress text takes up the point stressed in the Directory concerning adult catechesis 'it is to be regarded as the main form of catechesis to which all others are ordered'. Parents are given a special mention. They should be helped in the fulfilment of their role as the first educators of their children and in the task of sharing the faith with them since 'this is what it means to baptise children in the

---

4 ibid. p.72

faith of parents and the faith of the community'. Adult religious education best takes place within small groups. The text affirms the importance
of Scripture as 'the source and object of catechesis'. The attempts to
adapt the message in relation to the real lives of people should be undertaken 'under the direction of the Church's shepherds'. This is the guarantee that all Christians and local churches will participate in the faith of the
one Church of Christ.

> In the light of these affirmations, we can place in relief the cri-
> teria that should inspire the identification and presentation of
> content, which can be expressed with the global formula –
> fidelity to God, fidelity to people.[5]

Conclusions presented by Third World delegates

The Third World delegates spoke of the 'critical situation of depend-
ence and exploitation' in Latin America, Africa and Asia. In the
course of the past few years, bishops' conferences in these continents
gave Christians 'the urgent mandate to involve themselves fully in the
development and liberation of our people, especially the young and the
poor'. They recognise risks and dangers inherent in this.

> In looking for an immediate solution to these problems, there
> is a danger that we become absorbed in purely material devel-
> opment, such as could be provided by any aid programme
> whether Christian or non-Christian.
>
> To avoid this danger, we must reveal through our catechesis,
> beyond the economic and cultural aspects, the full dimensions
> of the true liberation and development which can only be
> offered by the Risen Christ.

Catechists should lead those they are catechising to become aware of the
real situation in which they live and help them 'become personally

5 ibid. p.76

responsible for the purposeful development of their lives in their concrete situations'. Given the emphasis on the role of the family in these cultures, the delegates declare 'we realise that our catechesis should focus on initiation through an experience of living with a truly Christian group'. They stress the importance of a welcoming, supportive Christian community in the task of educating to and in the faith.

> *This calls for a profound conversion of mentality and attitude of all Christians towards our areas. Together we must build up a true human solidarity in Christ without which the world cannot liberate itself from all the dominating forces that prevent humankind from realising its full capacity in the plan of God.*

The delegates declare as an urgent need the setting up of 'special institutes and centre for formation and research' which will undertake 'unceasing search for a catechesis adapted to our particular situations'. The text asks that 'the elements of divine revelation latent in our indigenous cultures and traditional religions' be seriously studied so that they may ensure 'a full flowering of the riches planted by God in the heart of every man and woman and in the authentic aspirations of every people'[6]. There are echoes here of what is said in the Directory, and quoted in the previous chapter, about the feeling of some Christians that the 'traditional faith is bound too much with ancient and obsolete formulations and too much tied to Western cultures'. For many Catholics such sentiments appear dangerous and destructive of the unity of faith and beliefs.

Conclusions presented by the English-speaking delegates

The English-speaking group commended the Directory 'for its concern to promote a variety of catecheses for local needs and cultural differences'. They requested that the bishops declare that the Directory is 'a service document promulgating guidelines and is not legislation'. They speak of two concepts of revelation found in the Directory. The first understands revelation as a communication of truths couched in conceptual terms and accomplished in structured situations such as classrooms.

---

6 ibid. pp.78 & 79

The other perceives revelation as the self-communication of God, proceeding from an incarnational point of view.[7]

In this context the group report refers to the paper read to the congress by Fr Amalorpavadass. His paper was entitled *'Catechesis as a Pastoral Task of the Church'*. According to Warren this address has 'become a catechetical classic, especially for the way it delineates the relationship of catechesis to the other ministries of the Church'[8]. Amalorpavadass distinguishes two notions of revelation. One he terms an 'inadequate notion', which he describes as 'mostly notional and abstract, over-essentialist and objective, exclusively of the past and static, impersonal and individualistic'. Catechesis meant handing on the revealed doctrines. The emphasis was on what was to be communicated. The preferred tool was the catechism with its precise statements couched in theological language of a past age which are somehow considered immune from the normal limitations inherent in all human language, expressed, as it must be, in cultural categories of a given time and place. He spoke of a second understanding of revelation that, in his view, was a more adequate notion. It was personalist: 'what is revealed is not something but somebody'. It is about an interpersonal relationship between God and the individual. Revelation is also historical, subject to the conditions of time and space. It was first announced in the Old Testament through the prophets, promulgated by Christ, and finally preached by the apostles. Revelation 'takes place concretely and actually in the very events and trends of human history humanity stands at no time outside the process of revelation but always within it'[9]. If God's Word is revelation, humanity's word is faith. Catechesis, within such a conception of revelation and faith, is very much more than the teaching of doctrine to the young. It is 'education of faith', a process which seeks to enable Christians to respond freely and personally to the invitation and challenge of God who reveals and communicates himself in Christ as the source and purpose of human life. The English-speaking group found the second notion outlined by Amalorpavadass to be a 'richer view'. However, they were aware that there were other strongly held opinions and so they called for further study of the issues raised.

The English-speaking group upheld the central place of adult catechesis and the catechesis of parents. They spoke of the concern expressed by parents and

---

7 ibid. p.80
8 D.S. Amalorpavadass, 'Catechesis as a Pastoral Task of the Church', Warren op.cit., p.339
9 ibid. p.346

adults with regard to the religious education programmes and religious text-books because they are different from what they learned as children. They recognised the situation which 'in many ways is polarising the Christian community' and sought to reassure these groups 'about the great and valu-able progress made in religious education during the past quarter of a centu-ry'. They called for 'mutual charity, honest dialogue and sincere search for understanding and reconciliation among the varying views'. They set out some suggestions for the training of catechists. They made specific mention of the need to give attention to those working with the physically and men-tally handicapped. The sacraments of initiation were touched on and stress was placed on the need to prepare parents which flows from the understand-ing of baptism 'as a sacrament of initiation into a believing community'. They questioned the directives on first confession and communion as set out in the appendix to the Directory. These stated that for children the sacrament of penance should precede the reception of the Eucharist. The English-speak-ing delegates put forward the opinion that 'children should celebrate the sacrament of Penance for the first time when they are personally ready'. This caused debate and disagreement. As regards Confirmation, they saw it as a theological problem and asked that further study of the theology of Confirmation should undertaken. As in the general conclusions, they also asked for further clarification regarding the key problems of the relationship between revelation and experience, between catechesis and theology.

Wrenn is highly critical of much of the work of the Congress and the lan-guage groups, particularly the English-speaking group. He has little time for their appeal for mutual charity and dialogue because he sees it as paper-ing over the real problems. For him 'the whole debate over doctrinal con-tent in religious education had already reached the point where the debaters were simply talking past one another; it was truly a dialogue 'of the deaf'.

The 1971 International Catechetical Congress in Rome served to demonstrate how ecclesiastical authority was not really coming to grips with a religious education establishment by then more or less operating autonomously and taking its pri-mary direction from the catechetical movement and from free-wheeling theologians and other theorists rather than from the magisterium of the Church.[10]

---

[10] Wrenn op. cit., p.102

There are signs here of tensions which would lead to heated debates which still continue and are given expression in some criticism of 'new' developments.

Critique of the reprinted Penny Catechism, 1971

In 1971 the Catholic Truth Society published a revised version of the Penny Catechism, *A Catechism of Christian Doctrine*. On the cover it was stated that it was 'approved by the Archbishops and Bishops of England and Wales and directed to be used in all their dioceses'. In the words of the Catholic Truth Society itself, the revision contained, 'a few minor amendments'. Many of those who had responsibility for catechesis and religious education were surprised that the catechism should be published with these minor alterations when it was no longer quite so widely used in schools. They questioned why it should be reprinted in the same year as the *General Catechetical Directory* was issued which called for more radical renewal in catechesis, renewal which went beyond 'eliminating ignorance of doctrine which must be taught'. According to Ritter, the General Secretary of the society, the bishops had agreed in their Low week meeting that the catechism should be revised. They left the details to Cardinal Heenan who, says Ritter, gave his approval and personal imprimatur to the revised version. Ritter claimed that it was a misunderstanding to speak of a re-issue of the catechism because, he maintained, it had never gone out of print. It was for this reason, he suggested, that there had been no need to consult diocesan directors of religious education. He did, however, say that a much more radical revision was called for and that the revision was only an 'interim measure pending the production of an entirely new catechism'[11]. Even now as we begin a new century, some thirty years later, no such radical revision of the Penny Catechism has appeared.

In a review of the revised catechism published in *The Tablet*, Drinkwater argued that the text was still 'basically eighteenth century, with extensive mid-nineteenth century additions'. The alterations were slight. There were questions and answers without any explanations. It included new answers on Our Lady's Assumption. There were changes in the promises

---

[11] T. H. Ritter, letter to the editor, The Tablet, 9th October 1971, p.991

made by Catholics in a mixed marriage and some slight changes in the teaching about mortal sin. According to the new text Catholics did not endanger their faith if they took part in the services and prayers of another faith. Otherwise, in his view, it was exactly the same. He was critical of the text from other points of view including what he described as 'all its unattractive bare bones, its lack of any account of Our Lord's life', 'its gloomy negative moral and sexual outlook, its penal-days picture of spiritual and liturgical life'. He disliked what he called 'its general presupposition of a threatening God waiting to catch you out'. In the hands of skilled teachers it could be a useful tool but he saw it as more of a hindrance. Referring to the current controversy he considered that 'catechetics has become the centre for the storm clouds gathering over the Church, nor have we seen the climax yet'[12].

In October of 1971 the Board of Religious Inspectors and Advisers, those appointed by each bishop of England and Wales to direct the work of catechesis and religious education in their respective dioceses, met and discussed the question of the revised catechism. They expressed concern that the decision to republish the catechism had been taken without consulting the Board. From the minutes of the meeting it is evident that 'there was a strong general reaction to republication' because 'the catechism was seen as being theologically, psychologically and pedagogically deficient – if not erroneous'. It would appear from these minutes that the Board was under the impression that the Catholic Truth Society had taken the initiative and had approached the bishops rather than the other way around. It was suggested that a draft letter be prepared which might eventually be sent to the bishops. The draft text states that the Board considered the catechism to be theologically deficient because, among other points, the Resurrection was only referred to on two occasions; there was no direct reference to the Bible; the approach to the sacraments was too mechanistic; there was no reference to Vatican II. The majority of the diocesan directors considered the text to be educationally 'disastrous'. There were very few changes and the revised text seemed to disregard the guidelines set out in the *General Catechetical Directory*. A minority of directors did not share this view. There were clearly divisions among the members of the Board.[13]

---

12 F.H. Drinkwater, 'Penny Catechism Redivivus', The Tablet, 9th October 1971, p.991
13 These remarks are quoted from the minutes of the Board dated 16th October 1971.

Over the months that followed the publication of the revised Penny Catechism there was considerable debate conducted mainly through the Catholic press. In May of that year Cardinal Heenan had defended the 'new catechetics' in an address to the Westminster Pastoral Council. He acknowledged that in the aftermath of the council there was certain disunity in the Catholic community. He referred specifically to the 'contemporary outburst of sectarianism in the field of catechetics'. New methods, he argued, were necessary in the teaching of religion as in other subjects such as mathematics. People, he said, might not like the changes but it was hardly just to accuse teachers who advocated them of subversion or of undermining the faith of their pupils. He accepted that there could be disagreement with 'current theories of religious education' because mistakes could be made especially in a time of some experimentation after the council. It was, however, 'intolerable' that many who were conscientiously trying to pass to children the new understanding of Catholic doctrine which came from the Second Vatican Council should be accused of heresy.[14] Already there are signs of tension and even profound disagreements concerning the understanding and practice of catechesis and religious education in the light of developments endorsed by Vatican II and in the interpretation of the principles and guidelines set out in the Directory.

Corpus Christi College

It is probably true to say that the controversy in the late sixties and early seventies focused on Corpus Christi College, London. The college was founded by Cardinal Heenan of Westminster in 1965 as a training college for catechists and teachers of religion in Catholic schools. It went through a crisis period in 1971-72 during which the staff resigned. Other staff members were appointed but the college ceased to exist in 1975. They were exciting and turbulent years. Damian Lundy has a lengthy chapter on the history of the college in his doctoral thesis in which he examines critically the 'Corpus Christi experiment'. He places the 'experiment' in the context of the history of catechesis in the twentieth century.

---

[14] J. Heenan, 'In Defence of the New Catechetics', The Tablet, 22nd May 1971, pp.514-515.

A frequent term of abuse chosen by the critics of the Corpus Christi staff to condemn the progressive tendencies of the new catechetics was 'neo-modernist'. Corpus Christi may be regarded as the classic British instance of the painful but inevitable conflict which had occurred at virtually every stage of the twentieth century catechetical movement.[15]

In March 1965 Cardinal Heenan issued a statement from Archbishop's House, Westminster, in which he announced the setting up of the London College of Catechetics in premises given by the Daughters of Zion in Notting Hill. It was intended that the college would address 'home conditions' in ways that centres in Europe could not meet the particular situations and needs in England and Wales. The plan was to enroll 120 graduate students each year, students who had experience in the fields of catechesis and of teaching religion in schools. Lundy quotes the Cardinal's view on the purpose of the college: 'the London College of Catechetics will aim at the same high scholastic level of lectures (as European centres) but will specialise in giving practical experience of teaching to the students taking the course'[16]. Its director was Fr Hubert Richards, a scripture scholar, who led an experienced team. Students came from many English-speaking countries, particularly the Commonwealth countries, Ireland and the United States of America. For the staff, the Vatican II constitution on the Church in the Modern World, with its invitation to accept personal responsibility for the development of modern world, was a key document that gave direction to their whole approach to the task in hand. Lundy points out that 'Richards enthused about the continental catechetical institutes, which Heenan's statement had implied were insufficiently practical'. A number of key figures in European catechetical institutes would be invited to Corpus Christi as visiting lecturers. The staff would draw heavily on the thought of European and American catechetical theorists. The cardinal was very much concerned with the pastoral ministry and wished it to be a special feature of the London College. He implied that this practical, pastoral aspect was lacking in European institutes. He also expressed grave concerns about the writings of many theologians in Europe. In his second volume of

[15] M. A. Lundy, doctoral thesis Adult Catechesis in the Roman Catholic Church in Britain since the Second Vatican Council, Manchester University, 1990, p.212.
[16] ibid. p.222

autobiography, Heenan observed that England was 'theologically and geographically cut off from the Continent. We had no idea of the religious metamorphosis which had taken place in Europe'. He noted that the English bishops were quite unprepared for the kind of council other northern Europeans were planning because they were unfamiliar with the changed thinking in Europe since 1945.[17] Taking note of these and other observations Lundy concludes:

> *From the very beginning of the Corpus Christi experiment, a collision was inevitable between the cardinal and those who would seek to justify radical changes in theology and education, in particular in ecclesiology and catechetics, with reference to certain emphases of the Vatican II texts.[18]*

Content and approach in the college curriculum

However, the opening of the college aroused considerable enthusiasm among many Catholics: 'in 1965 as Corpus Christi began its life under the attentive and sometimes suspicious gaze of a variety of onlookers, the mood was one of extraordinary enthusiasm'[19]. The Catholic Herald of 19th March 1965 quoted Richards as saying that the college would offer teachers of religion 'awareness of what they are going to teach, of whom they are going to teach and of how they are going to teach'. An awareness and appreciation of developments in the theory and practice of catechesis and religious education are in evidence in this statement of principle. The influence of the kerygmatic approach with the four sources or languages of the faith can be seen in Richard's description of the Corpus Christi course:

> *The basic ingredient of a catechetical course will therefore be a study of how the Good News is revealed to us in Scripture , is systematised in theology, is made actual in the liturgy, and is lived in the life of the Church.*

[17] J. C. Heenan, A Crown of Thorns, Hodder & Stoughton, London, 1974.
[18] Lundy op. cit., p.225
[19] ibid. p.248

However, Duckworth says that the staff members soon realised that, within a broader understanding of revelation as an ongoing process, the salvation history approach had its limitations and, consequently, they advocated a greater experiential approach to religious education in Catholic schools and in the catechesis of adults.[20] Many clergy and others were suspicious and critical of the life-experience stress of this 'new catechetics'. In the college courses importance would be given to educational psychology so that students would be aware of the mentalities and thought processes of different age groups. Students would specialise in the catechesis and religious education of a particular age group: children, adolescents, young adults and adults. Seminars in adult education were fairly uncommon at that time. While many of the students were involved in religious education in Catholic schools and wished to prepare themselves better for that task, the college staff took seriously the call for adult catechesis and were probably among the first to arrange courses which addressed the needs and experiences of adults. Lundy describes the work of Corpus Christi as a 'significant attempt to promote adult catechesis in the post-Vatican II church at a critical time in the history of the catechetical movement'[21]. The methods used and encouraged in the college courses included audio-visual aids and activity methods which were accepted as normal and necessary in educational circles. In 1970 the college underwent an HMI inspection and received high praise for its content, the methods employed, the enriching balance of theory and exploration on the one hand, and, on the other, the valuable practical experience in schools, in youth and adult groups.

Crisis and controversy

From the start the College attracted considerable curiosity and criticism from many in the Catholic community. According to Cardinal Heenan, many finally lost confidence in the work of the college when in 1968 Fr De Rosa, vice-principal and theology lecturer, circulated a letter attacking the teaching in the papal encyclical *Humanae Vitae* on birth control. In that year fifty priests signed a letter and sent it to *The Times* expressing their concerns and disagreement with the papal teaching.

---

[20] R. Duckworth, op. cit., p.386
[21] Lundy op. cit., p.212

Despite his deeply held personal conviction, De Rosa undertook not to lecture on the subject. Three years later he decided to resign the priest-hood and Fr John Perry, another member of staff, resigned at the same time. This caused a crisis at the college and led critics to renew their attacks and recriminations against staff members and past students and on the whole of 'new catechetics'. The crisis came to a head when the staff refused to remove five eminent scholars from the list of visiting lecturers. This led to an inevitable confrontation with the cardinal. In August 1971 the staff tendered their resignations. The account of events after that time are described and interpreted somewhat differently by the cardinal and Fr Richards in their statements to past and present students.

In his statement the cardinal did not accept that he had 'crushed a body of zealous catechists through fear of their honest search for truth'. For him, it was not so much a question of academic freedom as a question of academic responsibility. He made it clear that although many were 'far from happy' with the theology taught in the college, he himself had 'never worried about its orthodoxy'. He did not consider the theological course to be in error though he did think that it was in certain aspects 'inadequate'. The cardinal pointed out that he had on occasions defended the college and contemporary catechetics. He spoke, rather, of certain 'dangerous attitudes' such as a wrong attitude towards the Church, a somewhat easy-going lifestyle, group dynamics which he viewed as 'a dangerous form of experimental psychology'. He accepted that 'to be at Corpus Christi was, in some quarters, to become an object of suspicion'. He felt that this was due in some part to the indiscretion of some stu-dents.[22] In his address to past students, Fr Richards maintained that the central issue was 'the kind of religious education appropriate for the world we live in'. He argued that the college had been founded 'to inves-tigate how the understanding we received from the Christian community of yesterday can be faithfully and effectively communicated to people living today'. In his understanding 'that is what catechetics is all about'. He claimed that the *General Catechetical Directory*, 'a rather cautious document', affirmed this view of the modern world and 'the challenges it offers to today's educators'. The questioning of today's students and adults cannot, he insisted, be short-circuited by predetermined textbook

---

[22] J. C. Heenan, 'Address to the Students of Corpus Christi College', The Tablet, 15th January 1972, pp.44-46.

answers. He rejected talk of *a* Catholic theology since there had never been a single Catholic theology: 'there is a Catholic faith and this has been expressed in various theologies, never more so perhaps than in the present age'[23].

The crisis at Corpus Christi heightened the whole catechetical controversy. Many of the more conservative elements in the Catholic community spoke out angrily against the dangers that they saw in the approach to religious education and catechesis inculcated in the college. Some began openly to question the orthodoxy of former students who by this time held posts of responsibility in dioceses, Catholic colleges and Catholic schools. Archbishop Beck of Liverpool wrote a letter in January 1972 to all head teachers of Catholic schools in the archdiocese expressing confidence in the orthodoxy of his catechetical team – four out of six were former students of Corpus Christi. Some very conservative groups such as the Catholic Priests' Association were especially critical of the college and its students. Fr Telford, director of religious education in the archdiocese of Southwark, was also highly critical. He claimed that what was at stake were conflicting views of revelation: on the one hand, the view outlined by Moran and adhered to by the college staff, and, on the other hand, the view described in the *General Catechetical Directory*.[24] Different groups claimed to be vindicated by the Directory. While the Directory is to some extent ambivalent on this question, it seems to me that it can be argued that the Directory is more in line with the general approach taken by the college. The same opinion was expressed by a correspondent in *The Tablet* at the time: 'the General Catechetical Directory is a cautious and carefully balanced document' yet 'it would be very difficult to deny that it leans towards the Corpus Christi approach'[25]. Not all Catholics agreed.

Conclusion

The Roman international congress, as we have seen, called for further study and greater clarification of the relationship between catechesis and theology, between revelation and experience. Many today are wary of the

---

23 H. Richards, 'Address to the Past Students of Corpus Christi College', The Tablet, 22nd January, 1972, pp.70-71.
24 G. Telford, letter to the editor, The Tablet, 5th February, 1972, p.114
25 The Tablet, 19th February, 1972, p.154

apparent blurring of the distinction between the sacred and the secular, between the divine and the human. They see the stress on the experiential as a sort of humanism. Others maintain that since faith is the human response to God's self- revelation in Christ, catechesis must also be involved with the questions and searching of people and with the interpretation of human life in the light of God's self-revelation in Christ. There should be no absolute dichotomy between the sacred and the secular, between the human and the divine. Again, it is important to bear in mind the two interlocking aspects of faith: the 'fides quae' and the 'fides qua'. There is, on the one hand, the faith of the Church, what the Christian community believes and acclaims every Sunday in the Eucharist. There is also the unique personal journey to and in faith, with the consequent stages and degrees of commitment of the individual Christian. Catechists should seek to bridge the two. Once more it is a matter of holding in a delicate yet necessary balance the poles of the 'twofold fidelity' – fidelity to God and fidelity to people in their particular situation. In practice, as we see from this brief historical overview, it has proved and continues to prove a difficult yet necessary task.

Some readers, especially R.E. teachers and parish catechists, may be somewhat baffled and even put off by the terminology used when speaking of aspects of the process of educating to and in the faith. In the various documents and opinions considered in this and previous chapters there has been frequent mention of the terms 'catechesis' and 'catechetical instruction', 'the teaching of religion' or 'religious education'. For the most part they seem to be used interchangeably while speaking of the different contexts of parish, voluntary groups and of the situation in classrooms in our Catholic schools. The attempts to bring out the distinction and the relationship between the terms and what they stand for will also lead to tension and controversy. Yet it is essential that we give consideration to these fine nuances because they help to clarify the different and complementary roles of specific people and ministries in the work of educating to and in faith. This will be considered more in later documents and discussions and in the reflections in Part Two. The 1997 Directory will speak of these terms and will recognise that, while they can be finely distinguished when discussing theoretical issues and questions, in practice they often have to exist together.

Chapter Seven

Synod Documents:
Evangelisation and Catechesis

I do not think it is being too dramatic to suggest that the direction of the catechetical movement has been turned towards a much more outward looking perspective. If the postwar catechetical movement can be summed up initially in the slogan 'from catechism to catechesis', then I think the new emphasis might well be 'from catechesis to evangelisation'[1]

The thirty-year period between the conclusion of the Second Vatican Council and the threshold of the millennium has been a time in which the evangelising vigour of the original Church has in some ways re-emerged.[2]

In the years since the publication of the General Catechetical Directory in 1971 there have been a number of Church documents concerned with important aspects of the theory and practice of educating the young and adults to and in the faith. A number of these texts were published by departments of the Roman Curia and others by various national conferences of bishops. By way of completing these historical sketches I shall refer only to the documents which were the result of the two international synods held in Rome, *Evangelisation in the Modern world* (1975) and *Catechesis in Our Time* (1979). In the course of the reflections on recent trends and issues in part two I shall make reference to other documents. For example, *The Rite of the Christian Initiation of Adults* is a key document which gives insights into the whole process of evangelisation and catechesis. The Congregation for Catholic Education has issued several documents on the value and purpose of Catholic schools in which they also speak of the catechesis and religious education within the school context. The International Council for Catechesis set out principles and guidelines in the text *Adult Catechesis in the Christian Community*. The bishops

[1] G. Rummery, '1970-80: the Decade of Directories', Voice of the Hidden Waterfall, K. Nichols (ed), p.20
[2] General Directory for Catechesis, n.2

of England and Wales have made statements and authorised publications giving direction to the work of catechesis and religious education.

The Synod of Bishops and Synod Documents

This is not the place for a detailed study of the synod of bishops. However, if these documents are to be appreciated, a brief word on the topic will be helpful. The synod of bishops is a direct result of Vatican II. Many bishops found the council an enriching experience for themselves and for the Universal Church. They wished to make the exercise of 'collegiality' – the close working together of the Pope and the college of bishops throughout the world – a more frequent practice. The synods held every few years in Rome are a structured form of this 'collegiality'. Most of the bishops (about 85%) who attend the synod are elected by their fellow bishops in each national conference. On occasions it is the presidents of the conferences who attend. The bishops meet for a period of about a month to discuss the theme of the synod. Prior consultation will have already taken place with the bishops' conferences and among others with expertise in the particular topic being considered. The bishops listen to a number of interventions in the general sessions and meet in language groups to discuss the issues raised. Reports are collated and presented in general sessions. The synod is a consultative body. The bishops make recommendations. The Pope takes note of the debates and suggestions made by the bishops and then he writes a document or exhortation on the subject. Synod documents are not systematic theological treatises giving the final word on the topics under discussion. They are, generally, an attempt to collate a variety of opinions and to give some directives and guidelines for the way ahead. The process that enables bishops from all parts of the world to exchange views and to face common challenges is clearly of immense value. The documents that are produced as the result of such an exchange speak to the universal Church and seek to build consensus and avoid more radical opinions and disagreements. They cannot directly address specific issues which may be of special significance in particular parts of the world. To say this is not in any way to devalue the directives they contain or to minimise their authority. It is an acknowledgement of an inherent limitation of this type of document. The texts often reflect the debates which took place during the synod rather than give a final solution to the questions posed.

Evangelisation in the Modern World (1975)

The General Assembly of the Synod of Bishops met in October 1974 to discuss the theme of evangelisation in today's world. The 1997 *General Directory for Catechesis* describes their reflections as 'a decisive milestone for catechesis'[3]. The propositions drawn up by the synod were presented to Paul VI who promulgated his Exhortation *Evangelisation in the Modern World* 8th December 1975.

> *This document enunciates, among other things, a particularly important principle, namely, that of catechesis as a work of evangelisation in the context of the mission of the Church. Henceforth, catechesis would be considered as one of the enduring concerns of the Church's missionary mandate for our times.[4]*

Warren sees the document as 'more a series of questions on the dilemmas still facing the work of evangelisation than any sort of position paper'[5]. It is not a neat composition and tends to be repetitive with major themes recurring in various places. Yet it is joyful and positive in tone. The Pope describes it as 'a meditation on evangelisation' which he offers to the Church after having heard 'the wealth of the synod'[6]. Snijders claims that it is a summary and evaluation of missionary theology as it has developed since Vatican II. He is of the opinion that the Pope wrote not as a theologian but as a pastor reconciling different views rather than defining terminology.[7] There can be no doubt that there were disagreements among the bishops. That is hardly surprising when you consider the variety of experiences, backgrounds and theologies of men from every part of the world. There are mixed feelings expressed about the document, especially about its failure to resolve several important issues such as the link between evangelisation and human liberation, between the spiritual and the secular.[8] As I have said before, it is unrealistic to expect a synod document to solve these theological questions. It is the task of theologians and other experts to study the matters in greater depth. Rummery describes that Pope's exhortation:

3 ibid. n.4   4 ibid. n.4
5 Warren op. cit., p.336   6 Paul VI, Evangelisation in the Modern World, (EMW) nn.5 & 40
7 J. Snijders, 'Evangelii Nuntiandi: the Movements of Minds', Clergy Review, LXII, 5, 1977, p.171
8 N. Greinacher & A. Muller, 'Evangelisation in the World Today' (EN), editorial in Concilium, 114, 1979

> *It is an important illustration of the principle of collegiality operating in the post-Vatican II Church: there is a two-way flow of ideas, from the Church to the Pope, and from the Pope to the Church, and, in between, the very important process of discussion, clarification and new syntheses'[9]*

The text does point in a fairly definite direction which has important implications for the theory and practice of educating to and in the faith.

Evangelisation in a broader perspective

Whatever the limitations of the document as a theological exposition, Rummery considers that it is 'among the powerful incentives to change' in so far as it has helped the catechetical movement turn towards 'a much more outward looking perspective'[10]. Beozzo agrees with this view and says that the document enabled Catholics to look to 'the face of the Church that turns to the world outside its frontiers'[11]. Snijders and Rummery maintain that it broadens the Church's understanding of the missionary and catechetical activity by turning from a narrow concern for the conversion and instruction of individuals to a wider concern for all people and the quality of life in today's world. Evangelisation is seen as an umbrella concept and not simply as a stage in the faith journey which precedes catechesis. According to these writers, it delineates, however unsatisfactorily in the view of some, a conception of the Christian message of salvation which includes the proclamation of human dignity and freedom as part of building the Kingdom. As Rummery states, this implies that 'the security of being a Christian and of being on the road to personal salvation is not enough'. Conversion, which the text declares as the aim of evangelisation, involves 'both the personal and collective conscience of people, the activities in which they engage, and the lives and concrete milieux which are theirs'[12].

[9] Rummery op. cit., p.20
[10] ibid. p.20
[11] J. O. Beozzo, 'Evangelisation and History', Lumen Vitae, 33, 3, 1979, p.227
[12] ENW, n.18

> *For the Church it is a question not only of preaching the Gospel in ever wider geographical areas or to even greater numbers of people but also of affecting and as it were upsetting, through the power of the Gospel, mankind's criteria of judgement, determining values, points of interest, lines of thought, sources of inspiration and models of life, which are in contrast to the Word of God and the plan of salvation'.13*

From the context of the document it is clear that such determining of values etc. is not to be done by way of imposition but rather by proposing 'with complete clarity and with total respect for the free options which it represents'. This 'respectful presentation of Christ and his Kingdom' is the right and duty of those called to evangelise.14 It is a task of service and of solidarity in which Christians are motivated by the Christian concept of the 'Kingdom of God' and 'the loving plan of salvation' which are seen to encompass 'liberation from everything that oppresses people'. The message must also be proclaimed and explained. Even prior to that, and possibly of more value, is the 'wordless witness' which Christians can give to others.

> *In the midst of their own community of culture, Christians show their capacity for understanding and acceptance, their sharing of life and destiny with other people, their solidarity with the efforts of all for whatever is noble and good.15*

Commenting on this text Saris suggests that evangelisation is putting the Gospel into practice in the place where one happens to be: 'it does not mean that one goes around talking on every possible occasion, incessantly, about God, Jesus and the Bible'16.

Evangelisation and human liberation

Evangelisation is linked with the struggle for human liberation, with people's struggle 'to overcome everything which condemns them to remain on the margin of life'. The text specifically mentions famine,

---

13 ibid. n.19   14 ibid. n.80
15 ibid. n.21   16 W. Saris, Living the Faith Together, Collins, 1985, p.112

chronic disease, illiteracy, poverty, injustices in international relations and especially in commercial exchanges, situations of economic and cultural neo-colonialism. The Pope states that the Church has 'the duty of assisting the birth of this liberation, of giving witness to it, of ensuring that it is complete'. Such action, he says, 'is not foreign to evangelisation'[17]. The development of this line of thought is somewhat untidy in so far as it leaves loose ends which allow those who hold opposing views to make a case for their particular opinion. While the Pope speaks of the necessary link between evangelisation and human liberation and development, he also stresses that the Church cannot reduce its mission to the dimensions of a simply temporal project. The text, on the one hand, declares that the Church cannot restrict its mission to the purely religious field, dissociating itself from temporal problems, and, on the other hand, it reaffirms the primacy of the Church's spiritual vocation. The two poles of the tension are highlighted, but, in the view of many, there is no coherent theological argument presented which brings them together in a consistent fashion. Those who oppose this approach as being too 'political' and, therefore, not the domain of the Church or the concern of those involved in the work of catechesis, can claim to make some case for their stance. This is the reason why others, particularly catechists in the Third World, find the document unsatisfactory. However, there is definite evidence of a shift of emphasis from a narrow understanding focused on individual conversion and faith to a broader understanding of our part, under grace, in the service of the Kingdom. Paul VI declares that there are 'profound links' between evangelisation and human advancement. In the final text he quotes his own speech made at the opening of the synod.

We ourselves have taken care to point this out, by recalling that it is impossible to accept that in evangelisation one could or should ignore the importance of the problems so much discussed today, concerning justice, liberation, development and peace in the world. This would be to forget the lesson which comes from the Gospel concerning love of our neighbour who is suffering and in need.[18]

---

17 ENW, n.30
18 ENW, n.31

Evangelisation as a complex, multi-dimensional activity

The Pope insists that it is vital to hold together several essential elements or aspects of evangelisation. At times one or other of these is identified with evangelisation but, in the Pope's words, this runs the risk of impoverishing 'the reality of evangelisation in all its richness, complexity and dynamism' or even of distorting it.[19] Among its varied elements he lists the following: the renewal of humanity, witness of life, explicit proclamation, inner personal adherence, entry into the Christian community, taking up the task of evangelising others. Much of what has been said in the previous paragraphs deals with the element of renewing humanity. Witness is an essential element which involves 'presence, sharing, solidarity'. It is generally the first element in the process of evangelisation. It is important to bear this element of witness in mind when considering the contexts of home, parish and school. People should first of all experience the witness of a lived faith in the community. In Catholic schools, for example, pupils should experience a welcoming atmosphere which is inspired by the Gospel values of acceptance, respect and freedom. This 'silent witness' can have a profound influence on pupils. Generally, as the text says, this is the first and a necessary stage in the journey of faith. It must be backed up with the proclamation of 'the name, the teaching, the life, the promises, the kingdom and the mystery of Jesus of Nazareth, the Son of God'. The Pope points out that this proclamation – preaching or catechesis – is often identified with evangelisation and yet it should be seen as only one aspect, not the whole of evangelisation. This proclamation reaches fuller development when it is listened to and accepted, when there is personal adherence to the message and person of Jesus. Such adherence leads to the entry into the community of believers and participation in the life of the Church. Finally, 'the person who has been evangelised goes on to evangelise others'. The document invites us 'to relate these elements rather than to place them in opposition one to another'.[20]

---

[19] ibid. n.17
[20] ibid. nn.17-20

Content of Evangelisation

Throughout the document the Pope constantly states that the heart of evangelisation is the proclamation of the love of God that comes to us in Jesus Christ.

> *To evangelise is first of all to bear witness, in a simple and direct way, to God revealed in Jesus Christ, in the Holy Spirit; to bear witness that in his Son God has loved the world – that his Incarnate Word has given being to all things and has called all people to eternal life.*[21]

Evangelisation includes the preaching of hope, the preaching of God's love for us, the preaching of love for all people, the preaching of the mystery of evil and the search for good. Included too are the call to prayer and the celebration of the sacraments. However, we are reminded again that evangelisation would be incomplete 'if it did not take account of the unceasing interplay of the Gospel and the real life of people both personal and social'[22]. Snijders says that the Pope gives a warning to theologians and those involved in evangelisation 'to ensure that doctrine always remains a meaningful message, and that the message should always be anchored in sound doctrine'[23].

Methods of evangelisation

In the fourth part of the document the Pope addresses the question of 'how to evangelise?' In this section there is a fair amount of repetition of points made elsewhere in the document. He again talks of the witness of a Christian life 'given over to God and at the same time given over to one's neighbour with limitless zeal'[24]. Preaching is another key method of evangelising . He acknowledges that it is not easy in an era when 'modern man is sated by talk, often tired of listening and, what is worse, impervious to words'. Therefore modern means should be employed. He speaks positively of the use of the mass media and declares that the Church can find

---

21 ibid. n.26   22 ibid. nn.22 & 23
23 Snijders op. cit., p.172   24 EMW n.41

in it 'a modern and effective version of the pulpit'[25]. The importance of the homily in the eucharist and on other occasions is highlighted. He refers to it as 'evangelising preaching' which takes on many forms. Another important means of evangelisation is catechetical instruction.

> *The intelligence, especially of children and young people, needs to learn through systematic religious instruction the fundamental teachings, the living content of the truth which God has wished to convey to us and which the Church has sought to express in an ever richer fashion during the course of her long history. No one will deny that this instruction must be given to form patterns of Christian living and not to remain only notional.[26]*

This calls for suitable texts and resources 'updated with wisdom and competence, under the authority of the bishops'. As in other documents, it is stressed that 'methods must be adapted to the age, culture and aptitude of the persons concerned'. Such resources and methods 'must always seek to fix in the memory, intelligence and heart the essential truths that must impregnate all life'. Teachers and catechists should receive a thorough training for this task. Without neglecting the children, efforts must be made to address the needs of young people and adults. The proper celebration of the sacraments has a crucial part to play in the process of evangelisation. This flows from the broad perspective on evangelisation as set out in the text.

> *One can never sufficiently stress the fact that evangelisation does not consist only in the preaching and teaching of doctrine. For evangelisation must touch life: the natural life to which it gives new meaning, thanks to the evangelical perspective that it reveals; and the supernatural life, which is not the negation but the purification and elevation of the natural life'.[27]*

This understanding of human life, the 'natural' life, in relation to the Good News of the Kingdom and the promise of supernatural life is both embodied and given expression in the signs, symbols and rituals of the

[25] ibid. n.45
[26] ibid. n.44
[27] ibid. n.47

Church's celebration of word and sacrament. This is the wonder and the beauty of sacramental celebrations. To avoid mere 'sacramentalisation' which is unrelated to evangelisation there is need for 'the solid support of catechesis' which enables people to 'live the sacraments as true sacraments of faith – and not receive them passively or undergo them'.

Evangelisation is for everyone

The proclamation of the Good News to the whole of creation, to all peoples, has been the constant duty of the Church from the beginning until today. It is addressed to those who have not yet heard the Good News of Jesus Christ. There are immense numbers of people who profess other religions. We are reminded that 'the Church respects and esteems them because they carry within them 'the echo of thousands of years of searching for God'. They have 'an impressive patrimony of deeply religious texts'. They 'are all impregnated with innumerable seeds of the Word'. Still, the Church should not withhold from these people the proclamation of the Word. The Pope recognises that such a situation 'raises complex and delicate questions' that call for further study.[28] There are many in the Church who, although baptised, do not follow a Christian way of life. These too must be approached. At the same time the Church constantly seeks to 'deepen, consolidate and make ever more mature' the faith of the believing, practising members. The text declares that 'the phenomenon of the non-pracitising is a very ancient one in the history of the Christianity'[29]. It may be helpful to realise that 'non-practice' is not an entirely new phenomenon despite the outcry of some 'prophets of gloom', as Pope John XXIII called them. There are those who would have us believe that 'our era in comparison with past eras, is getting worse, and they behave as though they had learned nothing from history'[30]. Of course, we are faced with very real problems today and we cannot ignore them or wish them away. Still, we should take care not to be over simplistic in our judgements or too readily place the blame for every ill in the Church on one particular feature of Church life – 'new catechetics', for

---

28 ibid. n.53   29 ibid. n.56
30 John XXIII, opening speech at Vatican II, Abbot op. cit., p.712

example, – or on some particular groups. While a particular feature or group may not be without some blame, the situation at any given time is usually more complex and complicated. 'Non-practice' has been a feature of Church life throughout its history. It can be dangerous and less than helpful to harp back to some imagined 'golden age'. Each age had its problems and we have ours. This is the time and place in which we are asked to proclaim and be witnesses to the Good News. In his concluding paragraphs the Pope encourages us to overcome obstacles in the same way as the great preachers and evangelisers of the past did. He exhorts us not to lack 'spiritual fervour'. As we have already noted, in the Pope's view this lack of fervour manifests itself 'in fatigue, disenchantment, compromise, lack of interest and, above all, lack of joy and hope'[31]

Catechesis in Our Time (1979)

Paul VI called the fourth General Synod of Bishops to meet in Rome during October 1979. He chose the topic of catechesis with special reference to children and the young. While there were many other crucial issues which the bishops might have been invited to discuss, Paul chose the topic of catechesis because it would provide continuity with the 1974 synod on evangelisation. In preparation for the synod, as with others, working papers and questionnaires were sent to the conferences of bishops. From the responses the preparatory document for discussions was drawn up. The theme provided an opportunity for the bishops to air key concerns about the strengths and weaknesses in the theory and practice of catechesis throughout the Church. In reassessing progress they gave general approval to many recent developments but also pointed out some deficiencies. At the conclusion of the synod the bishops left thirty-four recommendations for the Pope to consider when writing the official synod document. PaulVI died before he wrote the document. John Paul II, who as Cardinal had taken part in the synod, issued the text *Catechesis in Our Time.*

---

[31] EMW n.80

A background of still unresolved tensions

The bishops and those whom they consulted were very much aware of the concerns and tensions that were being experienced and expressed by many in different parts of the Church. Marthaler even speaks of 'overt lobbying' of synod members by individuals and groups 'who linked what they perceived as the crisis in the Church to the direction of catechesis in the post-Vatican II years'[32]. Rummery says that 'attentive reading of many Catholic papers and journals during the decade would show the recurring theme of controversy about content, style and materials being used in catechetical work'[33]. As a consequence, a large number of initial interventions in the general sessions reflected something of the catechetical debates. In the United States the National Conference of Catholic Bishops circulated a questionnaire on the topic. The responses of the forty-five dioceses that replied formed the basis of their report in preparation for the synod. In what he terms 'a bare, unadorned summary' Wrenn outlines the findings in the report. These identify both positive and negative developments as perceived and experienced by some catechists and by some of the people being catechised.[34] It is important that such concerns and feelings are appreciated even if one cannot entirely agree with them. I think it is useful to give a brief outline of Wrenn's summary because it will serve to present something of the background to the debates and discussions in the synod. The positive and negative points listed are not unlike those experienced by many in England and Wales.

The report from the North American bishops indicated general acceptance of developments in scripture, theology, patristics, liturgy, social doctrine and ecumenism. There was a level of approval for the integration of psychology, education and other human sciences into catechesis. Many cited the use of experience, everyday situations and problems, which assured that 'catechesis would be more readily understandable, practical and liveable'. Inductive, experiential educational methods were generally accepted. The use of music, drama and art were appreciated as ways of 'producing a balance between the communication of content and the tapping of emotional, intellectual, physical and motivational potentialities'.

---

[32] B. L. Marthaler (ed), Introducing the Catechism of the Catholic Church, SPCK, 1994, p.8
[33] Rummery op. cit., p.22
[34] Wrenn op. cit., pp.193-199; see also Wrenn, 'Religious Education at the Crossroads:U.S.A.', Religious Education and the Future, D. A. Lane (ed),The Columba Press, 1986, pp.32-36

The professional training of catechists was an important development as was the emergence of graduate schools of religious education and catechetical institutes. The growing involvement of parents, especially in sacramental preparation of their children, was highly rated. There was appreciation of the shift to adult and family-centred catechesis. Another significant trend was the development of youth ministry. Other points mentioned favourably in the report included the realisation that catechesis is a life-long process that requires in the catechist or teacher an awareness of the stages of human development, and an appreciation of the fact that faith is a free choice rather than a matter of cultural identification.

The report goes on to mention some of the key developments which have hindered the work of catechesis since Vatican II. Some of these lie beyond the Church, some came from inside the Church. Chief among the first were the rapid cultural changes taking place in society, the fact that Christians now lived in a secularised society which led to deterioration in family life – divorce, abortions, one-parent families, drugs, and the widespread indifference to religion. From within the Church, among the 'most serious handicaps to effective catechesis' were 'confusion, ambiguity, distrust, fear and even hostility and anger' which many felt when faced with the changes in the Church in the wake of Vatican II. The report observes that 'religious education became one of the major battlegrounds for those who had opposing views on the Church and the world.' Such confusion often led to polarisation and serious tensions between 'progressives' and 'conservatives'. Often there appeared a disturbing division between theologians and the magisterium, with little or no distinction being made 'between matters of theological speculation and research and what is held and taught by the magisterium'. The blame for this confusion was assigned to the inadequate implementation of Vatican II, to ineffective communication of developments in the catechetical field. People were not helped to understand, internalise and participate in renewal. While some praised catechetical textbooks, others criticised them as lacking essential elements of doctrine and morality. There was continued tension regarding the cognitive versus the affective, the deductive versus the inductive dimensions of learning in catechesis. The neglect of memorising was considered unfortunate. Some thought that many catechists simply 'followed fads and used gimmicks, gadgets and novelties.' There often appeared little continuity in religious education and catechetical programmes. Many teachers and catechists were poorly trained and not up to the job. They lacked theological and educational preparation and qualifications. It was felt that the value of parish schools was being downgraded.

Having summarised the report, Wrenn expresses his opinion that what was 'a necessarily bland and impersonal report' did not give enough attention to what he described as 'doctrineless and experiential catechesis'. At the same time he notes that many of the positive factors mentioned in the report were quite accurate, although they were not the focus of his study. His own chief concern is with the danger of 'a creedless, doctrineless, non-cognitive' catechesis. In considering the text of John Paul II I shall touch on areas which seem to be more relevant to these concerns and issues.

Catechesis and evangelisation

John Paul II places catechesis within the pastoral and missionary activity of the Church. He himself says that he does not attempt to give any rigid, formal definition of catechesis. Briefly it can be described as 'education in the faith'. Yet, as has been said in other texts, here too it is recognised that in practice many come to parish catechesis and Catholic schools when initial evangelisation has not taken place. This means that catechesis must often concern itself not only with nourishing and teaching the faith but also with arousing the initial interest for the Christian faith. While recognising this fact, the text gives a description of an ideal situation.

> All in all, it can be taken here that catechesis is an education of children, young people and adults in the faith, which includes especially the teaching of Christian doctrine imparted, generally speaking, in an organic and systematic way, with a view to initiating the hearers into fulness of Christian life.[35]

Catechesis cannot be identified with evangelisation, nor can it be entirely separated from it. They integrate and complement each other. Catechesis is seen as one of the stages of the rich and complex reality that

---

[35] John Paul II, Catechesis in Our Time (CT), n.18

is evangelisation. The specific aim of catechesis is the 'reflective study of the Christian mystery'. This calls for a 'systematic catechesis' that is programmed, not improvised, deals with essentials and is an integral initiation into all the dimensions of Christian life. The Pope stresses the need for such 'a systematic Christian instruction because of the tendency in various quarters to minimise its importance'[36].

Catechesis: bridging doctrinal and the experiential dimension

According to the Pope there should no 'opposition set up between catechesis taking life as its starting point and a traditional, doctrinal and systematic catechesis'[37]. In stressing a systematic catechesis the Pope would appear to issue a warning to those who, while reacting to a narrow catechism approach, may well go to the other extreme of devaluing the important role of instruction in and understanding of the doctrines of the Christian faith. However, it cannot be seen as a simple recall to catechism learning. The bishops in their seventeenth recommendation imply as much when they say 'it is not possible today to conceive or put into motion catechetical studies only as a deepening of abstract truths formulated in a fixed, once-for-all manner'. The Pope speaks of a broad understanding of catechesis in which the initial option for the Gospel is gradually deepened, explained and channelled towards Christian action in the Church and the world. This broad understanding 'in no way contradicts but rather includes and goes beyond a narrower meaning which was once commonly given to catechesis in didactic expositions, namely the simple teaching of the formulas that express faith'[38]. With regards to methods used in catechesis and religious education, in their eighteenth recommendation the bishops say:

> *Some methods insist on a doctrinal approach, some are more experiential; some emphasise anthropological aspects, some are more centred on doctrine, some focus on political and temporal aspects, others stress spiritual formation. Any radical position will only be to the detriment of preaching the Gospel.[39]*

---

36 ibid. n.21   37 ibid. n.22
38 ibid. n.25   39 'Synod 1977: The Thirty-four Points', Living Light, 15, 1, 1978, p.77

The foundation of this necessary 'dialectic' between faith and life, doctrine and experience, is clearly expressed in a passage in which the Pope sets out the essential characteristics of 'authentic catechesis'. While spelling out what he means by authentic catechesis, the Pope enumerates what can be considered the main facets of a sound theology of revelation and faith, since it is in the context of revelation and faith that he here speaks of catechesis. Each of the facets or elements must be fully acknowledged, respected and related to each other in a manner which is consistent and upholds the value of each without minimising any other. I shall quote the passage in full but I shall divide it into separate sections in an endeavour to highlight and give greater emphasis to the various elements.

Authentic catechesis is an orderly and systematic initiation into the revelation that God made of himself to humanity in Jesus Christ,

a revelation stored in the depth of the Church's memory and in Sacred Scripture,

a revelation constantly communicated from one generation to the next by a living and active traditio,

a revelation which is not isolated from life or artificially juxtaposed to it but which is concerned with the ultimate meaning of life,

a revelation which illumines the whole of life to inspire and question it.[40]

I find this very helpful. It is possible to detect some of the ideas already expressed in the *General Catechetical Directory*, the Roman Congress, and by individuals within the catechetical movement. The passage gives a clear and coherent overview. It is true, of course, that those seeking to interpret and explain it may give different emphases to each of the facets. For what it is worth, I give here only a brief personal comment. I shall consider the matter more closely when reflecting on revelation and faith in part two. God reveals himself, not simply truths about himself. God reveals himself as the origin and goal of all human life. We are all invited to a dynamic and life-giving interpersonal relationship. For Christians the foundation of this belief is the event of Jesus Christ. The revelation experienced in the event of Jesus Christ is stored in the depth of the mem-

---

[40] CT n.22

ory of the Church and in Scripture. 'The depth of the Church's memory' comprises not only the verbal formations or creeds but also the symbolic, ritual expressions in prayer, liturgy and sacrament, as well as in the way of life of the Christian community, including the example of parents, grandparents and others. A 'living and active traditio' implies a creative dialogue and interplay between the revelation stored in the memory of the Church and in Scripture and reflection on contemporary human experience. Catechesis seeks to initiate people into the revelation which illumines and gives meaning to their existence, in a way which both inspires and at the same time questions and challenges the values they hold and which influence how they live their lives. Reflection on this passage of John Paul will help towards a more consistent understanding of the 'dialectic' between Christian faith and beliefs and the joys, hopes and burdens of human life. They belong together. If catechesis is 'education in the faith' and faith is understood as the free human response to revelation in Jesus Christ then catechists can be described as 'instructors (of human beings and their life) in the faith'.

Catechesis: a variety of responsibilities, a variety of settings

The synod text emphasises that all Christians, the whole community, share responsibility for catechesis: 'catechesis always has been and always will be a work for which the whole Church must feel responsible and must wish to be responsible'[41]. Members of the community have different responsibilities that are derived from their specific role – bishop, priest, parent, grandparent, godparent, teacher, catechist and so on. Catechesis also takes place in a variety of settings, particularly, though not exclusively, in the family, the parish and the school. The text has something to say about all three.

The parish is reminded that it has the duty not only to instruct its members but also to welcome them into a suitable, friendly environment in which they can 'live as fully as possible what they have learnt'. The importance of the community dimension is strongly underlined: 'catechesis runs the risk of becoming barren' without the support of a communi-

---

[41] ibid. n.16

ty of faith giving witness in Christian living. The Pope stresses that 'the parish community must continue to be the prime mover and pre-eminent place for catechesis'. He acknowledges that some now question the value and the viability of the parish, yet he maintains that 'it is still a major point of reference for the Christian people, even for the non-practising'. This rings true. Even for those who rarely darken the door of the Church there are special moments in their lives when the parish church is a key reference point. The funeral of relatives and friends is just one example. The Pope goes on to state that 'realism and wisdom' demand that energy be spent on renewing structures and giving new impetus to 'qualified, responsible and generous members'[42]. In the twenty-seventh recommendation of the bishops the parish is described as the 'community of communities' in so far as smaller groups can meet for specific needs and tasks in an atmosphere more conducive to sharing and providing support. They recognise that the community of the parish may be too large. They encourage the setting up of smaller groups which can more easily and more fully meet the needs of people in a more friendly, human way. Basic Christian communities seek to meet just such a need. In the case of young people the desire for such groups is very strong.[43]

The family's catechetical activity has 'a special character which in a sense is irreplaceable'[44]. Education in the faith by parents should begin very early in the child's life. This is mainly done through the witness of their lives, 'a witness that is often without words'. Catechesis takes place on the occasion of special family events – birth, sacramental preparation, at times of the celebration of anniversaries and feasts, in times of sickness and bereavement. The Pope goes on to urge parents to explain the religious significance of such events but he also says that this is still not enough: 'Christian parents must strive to follow and repeat, within the family setting, the more methodical teaching received elsewhere'. This reinforcing of what has been learnt in school or parish 'within a family setting impregnated with love and respect' will have a profound influence on the young. In the experience of many priests, teachers and catechists this will seem an ideal sometimes difficult to realise. Many family settings are far removed from what is envisaged in the text. Parents often

---

[42] ibid. n.24
[43] ibid. n.24 and Bishops' Message n.13.
[44] ibid. n.68

feel insecure in their own experience and understanding of the faith. They are frightened if we appear to ask them to be teachers as well as parents. This is one of the major issues that we face at the close of the century. Still, it is true that ideally 'family catechesis precedes, accompanies and enriches all other forms of catechesis'. In the mind of John Paul II, anyone who tries to help parents in this task performs a 'service without price'. In the light of this exhortation more time and resources need to be provided for the catechesis of parents both as adults with their own questions and searching and as parents who are enabled to live and share their faith with their children. We often blame them for the lack of practice and for the general behaviour of their children. We need to structure more helpful and realistic support systems for them.

The school is also seen as a setting which 'provides catechesis with possibilities that are not to be neglected'[45]. A school, it is said, would not deserve the name Catholic if it neglected or downplayed religious education, whatever its success in other areas. One of the chief reasons why parents should choose a Catholic school is precisely because of 'the quality of religious instruction integrated into the education of the pupils'. The text stresses that the pupils' freedom of conscience must always be respected. There should be no physical or moral pressure put on pupils especially 'in the case of the religious activity of adolescents'. Nonetheless, a Catholic school has 'a grave duty to offer a religious training suited to the often widely varying religious situations of the pupils'. In this brief sentence the Pope simply refers to the 'widely varying religious situations of the pupils', to the many different levels of religious interest and commitment among the pupils in our Catholic schools. This is a key issue when considering the potential and limitations of Catholic schools in the work of catechesis and religious education. More recent church documents and other studies will give greater consideration to this issue. R.E. teachers are keenly aware of the different levels of religious interests and commitment in their pupils. For this reason they look for resources that will arouse interest and involve pupils in reflection and discussion on the significance of religion and the Christian faith in their lives. The school, like the parish, must find ways of serving the needs both of the committed and of those who appear to be indifferent to religious questions. In this

---

[45] ibid. n.69

they need the support and encouragement of the Catholic community. Unfortunately, teachers are often too readily and unjustly blamed for the lack of knowledge and practice of the faith among the young.

The synod did not give a great deal of consideration to the school. Kevin Nichols attended the synod with the bishops from the English and Welsh conference. In his opinion, catechetical documents do not consider the school in any great detail because not all countries have a well-developed Catholic school system. He also detects a further reason: many bishops do not consider catechesis as a 'scholastic process' because the limitations of syllabus, compulsion and discipline 'are too great and overwhelm it'. He points out that the term 'religious education' was scarcely used and at times positively rejected because 'it implied too scholastic and detached a process insufficiently rooted in any community of faith'. In these documents a catechist is not generally considered to be a professional teacher but a person performing a ministry in the Church. Nichols maintains that this must cause British Catholics to raise important questions: are Catholic teachers, especially teachers of religious education, professional educators or are they performing a ministry? Can they do both? What is the distinction between catechesis and religious education, between catechists and teachers?[46] These questions need further consideration and clarification. I shall reflect on these issues in the final chapters of part two.

Catechesis in a pluralist society

The bishops in their message to the Church recognise that today's world is characterised by diversity: it is composed of people who have different visions of the world, different ethical principles, different social and political systems. Catechesis should prepare Christians to live in this world. The bishops advocate that Christians be educated to an appreciation of their own identity as members of the Church and, at the same time, they must be educated towards an openness which engages in real dialogue. Catechesis should be marked by an ecumenical dimension and should develop an attitude of reverence for and understanding of

---

46 K. Nichols, 'Continuity and Change in Catechetics', The Month, 11, 3, 1978, pp.86-89.

other religious traditions. The ecumenical formation of Catholics 'will enable them to understand better those who belong to other Churches or ecclesial communities while also preparing them for dialogue and fraternal relations with them'[47]. Van der Ven, however, considers that the synod text is 'very reserved in its attitude to other religions'[48].

Conclusion

The two synod documents are key texts for the understanding of the nature, aims and practice of the ministries of evangelisation and catechesis, including that of religious education in Catholic schools. They give a broad picture of the rich and complex pastoral activity of educating to and in the faith in today's Church. There are many dimensions in the task that include but encompass much more than instruction in Christian doctrine. These documents help and encourage us to unpack the richness contained in our beliefs and doctrines so that meaning of our human lives can be enlightened and interpreted by the Word of God, 'the Word who is life' (1 John 1:3). As Beozzo says, *Evangelisation in the Modern World* challenges Catholics to look to 'the face of the Church that turns to the world outside its frontiers'. Without fully solving the problems and dilemmas we face in the task of educating to and in the faith, *Catechesis in Our Time* advocates a healthy balance between the doctrinal and experiential approach. The necessary partnership of home, parish and school in the task is clearly and forcefully stressed. The importance of working with and for adults and parents is once again highlighted. These synod exhortations present a radical and dynamic view of Revelation incarnated in Jesus Christ and stored in Scripture and in the depth of the Church's memory. We are reminded that we are involved in the mission of communicating this Revelation to our generation as part of 'a living and active tradition'. We can all agree with the ideal set before us; it is in the practical working out of the ideal that disagreements arise. Still, that is very much part of the history of these ministries.

---

[47] Bishops' Message n.15
[48] J. Van der Ven, 'The Future of the Church as an Inter-generative Problem', Concilium, 174, 4, 1984, p.35

Chapter Eight

Catechesis and the Catechism of The Catholic Church

In two historic moments, at the Council of Trent and in our times, it was considered opportune to furnish a comprehensive presentation of the faith in a catechism of a universal nature, which would serve as a reference point for catechesis throughout the Church.[1]

The very purpose of the catechism precludes those adaptations of presentation and catechetical method which the variety of cultures, ages, spiritual maturity, social and ecclesial situations demands...these indispensable adaptations are the business of the derived catechisms, and of those who teach the faithful.[2]

In this final chapter of historical sketches and reflections I shall consider the renewed call for a universal catechism or for some sort of an official summary of doctrine in the spirit of Vatican II and the eventual publication in 1992 of the *Catechism of the Catholic Church*. Ever since the bishops at Vatican II opted for a directory with guidelines and directives rather than a catechism, there have been individuals and groups in the Church who have from time to time raised the question of a catechism. Already in the 1977 synod on catechesis the matter was considered in some language groups and mentioned in individual interventions. Some expressed the need for a text outlining fundamental doctrine. What form such a text might take and to whom it should be addressed were less clear. There was no general agreement. Paul VI in his concluding speech made no reference to a catechism. In the document *Catechesis in Our Time* John Paul II does seem at the very least to hint at the desirability of a catechism. It was in the course of the Extraordinary Synod of 1985 that approval was given to Cardinal Law's proposal 'to prepare a draft of a Conciliar Catechism to be promulgated by the Holy Father after consulting the bishops of the world'. In an attempt to answer the question 'How did this come about?' I shall briefly touch on some of the factors that may have influenced this decision of the 1985 synod.

[1] GDC n.114
[2] Catechism of the Catholic Church (CCC), prologue p.VI (Geoffrey Chapman, 1994)

Critical reservations regarding recent developments

From the reading of the previous few chapters it is evident that reservations have frequently and forcefully been expressed concerning the 'new catechetics', particularly of the anthropological or experiential approach of the late sixties and afterwards. Those who advocated the approach were deeply conscious of the need to communicate with people of a variety of cultures, many of whom lived in a secularised world in which there was widespread indifference to religion and the Church. For many people, Christian faith seemed superfluous; it had no significance for life, religion was, as far as they were concerned, a spent force. Religion was a purely private matter; take it or leave it was the general attitude. Indifference rather than any sort of militancy was the characteristic of the period. Many theologians addressed the questions that this raised. Some theologies took on a strong anthropological dimension.

Catechists sought to speak to people in the contemporary situation by attending to their questions and their aspirations. This approach was advocated by many scholars in the field of catechetics and endorsed in the catechetical study weeks, and, to a considerable extent, in a number of international and national Church documents. Notable among the latter is the Italian bishops' document, *Il Rinnovamento della Catechesi* published in 1970, the year before the *General Catechetical Directory*. The Italian and other national documents exercised an influence on those who wrote the Directory. The Italian text was translated into English and published by the Australian and the English and Welsh bishops.[3] I think it is useful to quote from this document - it has a special authority because it is published in the name of a national conference of bishops and accepted officially by other bishops' conferences.

> *Anyone wishing to have an effective discussion about God with people today must have human problems as the starting point, and must always keep them in mind when communicating the message. This is an intrinsic demand of every Christian dialogue on God. The God of Revelation in fact is 'Emmanuel' – 'God-with-us', the God who calls, who saves and makes sense of our life.*[4]

---

[3] Australian Episcopal Conference, The Renewal of the Education of Faith E. J. Dwyer, Sydney 1970; Bishops' Conference of England and Wales, Teaching the Faith the New Way, (TFNW) St Paul Publ., 1973
[4] TFNW n.77

The motivation and inspiration for this is found in the central Christian belief in the Incarnation.

The fundamental law of all catechetical method is that of fidelity to the Word of God and fidelity to the concrete needs of the faithful. This is the ultimate criterion by which catechists must appraise their work as educators. We are not dealing here with two different concerns but with one spiritual attitude... It is the attitude of the charity of Christ, the Word of God made flesh.[5]

General reservations concerning recent developments

Many Catholics were very unhappy with this direction in catechetical theory and practice. They were strong in their criticisms of this catechetical thinking and of the resources being produced by those who advocated this approach. Examples of such criticism and of the debates that took place, particularly in England and Wales, have already been considered. Another well-known example of this can be found in the reaction to the Dutch Catechism published in 1966. The text was commissioned by the Dutch bishops and written by the staff of the Higher Catechetical Institute at Nijmegen. It was a text meant for use in the catechesis of adults. In the foreword the Dutch bishops wrote that they hoped 'to present anew to adults the message which Jesus of Nazareth brought into the world, to make it sound as new as it is …in a form suited to the present day'. While the text was eagerly received and much appreciated by Catholics and others in many countries, other Catholics strongly disapproved of it. Questions were raised concerning its presentation of some aspects of Catholic doctrine. A group of Dutch lay people petitioned Paul VI to take action against the catechism which they considered to be dangerous. A meeting was arranged consisting of three theologians named by Rome and three selected by the Dutch bishops The result was a stalemate. Eventually the Pope appointed a commission of

---

[5] ibid. n.160

six cardinals to look into the matter. In their statement submitted in 1968 the cardinals spoke of the 'praiseworthy originality' of the Dutch text but, as Cardinal Ratzinger puts it, they 'found it necessary to render more precise, indeed to correct altogether, its affirmations regarding certain fundamental points'[6]. The Dutch Catechism was reprinted with the corrections made by the cardinals given in an appendix at the end. Ratzinger suggests that this debate may well have encouraged some to consider the question of producing a catechism for the entire Church. In his opinion the time was not yet ripe.

Speaking of the 'brouhaha that surrounded the Dutch catechism', Marthaler points out that it was not an isolated incident, as there were a number of others. He speaks, for example, of the opposition to the works of Moran in the United States and to the concept of 'ongoing revelation'. He mentions the debate over the publication of *Pierres Vivantes*, given the imprimatur by the French bishops, and he refers to the objections against the Argentinian text *Hoja de Ruta* dealing with social issues of concern to young people developed by the Salesian Catechetical Centre.[7] Many of the reservations concerning the anthropological, experiential catechetical content and methods have already been noted in the previous chapter. Among the main reservations was the fear that the approach was too 'horizontal', too taken up with human concerns with no real dialogue with the beliefs of the Christian faith. There seemed little sensitivity to an integral, orthodox content of faith. Concern for human questions and problems led to an over preoccupation with the 'fides qua' with much less attention paid to the 'fides quae'. Many placed the blame for the crisis of faith squarely on the 'new catechetics'. The solution lay in getting back to basics. Knowledge of the faith would overcome the crisis. Whether people actually fully agreed with such a bald statement or not, many were of the opinion that an authoritative catechism that presented doctrine, particularly in the light of Vatican II, might provide a resource that would go some way towards resolving the tensions. It would, they thought, help to build bridges between those who held opposing views. However, there was diversity of opinion when faced with certain questions - 'what sort of catechism?', 'which audience should it address?', 'how should it be

---

6 J. Ratzinger & C. Schonborn, Introduction to The Catechism of the Catholic Church, Ignatius Press, 1994, p.12.
7 B.L. Marthaler (ed), Introducing the Catechism of the Catholic Church, pp.12-13

used?', 'where would it stand in the context of catechetical developments?', 'how would it encourage and respect local adaptation?'.

Some more official reservations

Already in some official documents one can detect some inkling of a
wish for some sort of catechism or text which would have universal
influence. In *Catechesis in Our Time* it is possible to see general approval
for recent catechetical developments, including the anthropological direction, while at the same time being aware of certain reservations. The text
seeks to hold the doctrinal emphasis in balance with the life-experience
emphasis. However, Pope John Paul does stress the need for 'organic and
systematic Christian instruction' because of the tendency in some places
to minimise its importance. The Pope urges due respect for the integrity
of doctrinal content in catechesis. He warns catechists that 'no true catechist can lawfully, on his own initiative, make a selection of what he considers important in the deposit of faith as opposed to what he considers
unimportant, so as to teach one and reject the other'. He praises the
Catechism of Trent as 'a work of the first rank as a summary of the
Christian teaching and traditional theology for use by priests'[8]. He
expresses gratitude for the work of Borromeo, Bellarmine and Canisius
in producing catechisms that 'were real models for that period'. He
expresses the hope that 'the Second Vatican Council may stir up in our
time a like enthusiasm and similar activity'. Marthaler thinks that this
paragraph outlines the scenario for the catechism that would come later.[9]

Cardinal Ratzinger became the Prefect of the Congregation for the
Doctrine of Faith in 1982. He had already expressed strong criticism of the
Dutch Catechism. In 1983 he gave a widely publicised address on the subject of catechesis delivered in Lyons and Paris in which he berated aspects
of the new catechetics. In particular he lamented the abandonment of catechisms. In his view it was a grave error to do away with catechisms as
outdated forms of catechetical literature. This led, in his opinion, to the
fragmentation and to certain arbitrariness in presenting the Christian message. Others maintain that it is not entirely correct to say that there was an
'abandonment of catechisms' since a number of national and other cate-

---

[8] CT n.13
[9] Marthaler op. cit., p.11

chisms were published before and after Vatican II. The cardinal was also critical of some of the aspects of new educational theory and practice, of the 'infiltration' into theology and pastoral practice of some modern philosophies (neo-Marxism, positivism) and of the predominant influence of anthropology and sociology on the teaching and understanding of the traditional faith. The consequence of this sort of catechesis was the side-tracking of dogma and the building of faith directly on the bible. In this approach dogma was downgraded. Reactions to the cardinal's lecture were divided. Some were full of praise for his stance; others reacted negatively.

In his *Introduction to the Catechism of the Catholic Church,* Cardinal Ratzinger expresses some of these concerns. He speaks of a letter that he received after his lecture in France from a parent worried about the quality of catchetical instruction given to her child. She decided to examine the catechetical materials 'with an eye to their content' and discovered that the 'catechetical programme, which was pedagogically so refined and up-to-date, had almost no content at all but simply revolved around itself'. He admits that this is 'an extreme case' and did not wish to generalise. He then forcefully declares that 'content had to win back its priority'[10]. Many letters in the Catholic press lament the apparent lack of solid doctrinal content in recent resources for religious education in Catholic schools. One is left with the question, 'what about the balance between doctrinal emphasis and the life-experience approach?' These are two poles of the tension and neither can be de-prioritised. The Pope in *Catechesis in Our Time* emphasises this point. And so the debate continues. However, according to Cardinal Ratzinger and others, it was because of the 'the problematic situation of catechesis in the seventies and early eighties' that 'the bishops present at the 1985 synod gave voice to this realisation: the time for a catechism of the Second Vatican Council was ripe'[11].

The 1985 Extraordinary General Assembly of Bishops

In 1985, twenty years after the closing of the Second Vatican Council, John Paul II convoked a special or extraordinary synod to which he invited the presidents of the national conferences of bishops. In the Catholic press some expressed fears that the intention of the Pope and

---

10 Ratzinger & Schonborn op. cit., p.14
11 ibid. p.14

others was to backtrack on the developments since the Council. Many bishops gave assurances that the synod would not and could not turn its back of the reforms of Vatican II. It had no such authority. Paul VI had, in fact, considered the Second Vatican Council to be the great catechism of our time. In response to these misgivings, Cardinal Carter, Archbishop of Toronto, wrote a pastoral letter on the topic. The Cardinal, considered to be a liberal, had attended the Council. Rejecting the negative interpretations put on the summoning of the synod by John Paul II, he states: 'for me it is a logical, nay an almost required, underlining of the most important ecclesial event of the twentieth century'[12]. In his letter, Carter expresses regret for 'unfortunate exaggerations' that had taken place in the years since the Council. He expressed the hope that the synod would 'speak clearly to theologians, to catechists, and to all the faithful concerning the right of the magisterium to teach and to bind all of the Catholic faithful'. There is a strong hint here and in other writings of the time that there was much to celebrate in the aftermath of Vatican II while, at the same time, there were some negative developments that needed to be checked. The Pope spelt out some of his reasons for calling a special synod twenty years after the Council. In the first place, it was 'necessary to refresh ourselves at that fountain and to relive in some fashion that extraordinary atmosphere of ecclesial communion which marked the ecumenical council'. Secondly, it would be useful 'to exchange and deepen experiences and information on the application of the council, both at the universal and local level of the Church'. Thirdly, it was necessary to ensure that the spirit and teachings of the council should continue to influence the life of the Church while taking account of fresh demands.[13]

The proposal for a catechism

It would appear that in the preparatory stages of the synod and in the responses received from the national conferences of bishops, that a small minority asked for a catechism or some similar text. Cardinal Daneels of Brussels, who chaired some of the plenary sessions, alluded to the fact that some conferences saw the need for a catechism which would

12 Quoted in Wrenn op. cit., pp.17-18
13 John Paul II, address to the Curia, 'Implementing the 1985 Synod', Origins, N.C. Documentary Service, 14th August 1986

address the needs of the Church after Vatican II in the same way as the Roman Catechism had after the Council of Trent. The theologian Walter Kasper, general secretary of the synod, said that the call for a universal text came not from the Roman Curia – not from a centralist mentality – but from the bishops of the Third World and had been backed by bishops from Europe and North America. This statement is called into question by some.[14]

A few individual bishops in their interventions raised the matter of a catechism. It was in the fourth general session that Cardinal Law, archbishop of Boston, put forward his proposal that a preliminary draft of a Catechism of the Council should be drawn up and sent to the bishops for their comments and then to the Pope for his approval. He saw this as necessary because 'in a shrinking world – a global village – national catechisms will not fill the current need for clear articulation of the Church's faith'. The idea was taken up in the language groups and by the end eight out of the nine groups backed the proposal. The final synod report recommended a catechism.

> *Very many have expressed the desire that a catechism or compendium of all Catholic doctrine regarding both faith and morals be composed, that it might be, as it were, a point of reference for the catechisms or compendiums that are prepared in various regions. The presentation of doctrine must be biblical and liturgical. It must be sound doctrine suited to the present life of Christians.[15]*

In his closing address at the synod the Pope acknowledged the bishops' desire for a catechism or compendium expressed by the bishops. Soon after the close of the synod he set in motion what would prove to be a long and complex process of the writing of the catechism. As Cardinal Ratzinger put it: 'it was easier to assign the charge than to carry it out'.[16]

---

[14] See Concilium 25, 1989, pp.599-603.
[15] 'Final Report of 1985 Extraordinary Synod of Bishops', Origins, N .C. Service, 19th December 1985
[16] Ratzinger & Schonborn, op. cit., p.15

152 Soil for the Seed

Preparation and publication of the catechism

In July 1986 the Pope appointed a commission of twelve bishops and cardinals to undertake the task. Cardinal Ratzinger was to head the commission and the other members were from various departments of the Roman Curia along with some diocesan bishops representing different cultures. They found themselves faced with a very difficult task since the mandate from the synod was rather vague or, as Ratzinger described it, 'rather indefinite in its contours'. Certain points were to some extent clear: it was for the whole Church; it was to be a point of reference; its presentation of doctrine should be biblical, liturgical, sound and suited to Christians of today. Beyond that there was nothing very definite.

Work on the production of the catechism would take another six years to complete. It was hoped that the final text could be presented to the bishops at the 1990 synod, twenty-five years since the close of the Vatican II. The text was not ready by that date and all that Cardinal Ratzinger could do was to give a report on the progress so far and to set out a revised schedule. It is not feasible here to examine all that took place in the production of the final text. I can only mention some salient aspects of that long and complex process. Several working groups were set up. There was in the first place the commission of twelve with Cardinal Ratzinger in the chair. Next a commission of writers, an editorial committee, was appointed. This consisted of seven bishops, among these was Bishop Konstant of Leeds. The Dominican friar, Christoph Schonborn, was appointed secretary to the editorial committee. It was their task to write the different sections of the planned text. At first it was decided to have three parts to the catechism: the creed, the sacraments and the moral life. The bishops of the editorial board were divided into three groups with each group given the task of writing one of the three sections. Later it was decided to add the fourth section on the Our Father and prayer in general. Besides these two working groups, some forty expert advisers were nominated. A number of preliminary drafts were drawn up and amended.

In November 1989 a draft text of some four hundred pages was sent to the bishops. It may be of interest to note that the draft and final texts of the catechism were written originally in French, not in Latin. The bishops engaged in the work could speak and understand French, and it was easier to translate from one living language to another rather than from Latin[17] The draft text sent to the bishops was originally entitled *Catechisme pour l'Eglise universelle. Project revise. Text provisoire.* Each episcopal conference organised its own consultation process. The bishops of England and Wales together with a number of advisers met with Christoph Schonborn, then secretary of the editorial committee, to be briefed on the nature, the structure and purpose of the catechism and also to share comments on the draft text. The bishops nationally and locally held consultations with a large number of people. More than a thousand bishops responded to the revised draft text. It is not hard to believe that twenty-four thousand suggested amendments and comments were sent to Rome.

Clarifying the mandate given by the synod

It is worth noting some of the issues that the working groups had to face in planning and writing the catechism. Cardinal Ratzinger speaks of them in the book introducing the catechism. I shall touch on some of points discussed by the Cardinal. Because the sections of the catechism were being written by three different groups of bishops on the editorial committee, it was important that the style and thought of each group should be harmonised. This was the main task of the secretary of the editorial committee. Ratzinger expresses admiration for the result: 'it is still a sort of wonder to me that a readable, for the most part intrinsically unified and, in my opinion, beautiful book arose out of such a complex editorial process'.[18] Not everyone would agree with the Cardinal's view. The publication of the official English translation was delayed for some considerable time due to disagreement over the use of inclusive language. This aroused strong reactions among many. The Tablet published several articles and commentaries on the differences of opinion concerning the English translation of the Catechism.[19]

The question was raised concerning the meaning of the terms: 'cate-

---

[17] ibid. p.24; D. Konstant, 'Understanding the Catechism', Priests and People, June 1993, pp.213-219
[18] ibid. p.25
[19] The Tablet, 'Translators at Odds', and 'The English of the Catechism', 19th March 1994; 'Doctoring the Catechism', 21st May 1994; 'Launching the Catechism', 28th May 1994
Flawed Expectations, Ignatius Press, 1996, pp.129-163, M.J. Wrenn & K.D. Whitehead

chism' and 'compendium'. The word 'compendium' seemed to bring to mind works intended for 'scholarly libraries but not for normal readers'. The term 'catechism', on the other hand, spoke of a 'specialist literature offering not technical knowledge but proclamation'. Since the catechism was seen as a work of proclamation it was decided that 'it should be written, not by scholars, but by pastors drawing on their experience of the Church and the world'. The debate about the type of text – catechism or compendium – led to the all important question: for whom was the work intended? It is important to bear in mind what Cardinal Ratzinger says on this point:

> It was clear from the beginning there could be no question of a textbook for immediate use in catechesis in parishes and schools. Inasmuch as cultural differences spawn a corresponding diversity of teaching methods, such a common textbook is simply not possible... We agreed that it should be written first and foremost for those who keep together the whole structure of catechesis: the bishops. It should first serve the bishops, together with their responsible collaborators, for the formation of catechesis in the various local churches.[20]

Its aim would be to 'foster internal unity in the faith and its proclamation'. It was the task of the bishops to 'guarantee the right transposition of the common deposit into local situations'. However, the catechism was not intended only for a select few. It should be accessible to interested lay people *'as a tool of their Christian maturity and of their responsibility for the faith.'*

> In the confusion generated by the vicissitudes of theological hypotheses and by their often highly questionable diffusion in the mass media, many lay people want to know for themselves what the Church teaches and what she does not.[21]

---

[20] Ratzinger & Schonborn op. cit., p.17
[21] ibid. p.18

The Cardinal also points out that 'the catechism should serve the original task of catechesis: evangelisation'. Among its intended readers are 'agnostics, seekers, and inquirers' to whom it is offered 'as a help to becoming acquainted with what the Church teaches and tries to live'.

Another crucial issue had to be faced: how to balance the charge to communicate the faith and the task of expressing it in such a way that it becomes accessible to people in the present reality of today's world. Ratzinger acknowledges that 'it was not easy to bring together the two tasks'. There was much discussion about the proper starting point: the human situation in the contemporary world leading to God, or starting with 'the faith itself, in order to unfold it according to its own inner logic, that is, not so much 'argue' as bear witness'. There was always the danger that if the catechism did not begin with a description of the modern world it would appear 'ensconced in a mere world of ideas, far removed from concrete reality'.

> *Finally, however, we agreed that analyses of the present situation are always somewhat arbitrary, depending all too much on the angle of vision selected. We concluded further that there is no one global state of affairs. In fact, the context of a man living in Mozambique or Bangladesh (to adduce random examples) is entirely different from that of a man whose home is in Switzerland or the United States... It is indeed necessary to carry on dialogue with the mentalities of the day, but such dialogue is among the responsibilities proper to the local churches, whose field of action calls for great variety and flexibility.22*

The Cardinal rebuffs the opinion that, in this context, the catechism tries to be 'super-temporal'. In his view, that is not the case, 'it simply avoids binding itself too tightly to any actual arrangement of things'. Here we have a statement about the precise purpose of the catechism: it is a 'point of reference' for the work of catechesis that takes place in the many local churches throughout the world. It is a point of reference particularly for those engaged in writing catechetical texts, including catechisms.

---

22 ibid. p.21

The value and limits of the catechism in the task of catechesis

The Catechism is an authoritative and privileged instrument for catechesis. Unlike other catechisms, apart from the Catechism of the Council of Trent, it was authorised by the Pope and has been written with the collaboration of the bishops of the Church. John Paul II when promulgating the catechism stated:

> *The Catechism of the Catholic Church is a statement of the Church's faith and of Catholic doctrine, attested to or illumined by Sacred Scripture, the Apostolic Tradition and the Church's Magisterium. I declare it to be a sure norm for teaching the faith and thus a valid and legitimate instrument for ecclesial communion... This catechism is given that it may be a sure and authentic reference text for teaching Catholic doctrine and particularly for preparing local catechisms.23*

The Catechism is offered as an authoritative, contemporary summary of Catholic doctrine, of the faith of the Church. That is its unique strength and value. Inherent in this are certain limitations: as a document prepared for the whole Church, it cannot and does not take account of local circumstances or needs. It is not intended to replace local catechisms, it is meant to encourage and assist in the writing of new local catechisms. The *Catechism of the Catholic Church* and local catechisms provide valuable tools but are not the only tools to be used in the work of catechesis. The Catechism can help catechists, teachers, parents and others be more confident about the doctrinal content of the faith (fides quae), it does not provide the necessary expertise in developing and using appropriate methods and skills to help the young people and adults grow in the faith (fides qua). The text of the catechism makes this clear.

> *By design, this catechism does not set out to provide the adaptations of doctrinal presentations and catechetical methods required by the differences of culture, age, spiritual maturity and social and ecclesial condition among all those to whom it is addressed. Such indispensable adaptations are the responsibility of particular catechisms and, even more, of those who instruct the faithful.24*

23 CCC p.5   24 ibid. p.11

No catechism, including this most recent and most authoritative of catechisms, can replace or take over the work of catechists as they deal with a
variety of people in many different situations. In this context the Catechism
itself quotes the caveat given in the Catechism of Council of Trent:

> *Above all, teachers must not imagine that a single kind of soul
> has been entrusted to them, and that consequently it is lawful
> to teach and form equally all the faithful in true piety with one
> and the same method!... Those who are called to the ministry
> of preaching must suit their words to the maturity and under-
> standing of their hearers, as they hand on the teaching of the
> mysteries of faith and the rules of moral conduct.*

The structure and content of the catechism

It is not within the scope of this book to analyse the content of the catechism or to provide a critical review of it. These can be found in articles in catechetical and theological journals and in specific
commentaries. In the context of these historical sketches of catechetical
developments I shall touch only on some features of the catechism. The
plan of the catechism 'is inspired by the great tradition of catechisms
which build catechesis on four pillars: the baptismal profession of faith
(the Creed), the sacraments of faith, the life of faith (the commandments),
and the prayer of the believer (the Lord's Prayer)'[25]. These were features
of the ancient catechumenate and of some of the practices in the medieval
Church. These are 'pillars' or key dimensions of the Christian faith: its
expression in doctrines and beliefs, its celebration in liturgy, especially, in
the sacraments, its being lived in moral behaviour and social action and
in service of the Kingdom and in praying as Jesus taught us.

The Catechism has been described as 'a rich tapestry of different expressions of faith, both ancient and contemporary'[26]. The Catechism contains
matters that have been solemnly defined and others that have been officially taught with less formal authority. One of its main sources is, of

---

[25] ibid. p.9
[26] Bishops' Conference of England and Wales, 'Guidelines for the use of the Catechism of the
Catholic Church', in Briefing vol. 24 n.10, 26th May 1994, p.7.

course, the teaching of the Second Vatican Council. It makes extensive use of scriptural texts and references. In their guidelines for using the Catechism the bishops point out that Scripture is used in a variety of ways and they give some help in understanding the different genres of writing found within the Scriptures[27]. The catechism draws on the heritage of ancient and contemporary liturgical texts, of both eastern and western Catholic tradition. There are many quotations from the early Fathers as well as from leading theologians such as Thomas Aquinas and Cardinal Newman. Much of this material is 'illustrative, sometimes illuminating doctrine and sometimes offering spiritual insight'. Some of this material may be helpful for reflection, prayer and meditation. Amid this wealth of material which presents 'the Church's tradition as a varied and vibrant story', it is necessary, as the bishops point out, 'to discern the difference between this illustrative and additional material (often in smaller type-face) and the central expression of doctrinal points'[28]. At the end of each section of the Catechism there is a summary which is intended to help readers note and remember key points. The bishops warn that these 'are not intended as a balanced summary of the text but rather to highlight key points. They should not be separated from the full text or presented as if they stand alone'. There is just the danger that some people may make them into a shorter catechism. That is not their purpose.

The Catechism (content) and the Directory (process)

It is essential that those involved in the task of educating to and in the faith are aware of and have some understanding of the recent Directory, *The General Directory for Catechesis*, published in 1997, an updated version of the Directory of 1972. Whereas the Catechism presents an outline of Catholic doctrine, i.e. the beliefs of the Church community, the Directory looks more to ways in which catechists and others can accompany, encourage and challenge the individual believer on their personal journey of faith. As a consequence, the Catechism and the Directory must be seen as complementary tools or resources. I have already quoted

[27] ibid. p.6
[28] ibid. p. 8

Cardinal Ratzinger when he stressed that the Catechism is not 'a textbook for immediate use in catechesis in parishes and schools'. We read in the text of the Catechism itself that it does not set out 'to provide the adaptations of doctrinal presentations and catechetical methods required by the differences of culture, age, spiritual maturity and social and ecclesial conditions among those to whom it is addressed'. This is the task of the local Church and those who have direct contact with the various groups and individuals. The Directory offers theological and pastoral guidelines to meet 'the new situations and needs'.

> *The basic intention of the Directory was (and still remains) that of offering reflections and principles, rather than immediate applications or practical directives. This method has been adopted principally for the reason that defects and errors in catechetical material 'can be avoided only if the nature and end of catechesis, as well as the truths and values which must be transmitted, are correctly understood from the outset'.29*

Like the Catechism and other documents, the Directory is also the result of fairly wide consultation in the Church. In the aftermath of the publication of the Catechism and in the light of various synod documents, the international Committee for Catechesis felt that it was necessary to undertake a revision of the 1971 Directory. In 1993 a questionnaire was sent to the bishops who had responsibility for catechesis in the national conferences. It was also circulated to the main catechetical centres, to members of the committee and a number of leading experts. The questionnaire set out seven areas for consideration. In November of 1994, Cardinal Sanchez, prefect of the Congregation for the Clergy, invited two catechetical experts to draw up a draft revision. One of these, Mgr Estepa, had been involved in drafting the 1971 Directory; the other, Fr Cesare Bissoli, a Salesian, lectured in the Salesian University in Rome. They worked on the text during 1995 and the first draft was ready by the end of 1996. The Pope approved the final text in 1997 and the Directory was promulgated on 15th August of that year. In October 1997 an international Catechetical Congress was held in Rome organised by the Congregation for the Doctrine of Faith and the Congregation for the Clergy. The two main themes were the presentation of the Catechism and

---

29 GDC n.10

the new Directory. In the opinion of Bissoli, the Congress was more of a symposium than an opportunity for studying the texts. He maintains that more attention was given to the Catechism than to the Directory.[30]

During the discussions and consultation no one asked for a radical revision of the previous Directory. This is borne out in the similarities in the titles. Groome says of the latest Directory 'like its predecessor, it will be the official tone of catechesis for the coming era'. He maintains that it 'gives no solace to the restorationist sentiments' but rather 'gathers up wisdom from the Church's long-term and most recent experience as catechist – claiming the ground gained – and offers new horizons for the pilgrim people of God'[31.] The text is divided into five parts: catechesis in the Church's mission of evangelisation; the Gospel message; the pedagogy of faith; those to be catechised; catechesis in the particular church. There is considerable continuity with the 1971 Directory though there are some developments. Chief among these is the placing of catechesis within the context of the Church's mission to evangelise. Groome demurs about this stress and wonders whether it is not more suited to the missionary context where the Gospel is still 'new'. At the same time, however, he suggests that 'maybe seeing ourselves as evangelisers will give those of us in old enculturated faith traditions – like Ireland – that fire in the belly we need to catechise with enthusiasm (what Augustine called *hilaritas*)'[32.] There is a sense in which we in Britian and in Western Europe are very much in a missionary context, a context in which we need to summon people to the faith as well as affirm them in the faith. The Directory in its introduction acknowledges this fact.

These concrete situations of the Christian faith call urgently on the sower to develop a 'new evangelisation', especially in those churches of long-standing Christian tradition where secularism has made greater inroads. In this new context of evangelisation, missionary proclamation and catechesis, especially of the young and adults, is an evident priority.[33]

[30] C. Bissoli, 'Il direttorio generale per la catechesi: 1997', Salesianum, Editrice LAS, Rome, LX,3, July-September 1993, pp.521-547
[31] T. H. Groome, 'Hope for Dirty Hands', The Furrow, April 1998, p.221
[32] ibid. p.223   [33] GDC 26

In this regard the 1997 Directory is more realistic and helpful, whereas the 1971 Directory was possibly more optimistic about the task facing catechists and religious educators. The new Directory acknowledges that the conditions of the soil in which the seed of the Word is to be planted vary greatly and offers some useful guidelines that help us address these different situations. At the same time it speaks of the need to examine problems and difficulties in order to identify possible solutions. Some of these I shall consider in later chapters.

Some initial fears concerning a Catechism for today

As has already been pointed out, many in the Church were somewhat wary when John Paul II called the Extraordinary Synod. There were suspicions that there was a movement at the highest level in the Church to reverse or at least temper the direction for the Church which had been set out in the documents of Vatican II. On the whole such fears were removed by the synod's endorsement of the objective of renewal expressed in the Council documents, although even after the synod there was a certain apprehension about its proposal for a catechism or com-pendium of Catholic doctrine. This could appear as a reversal of the Council's decision to draw up a Directory rather than a catechism. However, in the thirty years since the Council it is obvious that many were concerned about certain features of the developments in catechesis. Would those who strongly expressed such concern seek to undo all the positive aspects of these developments? Would there be a return to the old idea of the catechism as a provider of both content and method. The con-stant tension that has been felt and expressed throughout the history of the Church concerning the proper process of educating Christians, young and adult, remains. Christians in every era are faced with the twofold demand of fidelity to the Word of God and of fidelity to the people to whom that Word is addressed.

The words of Donal Murray can be applied to many periods in the histo-ry of catechesis.

> *Some appear to believe that the Gospel could be effectively preached in the 1980s in the same way as it was in the 1880s. However blinkered and misguided it may be, such criticism can touch a raw nerve precisely because it expresses, even in caricature, a concern which no catechist can escape – the concern to be faithful to the unchanging faith in a changing world.[34]*

The 1997 *General Directory for Catechesis* is intended to assist catechists in addressing that concern in today's Church. The Catechism and the Directory *'are two distinct but complementary instruments at the service of the Church's catechetical activity'*. The Pope offers the Catechism as 'a point of reference for the authentic presentation of the content of the faith'. The Directory is 'an official aid for the transmission of the Gospel message and for the whole of catechetical activity'[35]. Yet I have a fear that the Directory is little known or read.

When it was announced that there would be a catechism following the 1985 synod I was invited to write an article and even to appear on TV expressing my views on the subject. I declined since I had no idea what sort of catechism would be produced. However, I was tempted to write an article entitled 'Awaiting the Catechism with hope, fear and indifference'. My hope was that a catechism based on the 'great catechism of Vatican II' would help bridge the gap between the more 'conservative' and 'liberal' schools of thought. It would address the concerns of those who criticised the 'new catechetics' for a lack of doctrinal content. If written in the language and thought patterns that would address contemporary issues, it would provide a necessary and useful reference for catechists and teachers struggling with the questions of today's young people and adults. My fear was that, despite the warning of Cardinal Ratzinger and others, many would see it as a textbook for immediate use in classrooms and parish programmes, also that it could be used as a big stick with which to 'clobber' teachers and catechists, and finally that as an authoritative text with its necessary emphasis on doctrinal content it might prevent to an even greater extent some 'traditionalist' Catholics from appreciating the need for adaptation and method. My sense of indif-

---

34 D. Murray, 'The Language of Catechesis', Religious Education and the Future, p.123
35 GDC n.120

ference was based on the belief that the Catechism would not of itself bring back the many for whom the Church had little meaning or significance in their lives. They would have no idea of the existence of a catechism and, if they were aware of it, they would find it difficult to comprehend and difficult to relate to the realities of their lives

Conclusion

The bishops at Vatican I voted for a universal catechism for use with children. The bishops at Vatican II opted for a Directory rather than a catechism. Throughout the twentieth century there have been calls for some sort of catechism or authoritative summary of Catholic doctrine. At the end of the century we have a Catechism, a text that is very different from the one envisaged by the bishops at Vatican I. Its publication is a milestone in the development of catechesis but it is certainly not the answer to every problem. The Catechism is certainly not the whole of catechesis. It is an authoritative and essential tool. Catechists and teachers will be helped and inspired by the Catechism and the Directory. These are authoritative documents that will assist us in presenting 'Christian doctrine in a manner adapted to the needs of the times, that is to say, in a manner corresponding to the difficulties and problems by which people are most burdened and troubled'. Vatican II reminded bishops that this was one of their primary duties. An example of such an approach is found in Jesus as he walked with the two disciples on the road to Emmaus.

Bernard Marthaler expresses some of my feelings and, I think, speaks for many catechists and teachers of religious education in Catholic schools.

Many (myself included) who have been lukewarm to the idea of a new generation of catechisms, are opposed not to catechisms in themselves but to the idea that new catechisms, however inspirational and informative, are perceived as a panacea for all that ails the catechetical ministry.[36]

---

[36] B. L. Marthaler, 'Catechetical Directory or Catechism? Une Question malpose', Religious Education and the Future, D.A. Lane (ed.), The Columba Press, Dublin (1986) p.57

It is for this reason that I stress the importance of the new *General Directory for Catechesis*. The Catechism and the Directory go hand in hand. I end these historical sketches and reflections with a quotation from the new Directory where it cites the Vatican II *Constitution on the Church in the Modern World* (n.14) and comments on it.

> The 'adaptation of the preaching of the revealed Word must always remain a law for all evangelisation'. There is an intrinsic theological motivation for this in the Incarnation. It corresponds to the elementary pedagogical demands of healthy human communications and reflects the practice of the Church throughout the centuries. Such adaptation must be understood as a maternal action of the Church, who recognises people as 'the field of God' (1 Cor. 3:9) not to be condemned but to be cultivated in hope'.[37]

The Directory, like the Catechism, is an authoritative document and the result of a wide consultation process in the Church. The directives and guidelines which it contains will form the basis of much of my thinking regarding some of the trends and issues in catechesis and religious education in part two of this book.

[37] GDC n.169

PART TWO

PASTORAL AND THEOLOGICAL REFLECTIONS

Our duty is not only to guard this precious treasure, as if we were concerned only with antiquity, but to dedicate ourselves with earnest will and without fear to that work which our era demands of us, pursuing thus the path which the Church has followed for twenty centuries.

The substance of the ancient doctrine of the deposit of faith is one thing, and the way in which it is presented another. And it is the latter that must be taken into consideration with patience if necessary, everything being measured in the forms and proportions of a magisterium which is predominantly pastoral in character.

John XXIII, opening address at Vatican II

The new historical situation now confronts the old task – old and ever new. Out of the fusion of task and situation will emerge the new service to which we are committed.

Karl Rahner

Chapter Nine

Faith, Doctrine and Life

The Word who is life – this is our subject (1 John 1:1)

Personal faith is sustained by the traditional statements of faith. Without attention to the primacy of the personal dimension of the act of faith, and all the struggle and doubt and darkness that are a natural part of that act of faith, we run the risk of passing on 'the faith' without faith.[1]

In these reflections we are concerned with the task of communicating and sharing our faith and beliefs, of educating the young and others to and in the Christian faith within the Roman Catholic tradition. It is only right, therefore, that we give some thought to what we mean by faith. It is important and, I think, useful, to bear in mind that many people have faith, there are many 'people of faith' who do not profess the Christian faith or indeed any religious faith. We cannot simply presume that these people are without 'faith'. I wish first to consider this notion of 'faith' understood in a wider, non-specific sense. I shall then look more closely at our understanding of 'the faith'. It is my hope that these reflections will help all of us who seek to live and share our Christian faith to reflect more honestly on how much what we profess is in fact the true inspiration and challenge for our lives. These reflections may be of some help particularly when we are faced with young people and others who appear to reject or who actually do reject Christian faith and beliefs. I hope too that they may be of help when we try to understand and respect people who sincerely search for or profess a different faith and hold other beliefs. My intention is to provide some pastoral reflections, not to give any deep theological exposition of the issues.

---

[1] D. A. Lane, 'The Challenge Facing Religious Education Today', *Religious Education and The Future*, D .A. Lane (ed), The Columba Press, 1986, p.161

Faith and the search for meaning

As Catholics we speak of 'the faith' referring to our Christian faith within the Roman Catholic tradition. In doing so we may tend to identify faith with 'the faith'. Yet the term 'faith' can be understood more broadly and, in this sense, it is not the prerogative of Christians or those who profess to be religious. Faith in the broad more generic sense is essentially related to an individual's and a community's search for meaning, purpose and significance in life. For the most part we seek some shape or pattern to our experiences of life. We instinctively want to make sense of birth and death, sickness and health, the joys and hurts of human relationships, good and evil in the world. We try to understand and interpret the universe and our place in it. This is part and parcel of being human. Broadly understood, faith is a deeply human quality. It is, as Maurice Wiles points out, 'not just a theoretical matter. It implies an attitude of ultimate confidence about the world, that does not simply ignore but can never finally be overwhelmed by many things that seem to make such an attitude unreasonable'[2]. Faith is rooted in a conviction about and a commitment to the significance and worth of human life. Understood in this way, faith is not some superstructure superimposed from outside the person; it essentially pertains to the deepest human aspirations. For Christians, of course, faith is not a purely subjective feeling, it is the response to God's self-revelation in Christ. Our God, however, is not some distant almighty Lord but rather 'Emmanuel': 'God-with-us, the God who calls, who saves and who gives sense to our life'[3]. If, for whatever reason, for certain individuals 'the faith' and our Christian beliefs, no longer seem to give sense to their lives, they may look elsewhere. They may appear to question, or even abandon, 'the faith' but they are not necessarily people without 'faith' or a hunger for the spiritual dimension of life. They may well still be searching for a 'faith' to live by. They may claim to have found a 'faith' which, in their view, does seem to give significance and meaning to their lives.

Some people have a religious faith that acknowledges the transcendent, something beyond human beings, as the source and end of the mystery of

---

[2] M. F. Wiles in Christian Believing, The Doctrinal Commission of the Church of England, SPCK, 1976, p.127
[3] Bishops of England and Wales, Teaching the Faith the New Way, (TFNW) St. Paul Publ., 1973, n.77

life. Some profess a humanistic faith and find meaning and significance in their experiences of life here and now without making any reference to any other reality, beyond life. Christianity together with Judaism and Islam claim that their faith-vision is founded on divine revelation. In the words of Dulles, they 'profess to devise their fundamental vision not from mere human speculation, which would be tentative and uncertain, but from God's testimony, that is to say, from a historically given divine revelation'[4]. Whatever they profess as the core of their faith, all communities express their faith in a set of verbal statements or beliefs about life. They celebrate their vision of the significance of life in a variety of rituals and symbols. They also seek to act out their faith and convictions in certain codes of conduct. Faith and the key beliefs that flow from such a faith are essentially concerned with the way we understand and live our lives, because a person's 'faith' is what gives meaning significance and worth to his or her experience of life.

Openness to 'faith' and the 'Mystery of life'

In the view of many scholars from a variety of disciplines, all human beings in so far as they go on living and seeking meaning and purpose in life can be considered to have faith. Among such scholars, theologians also speak of faith in more universal, generic terms. Lane says that faith is 'an activity in the life of the individual: it is a way of acting and living in the world', 'it is as much something we do as it is something we have'[5].Tracy describes faith as a fundamental commitment 'to the full affirmation of the ultimate significance of our lives in the world'. For him it is 'a basic orientation or attitude which determines one's cognitive beliefs and one's individual ethical action'. At this level, he speaks of a 'common faith'. He holds the view that 'the explicitly Christian faith can render intellectually coherent and symbolically powerful that common faith we share'[6].

Hebblethwaite, in an article 'Man's search for meaning' also considers it a mistake, when speaking of faith, to divide people into believers and

---

[4] A. Dulles, Models of Revelation, Doubleday, 1983, p.3
[5] D. Lane op cit., p.161
[6] D. Tracy, Blessed Rage for Order, Seabury Press, 1975, p.8

unbelievers. He writes, 'in practice everyone works by some simple scheme of values, or perhaps loyalties'. For example, for some people, Marxism offers, or at least appears to offer, a 'set of meanings in the meandering blur of world history'. In the view of Hebblethwaite, even the vast majority who may seem to drift, uninterested in the great questions about human life, cannot avoid some form of self-questioning especially in moments of failure, love, birth and death. Human experience is common ground for all and, consequently, 'there are not two sets of human experience, but there are different interpretations of it'[7]. Walter Kasper asks whether it is possible to ignore the question of meaning at certain focal points of one's life. He is of the opinion that one can force it out of one's conscious mind 'but in practice everyone lives by reference to a meaningful model of things'.

> *Hence, negatively speaking, no one can live without a certain answer to the question of meaning. Perhaps he or she does not speak of meaning, but what else does anyone have in mind when seeking for happiness, love, and fulfilment? In all these instances an individual is looking for harmony between self and the world, and for harmony between world and self. That is what we call meaning.[8]*

Shea, in his book *Stories of Faith,* expresses the opinion that 'faith is as common and unavoidable as the air'[9]. He speaks of the 'natural process of revelation and faith'. By this he means that the events of our lives bring us to the awareness of what he terms 'the Mystery of life in which they occur'.

> *People have become aware of Mystery in privies and parks, in beds and on mountains, at times of joy and despair, in interaction with both friends and enemies, battling against the larger systems of society and searching for the depth of the solitary self, gazing at the vastness of the sky and squinting at the intricacies which swarm at the other end of a microscope. There seem to be no rules for the arrival of this awareness.[10]*

7 P. Hebblethwaite, 'Man in Search of Meaning', The Month, 9,5,1976, pp.161-163
8 W. Kasper, An Introduction to Christian Faith, Burns & Oates, 1980, p.24
9 J. Shea, Stories of Faith, Thomas More Press, Chicago. 1978, p.44
10 ibid. p.18

On Shea's understanding, we are inescapably related to Mystery and we become aware of this ultimate Mystery in and through our history and the experiences of life: 'Mystery is not a reality we directly encounter. It is always mediated through our interaction with situations'. Any formulation of this Mystery and our relationship to it is always partial, yet the relationship is so inescapable and central that it inevitably finds expression.[11]

A community of faith and personal faith

According to these and other writers, openness to the Mystery of life and faith is considered to be a common feature of all human existence in the sense that it is linked with our human search for significance and meaning. It is a quality of human beings who seek and find reasons for living, who have a basic orientation in life which gives significance to their existence and in the light of which they order their actions and relationships with other human beings. Most individuals belong to a community of people who, to a large extent, share a common perspective on life, a common way of understanding, interpreting and living life. Any such vision which helps give significance to human existence can be termed 'faith'. The way of articulating the meaning of life and the way of living life that is consequent on such a faith is the belief system or tradition of the community which its members term 'the faith', 'our faith'. It is through such traditions and beliefs that faith is expressed, communicated, evoked, shaped and strengthened. In his book *The Experience of God* Dermot Lane argues that 'there is no such thing as pure or neat faith'. Faith does not exist without beliefs, however limited and partial they may be as expressions of the deeper reality that is faith.[12] For Lane faith is a way of life 'a way of being and behaving in the world that is informed by such complex factors as personal experience of existence, community and tradition'.[13] While scholars make distinctions between faith and beliefs, they generally agree that they cannot be separated. This is not the place to go into such deep discussion. The point I wish to make here is that 'faith' is normally given expression in the beliefs and the tradition of a community.

---

11 ibid. pp.16-19
12 D. Lane, The Experience of God, Veritas, 1981, p.60
13 ibid. p.54

However, conflicts and tensions can arise between individuals and the community. These can occur when, for whatever reason, the belief system of the community no longer seems to the individual to accord with or give true expression to his or her 'faith', his or her search for significance and worth in life. Some may reject or abandon the faith of the community because they are no longer prepared to face up to the challenges and demands inherent in it. At times a gulf can be created between 'the faith' and beliefs of a particular community and an individual's experiences of life, the individual's 'faith.' When this dichotomy occurs, then the faith of the community may be seen as a mere superstructure, a sort of imposition on the individual that fails to give meaning and significance. Using our Latin tags we might say that the bridge between the 'fides quae' – what the community believes, and the 'fides qua' – the personal search for a faith to live by, has collapsed. This can happen in any community with a belief system. As we know, this can and does happen within the Christian community, within our own families, as in other communities. The reasons for such a dichotomy can be many and varied. In an article that has some relevance in this context James Mackey discusses the choice that is faith. He imagines a conversation between a young Catholic couple out sailing on a Sunday afternoon. The girl suggests that it is time to turn back if they are going to the evening Mass. The boyfriend says that he is not going to Mass. When asked why he is not going, he announces that he has lost his faith. In the discussion that follows Mackey has the girl argue that it is possible to lose a wallet, patience or your wife, but not your faith. She declares that faith is not something you have, 'it is something you do. In fact, it's the way you live, the way you choose to live'. In her opinion, if a person no longer believed in anything that person would stop living, would have nothing to live for, would simply wither away or end it all. Somewhat bemused, he begins to reflect on the things which, in his view, make life worth living and explains some of the underlying principles and values by which he governs his life and actions. In the course of the discussion he rather impatiently retorts 'you know right well what I mean, I don't believe in the Catholic religion anymore'.[14]

---

[14] J. Mackey, 'The Choice that is Faith', The Furrow, 34, 2, 1983, pp.71-81.

Christian faith addresses the great human questions

These reflections on the wider understanding of faith and on the words of Kasper and others can be helpful when we reflect on our own faith. Do we really live our lives based on the inspiration and challenge of our Christian faith in Jesus Christ? Do we live our faith out of deep personal conviction, prepared to live out the implications of such faith in our relationships with people and our world? Or do we live and profess our faith more out of habit or custom? These are questions we have to ask ourselves if we wish help others come to and grow in Christian faith. Reflection on this wider understanding of faith can also be helpful when we are faced with young people and others who may seem disinterested in our faith – 'the faith' – or even in the great questions about life and its meaning. Yet, as Kasper says, what else do they have in mind when they speak of and look for happiness, love and fulfilment? If we have the ears to hear and listen with care and sensitivity, attempting to understand their questions spoken in their language, we may recognise those 'smoke signals of hope' in what may appear 'a burnt-out desert'. People, of course, can close themselves off from the openness to the Mystery of life and faith. Certain events of life and other people may blind them to it. Yet for the most part people, young and not so young, are seeking true significance in life in whatever way they may name it or search it out. We need to be more open to them if we wish to share our faith, 'the faith', in a true dialogue of hearts and minds in a way that might address, touch and challenge their searching and questioning. This is a duty that flows not only from a rational understanding of the nature and purpose of faith in a person's life. It flows also from our Christian faith vision of life and from our belief that every single person is uniquely created and loved by God and destined to share life with Father, Son and Spirit. We can discern the search for meaning, for happiness, love and fulfilment, as the search for God who is the origin and goal of all human life.

The bishops at the second Vatican Council in the *Pastoral Constitution on the Church in the Modern World* expressed their respect for and solidarity with all human beings in their search for the significance and meaning of life. They urged the followers of Christ 'to be aware of and understand the aspirations, the yearnings, and the often dramatic features of the world in which we live'. They acknowledged that, despite all modern developments 'there is a growing body of people who are asking the most fundamental of all questions or are glimpsing them with a keener insight: What is humanity? What is the meaning of suffering, evil, death, things which have not been eliminated by all this progress?' The bishops encouraged members of the Church to enter into dialogue with others because they share and are perplexed by these common human concerns. As Christians we believe that we are 'bearers of a message of salvation for all of humanity' because the Church believes that 'the key, the centre and purpose of the whole of human history is to be found in its Lord and Master'. The bishops declared that our Christian faith 'casts a new light on everything and makes known the full ideal which God has set for humanity, thus guiding the mind towards solutions that are fully human'.[15]

> *The Church is keenly sensitive to these difficulties. Enlightened by divine revelation it can offer a solution to them by which the true state of humanity may be described, its weaknesses explained in such a way that at the same time its dignity and vocation may be perceived in their true light.*[16]

In the light of this revelation 'the high calling and the deep misery which people experience find their final explanation'.[17] Faced with the mystery of good and evil, of birth and death, 'faith, with all its solidly based teaching, provides thoughtful people with answers to their anxious queries'.[18] For the bishops at Vatican II the Church's message 'is in harmony with the most secret desires of the human heart, since it champions the dignity of humanity's calling'. Citing the famous quotation from Augustine 'you have made us for yourself, O Lord, and our heart is restless until it rests in you', the bishops state that the Church's message, 'far from diminishing humanity helps people to develop themselves by bestowing light, life and freedom. Apart from this message nothing is able to satisfy the human heart'[19]. Our Christian message is that 'through Christ, and in Christ, light is thrown on the mystery of suffering and death which,

---

[15] Vatican II, The Church in the Modern World, nn.1-10. Flannery.
[16] Ibid n.12
[17] ibid. n.13
[18] ibid. n.18
[19] ibid. n.21

apart from his Gospel, overwhelms us.'[20] *The Catechism of the Catholic Church* speaks of Christian faith in this context of the human search for meaning.

> Before expounding the Church's faith, we must ask what 'to believe' means. Faith is man's response to God, who reveals himself and gives himself to man, at the same time bringing man a superabundant light as he searches for the ultimate meaning of his life.[21]

Communicating the message: Scripture, Tradition, Magisterium

On our Catholic understanding as expressed by John Paul II in *Catechesis in Our Time*, faith is the human response to the revelation that God made of himself to humanity in Jesus Christ. This revelation is stored in the Church's memory and in Sacred Scripture, it is communicated in a living, active tradition. The first disciples came in contact with Jesus. They were impressed, inspired and challenged by what he said and by what he did. What they experienced by being with him during his life and in the events of his death and resurrection brought new meaning and purpose to their lives. Gradually, inspired by the Holy Spirit, they became aware of the real significance of Jesus for themselves and for all people. They recognised him as 'the Christ', the one to whom the Old Testament prophecies pointed and the one in whom they were fulfilled.

> A particular experience stands at the beginning of Christianity. It began with an encounter. Some people, Jews, came in contact with Jesus of Nazareth. They were fascinated by him and stayed with him. This encounter and what took place in Jesus' life and in connection with his death gave their lives new meaning and significance.[22]

---

[20] ibid. 22
[21] CCC, n.26
[22] E. Schillebeeckx, Interim Report on the Books of Jesus and the Christ, SCM, 1980, p.10

Christians today are dependent on the memory of those first disciples, on their interpretive expression of that experience, on the tradition which has been handed on and which enshrines the memory of that experience. Schillebeeckx stresses that the foundation of the Christian tradition is not a doctrine but the history of an experience and that 'this history has to be communicated as carefully as possible if people are to make a Christian experience of their human experience'. This is the task of the Church who is at one and the same time 'disciple, guardian and interpreter' of the mystery revealed in Christ.[23] In the early Christian communities the apostles communicated the message in the first instance 'by oral preaching, by their example, by their dispositions'. In time they committed the message to various forms of writing.[24] The apostles in their preaching could be said to have inspired the criterion set out in the 1997 Directory: 'the selection of a particular order for presenting the message is conditioned by circumstances, and by the faith level of those to be catechised'.[25] This is borne out, as has been already noted, in the fact that there are four gospels originally written for different groups within the Church. We see it too in Paul's preaching to the Athenians and we recognise this approach in the letters in the New Testament, each with a particular community in mind.

As the Catechism states, it is our belief that the message of 'God's self-communication through Christ in the Holy Spirit remains present and active in the Church, firstly through the apostolic preaching and then through the apostolic succession of the bishops, successors of the apostles.'[26] Catechesis, in the words of John Paul II, is 'an orderly and systematic initiation' into God's self-revelation in Christ' and will draw its content from the living source of the Word of God transmitted in Tradition and the Scriptures. This is the 'deposit of faith', the 'treasure entrusted to the Church, the family of God, and she continuously draws from it things new and old'.[27] In the words of the Catechism 'this living transmission, accomplished by the Holy Spirit, is called Tradition'. It is distinct from, though closely connected to, Scripture. It is through this Tradition that 'the Church, in its doctrine, life and worship, perpetuates and transmits to every generation all that it is itself, all that it believes'.[28]

---

[23] TFNW, n.7
[24] Vatican II, Dogmatic Constitution on Divine Revelation (DV), n.7 Flannery.
[25] GDC, n.118   [26] CCC, n.79
[27] GDC, n.79   [28] DV, n.8

The 'deposit of faith' contained in Scripture and Tradition has been entrusted to the whole Church. The task of giving an authentic interpretation of the Word of God in Scripture and Tradition is 'entrusted to the teaching office of the Church alone – to the bishops in communion with the successor of Peter, the bishop of Rome'. This is referred to as the 'Magisterium of the Church'.

> *This Magisterium is not superior to the Word of God, but is its servant. It teaches only what has been handed on to it. At the divine command and with the help of the Holy Spirit, it listens to this devotedly, guards it with dedication and expounds it faithfully. All that it proposes for belief as divinely revealed is drawn from this single deposit of faith.*[29]

Scripture, Tradition and the Magisterium are the principle sources of catechesis, of educating in the faith. The Directory describes catechesis as 'nothing other than the process of transmitting the Gospel, as the Christian community has received it, understands it, celebrates it, lives it and communicates it in many ways.'[30]

A meaningful message for the human person

The Pope, in paragraph twenty-two of *Catechesis in Our Time*, also describes authentic catechesis as an initiation into 'a revelation which is not isolated from life... but which is concerned with the ultimate meaning of life', 'a revelation which illumines the whole of life to inspire and question it'. The interrelationship of faith, our doctrines and our human search for meaning is a constant theme in catechetical writings, particularly since Vatican II. I have highlighted this aspect when discussing the official documents in the historical sketches and reflections. Already in this chapter it is clear that the Vatican II *Constitution on the Church in the Modern World* was very concerned with this relationship. In fact, it states that the split between faith and life is one of the major problems of our age. Leading catechists have recognised in the spirit of this constitution a model of evangelisation which enters into dialogue with all human beings and brings the light of Christ to bear on the human

[29] ibid. n.10
[30] GDC, n.105

quest for significance in the mystery of life. The bishops, as we have seen, were urged to guard the doctrine faithfully while presenting it 'in a way that addressed the difficulties and problems by which people are most burdened and troubled'. The 1971 Directory stresses the need to be faithful to the teaching of the Magisterium while delivering the message in a way that is meaningful to people today.

> *It is necessary for the ministry of the Word to set forth the divine revelation such as is taught by the Magisterium and such as it expresses itself, under the watchfulness of the Magisterium, in the living awareness of the people of God. In this way the ministry of the Word is not a mere repetition of ancient doctrine, but rather it is a faithful reproduction of it, with adaptation to new problems and with growing understanding of it'.[31]*

When dealing with young people the Directory reminds catechists and religious educators they should help shed the light of the Christian message on the realities which have greater impact on the young. Paul VIth reminded those involved in educating to and in the faith that 'evangelisation must touch life: the natural life to which it gives new meaning'.

The 1997 Directory takes up this theme of the relationship between the Christian message and human experience and maintains that it is 'not a simple methodological question'. The text reiterates what was said in the 1971 Directory. Catechesis should make people more attentive to their more significant experiences and place the questions which arise from them under the light of the Gospel. The recent Directory spells this out with regard to different stages and aspects of evangelisation, catechesis and religious education.

- In any pre-catechesis the proclamation of the Gospel should be done 'in close connection with human nature and its aspirations'.

- In exploring the Bible, catechists should help people 'interpret present-day human life in the light of the experiences of the people of Israel, of Jesus Christ and the community of the Church'.

---

[31] GCD, n.13

- In explaining the Creed they should demonstrate 'how the great themes of the faith (creation, original sin, Incarnation, Easter, Pentecost, eschatology) are always sources of life and light for the human being'.

- In discussing moral issues as set out in the Gospel, the Beatitudes and the Commandments, catechists should 'root them in the human virtues present in the hearts of men and women today'.

- In considering liturgy they should 'make constant reference to the great human experiences represented by the signs and symbols of liturgical action'.[32]

As I pointed out in a previous chapter, this theme of faith and doctrines interpreting our human experience is almost laboured in these documents and other texts. This is because it is such a core feature of the different ministries which are concerned with educating people to and in the faith.

Doctrines speak of the significance of life

In his criticism of the catechism in the 1950s Jungmann complained that many in the Church looked upon doctrine as 'a string of dogmas and moral precepts' which they perceived as 'threats and promises, customs and rites, tasks and duties imposed upon unfortunate Catholics'[33]. They failed to understand the saving significance of these doctrines for their own lives. Drinkwater expressed a similar concern. Reflecting on religious education, he expressed admiration for the great devotion of so many dedicated teachers who taught the catechism as it was in his day. Yet he considered it a tragedy that 'the little book itself should be so dull and dry as dust in its content and wording'. He lamented its inadequacy despite such devotion among many teachers. He expressed his regrets: 'What a difference there could be if its words were more simple and direct enough to make the immediate impact on the human mind and heart which the tremendous News itself ought to make'.[34] We saw that a dominant characteristic of the anthropological phase of the catechetical movement was the interpretation of human experience in the light of the Gospel. Those gathered in Medellin for the catechetical study week recognised in historical situations and in authentic human aspirations an

---

32 ibid, nn.116-117
33 J. A. Jungmann, 'Theology and Kerygmatic Teaching', Lumen Vitae, 5,2-3,1950, p.258
34 F. H. Drinkwater, Telling the Good News, Burns & Oates, 1960, p.2.

important sign to which catechists should be attentive if they wished to help people discover God's plan for them in their lives.

Kasper compares the opinions of those who lay great stress on preserving the faith as handed down with those who stress the need for relevance in today's world. He points out the dangers in both positions if taken to extremes. He then goes on to say 'that dogma has to take effect as a form of the Gospel'.

> *Dogmas are to be interpreted as a form of glad tidings and not as ill tidings. They must be interpreted so that they can be understood as an offer of a more human form of human existence. Only thus can they become a challenge binding on conscience and a challenge to life and death.*[35]

Schillebeeckx makes something of the same point. In his view, if the Church hands on its long tradition of Christian experience in a set of concepts which are alien to our day, then 'most people never even begin to take up that particular searchlight as a possible interpretation of their experience'. At the same time he warns that 'no experiential catechesis can be effectively Christian if it is developed without the story of Jesus'.[36]

In what I consider to be a very remarkable and telling statement, the text of the Vatican Congregation for Catholic Education, *The Religious Dimension of Education in a Catholic School* declares that 'the human person is present in all the truths of faith'.[37] If we 'unpack' the doctrines of creation, of original sin, of redemption, of eternal life, they speak of the dignity of the person, the understanding of human weakness and failure, the hope of salvation amidst the mess of our world, and the hope of overcoming death. The 1997 Directory talks of an authentically Christian world view that encompasses the three key elements of creation, sin and redemption. The disciple of Christ, it says, deeply shares the joys and hopes, the sadness and anxieties of people today. The Christian looks on history and participates in it, not only from the standpoint of reason, but also from that of faith. Giving expression to our faith vision of the world and life are doctrines which speak to the aspirations and fears of people.

[35] W. Kasper, op. cit., p.110
[36] E. Schillebeeckx, op. cit., p.7
[37] Congregation for Catholic Education, Religious Dimension of Education In a Catholic school, (RD) Catholic Truth Society, 1988, n.84

In this world view all reality is marked by:

- the creative activity of God which communicates goodness to all beings;
- the power of sin which limits and numbs the human person;
- the dynamism which bursts forth from the resurrection of Christ;
- the hope of a 'definitive' fulfilment.[38]

It is not too difficult to relate some of the great human questions, anxieties and hopes to these Christian themes and doctrines.

Relating some doctrines to life

I recall an occasion when a somewhat perplexed mother approached me after a session on family catechesis. The woman expressed her gratitude for what had been discussed but said that she still had some worries. She explained that she had a four-year old son and that she was extremely anxious about what she should say to him when he asked her about the Trinity. A precocious child, I thought. Yet I could understand her anxiety. For many Christians the doctrine of the Trinity is among the most difficult to comprehend and explain. For too many people it seems more of a mathematical problem concerning the relationship of the numbers three and one. Evidently the woman was very dedicated to her family and to the child. She could not relate her understanding of Trinity to that experience. Yet is the doctrine of Trinity not about family, community, shared love that is also outgoing love? The recent Directory speaks of the doctrine of the Trinity and says that the presentation of God revealed by Jesus as 'the mystery of being one in essence and three in Person, has vital implications for the lives of human beings'.

It implies that humanity, made in the image and likeness of God who is a 'communion of persons', is called to be a fraternal society, comprised of sons and daughters of the same Father, and equal in personal dignity. The human and social implications of the Christian concept of God are immense.[39]

[38] GDC, n.16
[39] GDC, n.100; CCC, 2205

I imagine that the explanation of the Trinity that my anxious mother had in mind was not related to such a way of understanding this central mystery of our faith. To her and many others it is unfortunately an enigma, an abstract philosophical, theological concept, or worse, a mathematical problem. It is a useful and necessary exercise for catechists and R.E. teachers to 'illuminate' doctrines in this way and to mark out the great human issues to which they give a deeper significance. Bringing the two together is an essential part of their task. It is in this way that they connect the faith and doctrines of the Church with the individual's search. This is not simply a quest for relevance that looks to the latest fads and fashions, but rather the very serious search for significance that we believe is found in the person of Jesus, the Christ, the Incarnate Word of God.

I came across another helpful example of this 'unpacking' of doctrine in the intervention that Bishop Vincent Nichols, now Archbishop of Birmingham, made at the recent synod of European bishops. He spoke of the themes often referred to as the 'four last things' – death, judgement, heaven and hell. At first sight these may not appear easy themes to speak of with people of today. Bishop Nichols acknowledges that they are 'deeply set in the tradition of the Church' and that they are also themes 'which touch directly the fears, hopes, questions that, from time to time, fill the hearts of our contemporaries'. People have doubts and fears about death; they are puzzled over judgement. They are fascinated with heaven and have a dread of hell. During his intervention he spoke of the impact that the death of Princess Diana had on the people of Britain. People expressed their shock at death and their longing to reach beyond it by bringing countless flowers and lighting candles around the palace where she had lived and around Buckingham Palace. He spoke too of the outstanding example that Cardinal Hume gave in approaching death with a wonderful calm and sense of peace. His was a witness that opened up the 'horizon of transcendence' for very many people. What they understood from him was that death brings us to a meeting with God: 'the transcendent is not abstract, but the personal reality of the living God.'

The example of the Cardinal, who hesitated over accepting a high honour from the Queen because he wished to meet his God empty-handed, also gave him an insight to the Christian doctrine of judgement; 'our achievements, our successes, even our failures, are less important than our capacity to receive'. The doctrine of the last judgement invites us 'to live each day by generous giving, so that we may be filled with the gifts of the Lord'. Bishop Nichols believes that people today yearn for this Gospel truth. Too often people are imprisoned by notions of harsh judgement whereas the 'judgement of the Lord is a gift of understanding and mercy'. He urges the Church to announce and practice this judgement especially for those whose lives are wounded and broken. When it came to an understanding of heaven, he saw points of departure in a newspaper article entitled 'Weekends in Heaven'. The article was about holidays with time spent with loved ones, all desires fulfilled in serenity and beauty. He recognised this as 'fertile ground for the seed of the Gospel'. In our doctrine of heaven we can affirm that we are created for happiness and that such final happiness is attainable. In this way the Gospel of hope is made real. A true vision of heaven does not distract us from this world but rather guides our commitment to justice in the here and now. As for hell, Europeans had plenty of examples of the 'construction of hell on earth: in wars, prisons, concentration camps. Our fear of hell is real and profound'. The article of the Creed 'he descended into hell' speaks of the self-emptying of God in Jesus. In the opinion of the bishop, this doctrine could be 'the very core of the Gospel of hope' which proclaims that 'even the most terrible evil imaginable is not as powerful as the victory of the Lamb'. He ended his intervention by saying 'new ways of proclaiming these truths are needed if they are to be powerful messages of the hope and meaning so desired by people today.'[40]

Correlation of faith, doctrine and experience

The 1997 Directory addresses the question of the place of human experience in catechesis. Our human experience arouses in us interests, questions, hopes, anxieties, reflections and judgements. It is the task of catechesis 'to make people aware of their most basic experiences, to help them to judge in the light of the Gospel the questions and needs that spring from them, as well as to educate them to a new way of life'.

---

[40] V. Nichols, in Briefing, vol. 29n. 11, 10th November 1999, pp.20-21.

Experience also promotes an understanding of the Christian message. Jesus made good use of people's experience in his teaching. The Directory concludes that 'experience is a necessary medium for exploring and assimilating the truths which constitute the objective content of Revelation'. It states that 'interpreting and illuminating experience with the data of faith is a constant task' and acknowledges that it is a difficult one. It is possible to achieve this with 'a correct application of the correlation and interaction between profound human experiences and the revealed message'.[41] The modernist tendency in the Church caused many to be suspicious of experience. Emphasis on human experience could open the way to subjectivism and relativism. In the historical sketches we saw that catechists began to rediscover experience as an integral part of educating people to and in the faith. In recent years there has been a growing concern that in some ways the stress on experience was downplaying the role of Scripture, Tradition and the Magisterium. However, a delicate balance must be kept. There must be some form of critical correlation between human experience and the Gospel of Jesus Christ. Tracy and Schillebeeckx speak of the two sources of the theology as firstly, tradition or 'Christian fact' and, secondly, contemporary human experience. They argue that the two must stand together in some mutual and critical correlation. This is not, in their opinion, demanded by the search for contemporary relevance but by the claim that the Christian faith can only be accepted and developed when it is experienced as 'the liberating answer to the real questions that we ask'.[42] Tom Groome acknowledges that there has been considerable disagreement among catechists. Some argue that the prime emphasis should be on the biblical message and Christian tradition while others maintain that the stress should be on the experience of people today. He places himself within the 'experiential' school but declares that, more than others, he attempts 'to deepen the critical dimension of reflection on experience' and that he more deliberately sets out to hold experience and the Christian tradition 'in a dialectical and critical correlation'. This is the aim of his 'shared praxis' approach which he outlines in his book Christian Religious Education.[43] Mary Boys refers to the task of catechesis as making accessible the Tradition in a way that avoids 'the pitfalls of fossilisation and an uncritical pursuit of relevance' and

---

[41] GDC, n.152
[42] E. Schillebeeckx, op. cit., p.4; D. Tracy, op. cit., pp.43-45
[43] T. Groome, Christian Religious Education, Harper & Row, 1980, p.149

maintains that 'transmission and creation, paradoxically, must be held in tension'.[44] To fail to undertake this task is to hold an incomplete theology of revelation and faith and leads to a defective education to and in the faith. These theological terms are another way of speaking of the 'twofold fidelity: to God and to people' that is the constant refrain of catechetical documents and writings. If the Tradition is to be living and active, as the passage in *Catechesis in Our Time* suggests, there must be a constant dialogue between what is stored the Church's memory, Scripture and present-day experience. If such a dialogue does not take place then, as Shea puts it, the inherited language and tradition can become a priceless heirloom isolated from life, with little that is vital to say to the rough and ready contemporary scene.[45].

I bring these reflections to a conclusion with a quotation that has remained fixed in my memory for a long period of time. I find it disturbing, challenging and relevant to the present discussion. In his book *Free to be Faithful*, Anthony Padovano says that 'faith is impossible to many of us not because of its intellectual demands nor because of the personal sacrifices it requires'. In his opinion, 'the problem is that faith seems less than we are, smaller than life, unrelated to love and insufficient for hope'.[46] Properly understood and presented, the great Christian themes speak loudly and profoundly about the richness and value of life, love and hope. The recent Directory urges us to understand them, assimilate them and present them in that way.

Experience, assumed by faith, becomes, in a certain manner, a locus for the manifestation and realisation of salvation where God, consistently with the pedagogy of the Incarnation, reaches man with his grace and saves him. The catechist must teach the person to read his own lived experience in this regard so as to accept the invitation of the Holy Spirit to conversion, to commitment, to hope and to discover more and more in his life God's plan for him.[47]

---

[44] M. Boys, 'Access to Tradition and Transmission', Tradition and Transmission, O'Hare (ed), Religious Education Press Alabama, 1979, p.14.
[45] J. O'Shea, op. cit., p.31
[46] Padovano, A. 'Free to be Faithful', Pastoral Education Services, New Jersey, 1972.
[47] GDC, n.152

Chapter Ten

Head faith, heart faith, hands faith

A catechesis which inspires not only intellectual assimilation of the faith, but also touches the heart and transforms conduct is correct. Catechesis, thus, generates a dynamic life which is unified by the faith.[1]

Faith is a way of believing, a way of worshipping, and a way of living; it is cognitive, affective, and behavioural, engaging people's minds, emotions, and wills.[2]

An important development in the theory and practice of the mission of educating people to and in the faith is to be found in the renewed, wider theological understanding of revelation and faith that was evolving in the years before and after the second Vatican council. In writing about the recent *General Directory for Catechesis* Groome speaks of three great expansive horizons that the text lays out to inspire the ministry of catechesis. The first of these that he mentions is 'a holistic Christian faith': by which he means 'a broadening of Christian faith to engage the whole person – head, heart and hands – and inviting a wholesome and holy life after the way of Jesus'.[3] This understanding of Christian faith is to be found in Vatican II's *Constitution on Divine Revelation*. A fundamental feature of this document is the shift from an almost exclusive stress on the intellectual understanding and acceptance of truths revealed and set out in propositional form, in doctrinal formulations. The catechism of the council of Trent acknowledged that faith had a variety of meanings in Scripture but, in the context of the controversies of that time, the bishops focused on that particular aspect of faith 'by which we yield our entire

---

[1] GDC, n.205
[2] T. H. Groome, 'Hope for Dirty Hands', The Furrow, April 1998, p.225
[3] ibid., p.224

assent to whatever has been divinely revealed'. Within the Catholic tradition, this is upheld as an important, central dimension of the faith. However, many in the Church claim that in the post-reformation Church it has, for a number of reasons, been emphasised to the detriment of other key dimensions or features of our Christian faith. In this chapter I wish to reflect a little on the development of the understanding of revelation and faith, on key dimensions of faith and on some features of our task that follow on from this understanding. Again I shall refer to the recent Directory which makes frequent references to these themes.

A multi-dimensional understanding of faith

In the Vatican II constitution revelation is understood as the act by which God communicates himself in a personal way, revealing himself and making known his plan of love for human beings, inviting them into communion with himself.[4] This plan of the Father is fully revealed in Jesus Christ and is realised by the power of the Holy Spirit. Faith is described as the human response to revelation: 'by faith man accepts revelation, and through it he consciously becomes a sharer in the gift of God'.[5] Damian Lundy cites and summarises Bishop Butler's reflection on this development in the theological understanding of revelation as presented in the Vatican II constitution. Bishop Butler as auxiliary in Westminster attended the Council.

Butler sees it as a move from the image of an unseen divine philosopher in a schoolroom dictating abstract ideas to pupils of high intelligence to an infinitely loving God calling in friendship to humankind: the 'heart speaketh to heart' of Newman's motto.[6]

Understanding revelation and faith in this way, our task is to invite and enable people to come to an appreciation of God's loving design which is concerned with the true vocation and dignity of each person as created by God and destined to share the divine life. This does not set aside the tra-

---

[4] DV, n.2; GCD, n.10; GDC, n.36
[5] GCD, n.15
[6] D. Lundy, op. cit. p.45; B. C. Butler, The Theology of Vatican II, Darton, Longman & Todd London, 1981, p.27

ditional thinking with its emphasis on the assent of the mind to revealed truths. It rather situates such thinking within a renewed theology that considers a wider view of revelation and faith and which encompasses other aspects or dimensions of faith. Once the interest of people in Jesus and the Church has been aroused and an initial choice is made for some commitment, it is our task to accompany them and to help deepen their understanding of God's loving plan and to foster a free, personal, maturing response to that plan. Flowing from such a view of revelation, the task of educating people to and in the faith can be seen to have several key features or dimensions:

- to bear witness to and make known this call of a loving God and to encourage a personal response;
- to lead people gradually to a deeper understanding of God's plan in Christ;
- to enable them to celebrate this in liturgy and prayer;
- to encourage them to play a part in achieving this plan by working to build the Kingdom.

In taking up this multi-faceted, multi-dimensional task we engage in the mission of the Church. The Church sees itself as 'commissioned to safeguard and herald the revelation committed to it by Christ' and, believing itself called into being by this divine revelation, 'the Church claims to address its own members and all humanity in the name of the revealing God'.[7]

Towards a broader understanding of revelation and faith

In the historical reflections on developments in catechetical theory and practice, especially in the twentieth century, I pointed out that the theology of revelation was frequently seen as problematic. We saw this in the early critiques of the catechisms, in the renewed biblical and patristic emphasis of the kerygmatic movement and later in the anthropological stage with its emphasis on addressing human experience as an important

---

[7] A. Dulles, Models of Revelation, Doubleday, 1983, p.4

feature of evangelisation and catechesis. The delegates at the Roman Congress of 1971 recommended that the relationship between revelation and human experience be examined more fully. They asked that a more dynamic interrelationship should be explored. In the opinion of many, the controversy over Corpus Christi College in the 1970s was a controversy about two divergent views of revelation – the propositional and the experiential. The debates of the last decades concerning catechetical and religious education resources for parishes and schools were to a large extent debates about the doctrinal, cognitive approach, and/or a more personal, experiential approach. More recent official catechetical texts have tried to hold the two in proper balance and the recent Directory is no exception. In practice, this is still one of the crucial issues facing those involved in educating both the young and adults to and in the faith. The fear of an over reaction against a strongly doctrinal emphasis that might, in turn, play down the importance of the doctrinal, was one of the major factors in the demand for a catechism or compendium of Christian beliefs. This is not the place to examine in depth the issues involved in the theological understandings of revelation and faith. That is the task of those who are engaged in the study of fundamental and systematic theology. Dulles, for example, in *Models of Revelation* analyses what he terms five 'models, 'types' or 'varieties' of theological opinion on the subject in the twentieth century. Catechists must rely on the work of such scholars. A sound theology of revelation is the necessary basis for a proper and balanced understanding of Christian faith and of the task of educating people to and in that faith.

In his text on fundamental theology, O'Collins remarks that it is now commonplace to note the way theology, especially Catholic theology, has shifted ground on the question of revelation. He states that 'undoubtedly a massive shift has taken place from a propositional to a personal model of revelation'.[8] The 'propositional model' is the first which Dulles examines in his book. In this model 'objectively considered, the revelation is identical with the prophetic-apostolic deposit committed to the Church'. The appropriate response to revelation 'is faith in the sense of a firm assent to the revealed truths contained in the authoritative sources'. It is, he says, the theory 'most familiar because of its long history and its

---

[8] G. O'Collins, Fundamental Theology, DLT, 1981, p.54

unchallenged predominance in the recent past'.[9] Groome and others are of the opinion that the approach taken by the Council of Trent strengthened the popular Catholic understanding of faith as synonymous with belief, and belief as intellectual assent to officially stated doctrines. On this model, a distinction is made between 'natural revelation' and 'supernatural revelation'. Natural revelation is knowledge of God that human beings can deduce from observing the world around them. Supernatural revelation refers to divine communication concerning truths that are inaccessible to the unaided human mind such as, for example, the Trinity, Incarnation and Redemption. For Catholics and Reformers, faith was generally conceived as a firm assent to such revealed truths contained in authoritative sources. Catholics stressed the Church's teaching as the infallible guarantor of God's truths. The Reformers emphasised the role of the Bible as the inspired document that contained these divine truths. Faith was seen as reasonable because, although the human mind could not comprehend these truths, they were worthy of belief because of the fact that they came from God. The divine origin of such truths could be demonstrated by recourse to the miracles and prophecies.

The first Vatican Council discussed this question and in its conclusions it stated:

By divine and Catholic faith everything must be believed that is contained in the written word of God or in the tradition, and that is proposed by the Church as a divinely revealed object of belief either in a solemn decree or in the ordinary, universal teaching[10].

The Catholic position has to be considered within the philosophical and scientific context of that time. The text of Vatican I sought to avoid two extreme positions. On the one hand, it wished to reject an out-and-out rationalism which asserted that the truths of the Christian faith could be arrived at and proven by rational argument alone. On the other hand, it wished to avoid a pure fideism which totally rejected the role of human

---

9 Dulles, op. cit., p.45; p.36
10 Vatican I, Dogmatic Constitution 'Dei Filius', see Denzinger & Schonmetzer, Enchiridion Symbolorum, Herder, 1963 (32nd edition), p.590, n.3011

reason in matters of faith, because faith was pure gift and human reason played no part in it. Dulles, however, suggests that Catholic theologians were themselves 'infected somewhat by the very rationalism they were seeking to refute' and they portrayed revelation 'as a body of clear and distinct ideas from which conclusions could be drawn'[11]. It is, of course, easy to make sweeping generalisations that overlook delicate nuances and certain aspects of an issue. Nonetheless, many in the Church would claim that from the Counter-Reformation more or less to the present, Catholics have generally looked upon faith as a submission of the mind to the teaching of the Church through which God revealed these divine truths.

Reaction to the modernist movement

The Catholic position hardened further as a reaction against the spread of non-propostional theories of revelation. This is exemplified in the Church's reaction to the thinking of some theologians and others, termed 'modernists', towards the end of the nineteenth and at the beginning of the twentieth century. Modernism is a complex phenomenon. An exposition of the thinking of the modernist theologians and philosophers is not my concern here. I wish only to consider briefly the indirect influence that the movement had on catechetical theory and practice. In general terms it can be said that the modernists reacted against the identification of the Christian message with a body of truths and dogmas. They stressed inner religious experience which, they thought, could not be translated into human language. All attempts to express this inner, subjective experience in doctrines and dogmas were inadequate since these were conditioned by the thought patterns of a particular time and place. Modernists emphasised the individual and collective consciousness as the norm of Christian faith over and against the teaching of the Church. They rejected the central place given to scholastic theology with its rationalist abstractions. Influenced by the philosophies of the time, they stressed the value of lived experience rather than a priori conceptions. Some sought to distinguish faith from theological orthodoxy and assent to a system of dogmas. In the words of Roger Aubert 'they tried to replace scholastic

---

[11] Dulles op. cit. p.36

intellectualism by a doctrine which would involve the forces of the heart and the concreteness of actual life'[12]. Religious truth, they argued, could be deduced from the needs of human beings rather than from some supernatural source working from outside. They wished the Church and theology to be more open to the influence of modern philosophers and thinkers. They advocated a greater biblical approach in theology though Scripture was to be interpreted like any other historical document without reference to the magisterium of the Church.

In both the official teaching of the Church and in theological treatises Catholics reacted strongly against these views which 'seemed to imply a faith that was vague, imprecise, subject to the vagaries and waywardness of human emotions and completely lacking in objective validity'[13]. There was the danger of emotional subjectivity. It ran counter to the official stress given to scholasticism as the safeguard of Catholic theology. The teaching authority of the Church was questioned and even rejected. Pope Pius X officially condemned modernism in 1907. He did this very solemnly in his encyclical *Pascendi*. He describes their thinking as based on two fundamental and erroneous philosophical positions: 'agnosticism, which denies the validity of rational argument in the religious sphere, and immanentism, which derives religious truth from intrinsic needs of life'. The Pope also rejected their conception of biblical criticism, their purely subjective apologetics and their demands for reform in the Church and theology[14]. It is now fairly generally acknowledged that the movement, while erroneous, raised some vital issues that are being discussed among theologians today. Kasper suggests that the problems of modernism were more frozen than solved at the beginning of the century.[15] These are questions that I leave to others who specialise in this field of theological exploration. Moran, as a religious educator, claims that the modernists had a rather naïve conception of the relationship between experience and doctrine which 'made impossible its (modernism's) deepening of the Catholic understanding of revelation or its synthesising the objective and subjective, the personal and doctrinal, temporal and non-temporal char-

---

12 R. Aubert, 'Modernism', Encyclopedia of Theology, K. Rahener (ed), Burns & Oates, 1975, p.970
13 A. Shorter, Revelation and Its Interpretations, Geoff. Chapman, 1983, p.165
14 Aubert, op. cit. p.973
15 Kasper op. cit. p.21

acteristics of revelation.'[16] Damian Lundy maintains that a major consequence of the modernist debate was 'the outlawing of experience as a factor in religion, theology and spirituality'. In his view, 'the response to the Modernist's appeal to experience was to re-emphasise the intellectual character of faith and to reject vehemently the significance of experience in Christian faith and morals'.[17] In Lane's opinion there resulted 'a kind of apartheid' of experience that gradually came to be seen as inconsistent and there has been a recovery of experience as an integral element in the exercise of theology.[18]

Influences for change

It is possible to mention some of the principal influences that helped bring about what O'Collins called the 'massive shift from a propositional to a personal model of revelation'. Moran sums up the general opinion when he acknowledges that the 'primary factor' that influenced theologians was modern biblical scholarship. Dulles concurs and points out that sound biblical criticism called attention to the great variety of literary forms in the Bible and established that

Even passages that profess to be historical are shot through with poetic, legendary, and mythical elements, and that the biblical authors differ considerably among themselves in their religious views. Modern advances in science and historiography make it well nigh impossible to use the Bible any longer as an authoritative source of historical information, as was done in a pre-critical age.[19]

Mary Boys, referring to the Gospels, argues that modern biblical scholarship contradicts the 'blueprint mentality' in which it was assumed that Jesus left a specific and detailed plan for the Church. She maintains that modern biblical scholarship has provided Christians with insight into the 'fascinating and complex process by which the traditions of Jewish and

---

[16] G. Moran, Theology of Revelation, Herder & Herder, 1966, p.29.
[17] D. Lundy, op. cit. p.139; Lundy discusses the modernist crisis in his doctoral thesis, pp.111-144.
[18] D. A. Lane, The Experience of God, Veritas, 1981, p.5
[19] Dulles op. cit. p.49

Christian communities were remembered and reactualised'.[20] In the light of biblical criticism it is no longer possible to view the Bible as a series of heavenly truths directly revealed by God. Dale strikingly describes the heart of the Bible as a story: 'a story of a people learning the hard way what our rough human experience is all about and what are the things by which people really live'.[21] The Bible is seen as the articulation of a community's faith in the loving kindness of God which they perceived in their historical experiences, especially in the event of Jesus the Christ, a faith which came to expression in a complex process of development.

Another factor in the theological shift from a strict propositional model of revelation and faith is the application of the historical-critical method to the teaching and doctrines of the Church. This has led to a keener appreciation of the fact that doctrinal, credal formulations are always, as is the case with all language, conditioned by the historical, social, cultural settings in which they were expressed. This does not make them any less relevant or important in our day. However, we are more aware of the fact that they are shaped by the world view, the literary forms and philosophical presuppositions of a particular age. As a consequence they cannot escape what Dulles terms 'the limited horizons of their day'. In his book *Survival of Dogma* he speaks of 'the historical relativity of all doctrinal statements'. Dulles therefore, sees the task of contemporary hermeneutics as that of seeking 'to achieve fidelity to the given without rigid adherence to the approved verbal-conceptual formulation'.[22] Both General Directories see this as an essential, if delicate and difficult task. Whatever the dangers and risks, such a task must be undertaken if we are to speak from within a vibrant tradition that can still speak to young people and adults of the twenty-first century. Clearly, this must be done not on a purely individual basis but under the guidance of the community of the Church. Fidelity to our Catholic tradition does not simply mean the repetition of traditional formulas.[23] The bishops in the synod of catechesis rejected the view that catechesis was a matter of coming to a deeper understanding of 'abstract truths formulated in a fixed once-for-all manner'. At the same time they warned against adopting a radical position that set up an absolute opposi-

---

[20] M. Boys op. cit. pp.19-20
[21] A. Dale, 'The Art of Communication', A Source Book of the Bible for Teachers, R. C. Walton (ed), SCM, 1970, p.30
[22] Dulles op. cit. 49; see also Survival of Dogma, Doubleday, 1971, p.178
[23] GCD, n.11

tion between the propositional, doctrinal approach and the more experiential, personal approach.[24] Traditional formulas are to be respected and valued, they cannot be ignored. They are part of our living tradition and Christian heritage. While not ignoring them, however, we must seek to express them in language that can be understood by those being addressed today. The 1997 Directory sees this as a linguistic task that is a consequence of the need for inculturation of the faith.

> *This implies that catechesis respect and value the language proper to the message, especially biblical language, as well as the historical-traditional language of the Church (creed, liturgy) and doctrinal language (dogmatic formulations)... Catechesis should not be afraid to use traditional formulae and the technical language of the faith, but it must express its meaning and demonstrate its existential importance.*

This calls for an appreciation of the context in which the biblical or doctrinal statement was made, a sense of the development of doctrine, as well as an appreciation of culture of the people being addressed today. It also implies that we are prepared and able to speak a language suited to today's children, young people and adults, a language suited to both the more and the less academic.[25] Introducing people to the traditional language of the Bible and dogmatic formulations can only be done gradually always bearing in mind the ability and the readiness of people.

Other factors that had some influence on this theological development can be found in some of the more personalist, existential philosophical thought and in the anthropocentric and existential thrust of some recent theologies. Ecumenism has been a significant influence in bringing about development in the theological understanding of revelation and related topics such as the relationship between Scripture and Tradition, the question of biblical inspiration and so on. Moran points out that the catechetical movement itself was one of the influences that helped bring about change in theological perspective on the question of revelation. He mentions particularly the work of Jungmann with his emphasis on the kerygma, the Good News, and his reaction to the rather arid, doctrinal approach of the catechisms and

---

[24] 1977 Synod, Bishops' propositions, nn.17 & 18
[25] GDC, n.208

scholastic theology of his time.[26] The works of Moran himself were influential in this regard. These are at least some of the principal factors in the shift in the theological conception of revelation and faith.

Not either/or, but both/and

In considering the two 'models' of revelation, it is not simply a question of either accepting or rejecting one or other of them, the propositional or the personal model. O'Collins does not see the two as mutually exclusive. In his opinion 'talk of personal encounter' is not a way of distilling the essence of revelation into 'a set of indescribable experiences'.[27] Dulles is keenly aware of the limitations of the propositional model. At the same time, he suggests some of its merits and strengthens: it encouraged a loyalty to foundational documents and tradition, it provided a sense of identity and solidarity among believers and it made it relatively easy for them to give a clear account of their faith.[28] Pope John Paul II and others have expressed concern that these strengths may be somewhat weakened or discounted in the renewed emphasis on the inter-personal, relational aspect of Christian revelation. The Directories seek to avoid this dichotomy. There is constant reference to close relationship of the two aspects of Christian faith:

■ *faith as adherence, which is given under the influence of grace, to God who reveals himself; in this case the faith consists in believing the Word of God and committing oneself to it (fides qua);*

■ *faith as the content of Revelation and of the Gospel message; in this sense, faith is expressed in its endeavour to understand better the mystery of the Word (fides quae)*

The Directories state that 'both aspects, by their very nature, cannot be separated' and that 'a normal maturing of the faith assumes progress of both together'. However, they can be distinguished for reasons of methodology.[29] The cognitive, intellectual appreciation of the Christian mysteries of faith expressed in beliefs and doctrines is an essential feature of a maturing faith. The task of helping people to come to a fuller and richer understanding of these beliefs and their significance is a central

[26] Moran op. cit. p.36   [27] O'Collins op. cit. p.55
[28] Dulles, Models of Revelation, p.47   [29] GDC, n.92; GCD, 36

part of educating people to and in the faith. But as the passages that I cited at the beginning of this chapter make clear, it is one important feature of faith, not the whole of faith. As Groome's reflection on the Directory points out, faith is understood as involving the whole person: 'it is cognitive, affective and behavioural, engaging people's minds, emotions and wills'. This is clearly based on the text of the Directory when it speaks of three aspects of the content of catechesis: 'cognitive, experiential, behavioural'[30]. It also states that 'catechesis is correct when it inspires not only intellectual assimilation of the faith, but also touches the heart and transforms conduct'. I will now consider these characteristics or dimensions of the faith as described in official documents and in the writings of others concerned with the understanding and development of faith.

The Directory on the key dimensions of Christian faith

Since Vatican II there has been constant mention in official documents and other writings of what are variously termed 'dimensions', 'aspects', features' or 'characteristics' of the faith. These relate to 'dimensions', 'tasks' and 'duties' of the mission of educating to and in the faith. The Italian bishops' document of 1971 alluded to these dimensions when it stated that 'the aims of catechesis become more precise when we refer to the various dimensions of the Church, seen as community of faith, worship and charity'.[31] The *Rite of Initiation of Adults* employs almost the same terms when referring to the aim of the catechumenate stage of the process of conversion and coming to faith. At this stage the catechumens are 'introduced to the life of faith, the liturgy and the charity of the people of God'. All of this takes place within the community which offers help and support.[32] The terms 'community', 'faith', 'worship 'and 'charity' indicate the four generally recognised key dimensions which are called by other names in different texts. 'Community' indicates that we journey in faith with other disciples who make up the pilgrim people of God, the Church. 'Faith' relates to beliefs and doctrines, knowledge and understanding. 'Worship' embraces celebration, liturgy, sacraments, the

---

[30] GDC.n.35
[31] TFNW, n.42
[32] RCIA, n.98; The Rites of the Catholic Church, Pueblo Publishing Co. Nil. 1976, each dimension is discussed in turn in n.19 of the text.

use and appreciation of symbol and ritual. 'Charity' involves living out the faith in action, in commitment in a personal and public moral life, in service of others and taking up the cause of justice. Each of the four parts of the *Catechism of the Catholic Church* concentrates on one of these key dimensions: 'faith as believed, celebrated lived and prayed'.[33] The Catechism adds prayer in a separate section. In many other documents it is included under the notion of celebration and worship. The Directory speaks of these dimensions and the duties related to them.

> The duties of catechesis correspond to education of the different dimensions of faith, for catechesis is integral formation... In virtue of its own internal dynamic, the faith demands to be known, celebrated, lived and translated into prayer. Catechesis must cultivate each of these dimensions. The faith however, is lived out by the Christian community and proclaimed in mission: it is a shared and proclaimed faith'.[34]

In another place the Directory speaks of some important aspects of catechesis which must be regarded as fundamental. It states that within the community of the Church the 'proper nature' of catechesis must be respected 'by developing the richness of its content through the threefold dimension of word, memory and witness (doctrine, celebration and commitment in life)'.[35] Once again we have the same dimensions described in slightly different terms. This education of the different dimensions of faith calls for education *to* as well as *in* each of the dimensions. We must lead people - children, the young and adults - gradually to an appreciation and understanding of these dimensions in the hope that they may enter more fully into them and so mature in Christian living.

The need to educate people to and in the dimensions of faith

After enumerating these fundamental tasks of catechesis the Directory considers each in turn.

■ It speaks of 'promoting knowledge of the faith' as one of the fundamental tasks. Much has already been said about this task in considering the interrelationship of the propositional and personal

---

[33] GDC, n.122   [34] ibid. n.84   [35] ibid. n.262

models of revelation. Faith is recognised, as the giving of ourselves in trust to God who lovingly invites us in Christ to share in the divine life of Father, Son and Spirit. Taking the example of people in love, the Directory points out that in their trust and love for each other, people also wish to get to know and understand each other better. In much the same way people should be helped to come to a better knowledge and understanding of the Christian mysteries about God and his plan for us. People should be helped to a gradual understanding 'of the whole truth of the divine plan' by introducing them to the Scriptures and Tradition in a way that will nourish the life of faith and enable Christians to give an explanation of it to others. The RCIA speaks of the need for 'a suitable knowledge of dogmas and precepts'. The presentation of the teachings of the Church will obviously have to be in a language suited to age, ability and conditions of the people being addressed.

■ The Directory then speaks of 'liturgical education'. Christ is present in his Church especially in 'liturgical celebrations': the sacraments and above all in the Eucharist. Referring to the Vatican II constitution on the liturgy, it wishes that Christian be led to a 'full, conscious and active participation' in these liturgical celebrations. It is not only a question of promoting a knowledge of the meaning of the liturgy and sacraments but of educating people to a sense of prayer which can be expressed in thanksgiving and repentance.

■ Speaking of 'moral formation' the Directory recalls that conversion implies walking in the footsteps of Jesus Christ. The disciple undertakes a journey of interior renewal. For the Christian the Sermon on the Mount 'in which Jesus takes up the Decalogue, and impresses upon it the spirit of the beatitudes, is an indispensable point of reference' for such moral formation. This moral formation ensures that the word is not merely proclaimed but lived. It must also 'demonstrate the social consequences of the demands of the Gospel'.

■ Teaching to pray is another fundamental task of catechesis. It leads the disciple 'to assume the attitude of prayer and contemplation which the Master himself had'. The Our Father is the model of all Christian prayer since it is 'a summary of the entire Gospel'. Catechesis activity should be permeated by a spirit of prayer. This is particularly necessary when those being catechised are 'confronted with the more demanding aspects of the Gospel, when they feel weak or when they discover the mysterious action of God in their lives'.[36]

- Catechesis should also prepare Christians to live in community and to participate actively in the life and mission of the church. This call for education to the community dimension is rooted in the teaching of Jesus on community life as recounted in various sections of the Gospel of Matthew. In developing this community sense, an ecumenical dimension is to be fostered which includes the ability to give a clear expression of the Church's doctrine and 'a suitable knowledge of other confessions' with which there are shared elements of faith. Catechesis should nourish a 'true desire for unity'.

- The Directory also says that catechesis should be open to 'a missionary dimension': Christians should be present in society through their 'professional, cultural and social lives'. This includes a vocational dimension of lay people and one that encourages discernment concerning vocation to the priesthood and religious life. Mention is made of the need for 'inter-religious dialogue' which enables Christians to be capable of 'meaningful communication with men and women of other religions'. At the heart of this is the recognition of 'common origin and end of the human race' as well as 'the many seeds of the Gospel which God has sown in these religions. This calls for a proper balance between the 'proclamation of Christ' and 'interreligious dialogue'; 'dialogue does not dispense from evangelisation'.[37] The text stresses that all of these tasks are necessary. If one or other is omitted or neglected then 'Christian faith does not attain full development'. The tasks are interdependent and should develop together.

Reflections on the dimensions of the faith

Other writers speak of the dimensions of faith and the consequent duties of catechists and religious educators in a variety of ways. In *The Survival of Dogma* Dulles speaks of three key features of faith which he describes as 'conviction', 'trust' and 'commitment'.[38] 'Conviction'

---

[36] GDC, n.85 [37] GDC, n.86
[38] Dulles, The Survival of Dogma, p.16

refers to the cognitive, intellectual aspect of faith as assent to truth. 'Trust' refers to the personal adherence or giving of one's self to Christ as Good News and Saviour. 'Commitment' refers to the active living out of that faith particularly in social action for justice. Groome, in his book *Christian Religious Education* considers at some length what he terms 'the Christian faith in three dimensions: faith as believing, faith as trusting and faith as doing'.[39] He and others often speak of these dimensions as 'head faith', 'heart faith' and 'hands faith'. 'Head faith' denotes the intellectual aspect of faith, the need to come gradually to a deeper understanding of faith and beliefs. It refers to what we believe about God and about the purpose and significance of life in the light of such beliefs. 'Heart faith' embraces a loving, trusting response to the God who first loved us. It refers to an attitude of loving, prayerful respect and trust towards God, life and others. 'Hands faith' speaks of the demand that our faith makes on us to go out and play our part in the building of the Kingdom in the service of others especially those in greater need. It refers to the faith that motivates choices, actions. The terms 'head faith', 'heart' faith', 'hands faith' often appeal to catechists and teachers because children and the young especially can latch on to them and understand them more easily in relation to their own lives.

Pat Collins examines three models of evangelisation giving what he sees as their strengths and weakness. He speaks of 'didactic/sacramental evangelisation' which is 'head-centred'. It aims at orthodoxy, at mental assent to the doctrines revealed by God and taught in an authoritative way by the Church. For him it is still the predominant model in the Church. Its strength is that it is traditional and has worked in the past. It gives a clear sense of focus and purpose. He considers that it is not as well suited to needs of 'the existentialist era in which we live'. Nor does it necessarily mean that people 'have been evangelised in a primary way'. The second model he calls 'kerygmatic/charismatic' which is 'heart-centred'. Key features of this model are the fact that it is proclaimed and backed by personal testimony expressed in witness and joy. Its emphasis is on faith as trust. It is seen as biblical, is experiential and appeals to many today. Among its weaknesses is the fact that it can tend to individualism, being concerned about 'my salvation', 'my experience'. The Church's teaching can be ignored or to some extent neglected with greater significance

---

[39] T. H. Groome, *Christian Religious Education*, chapter 4, pp.56-81

given to personal feelings. His third model is 'political/developmental evangelisation' which is 'hands centred'. The stress is on Gospel inspired activity which seeks to liberate individuals and communities from all that oppresses them. It challenges and condemns the systematic causes of poverty. It is motivated by important biblical themes. It can, however, appear to neglect the importance of personal commitment to Christ. It can be too humanistic. Once again he argues that elements of all three are of value and necessary. [40]

New emphases on the different dimensions

Michael Paul Gallagher uses other terms for these dimensions of faith. He speaks of 'meaning', 'doing', 'listening' and also of 'belonging'. He refers to these as the 'pillars of faith'. He sees them as central to the very nature of faith and of the Church's mission from New Testament times as can be seen in the description of the early Christian community in the second chapter of the Acts of the Apostles. The experience of faith is built up when there is 'some convergence of genuine community, initiation into prayer, and the challenge of concrete service of others, especially of the wounded of the world'.[41] He maintains that these features of Christian faith are no less important today. In fact, he is of the opinion that they are 'called into new prominence by a time of secularisation'. However, he sees new emphases being put on them among different groups in the Church in ways that address the needs and aspirations of Catholics, particularly the young, today.

'Meaning' encompasses an understanding of Christian faith that gives significance to human life. In his opinion there is less attraction today to doctrinal or theological monologues that seem to give all the answers. There is greater interest in the common search and journey of discovery. There is stress on reflection on human experience and on being in touch with 'the hungers of the heart'. 'Listening' speaks of prayer as openness to God in trust. Gallagher recognises a search for new forms of spirituality as a reaction to 'vulgar exteriority and sensate life patterns' fostered by, for example, advertising and popular entertainment. He warns against

---

[40] P. Collins, 'Models of Evangelisation', Doctrine and Life, January 1998, pp.31-41
[41] M. P. Gallagher, 'The New Agenda of Unbelief and Faith', Religion and Culture in Dialogue, D. A. Lane (ed), Columba Press, 1993, p.148

escapist forms of prayer that seem to foster a withdrawal from reality. 'Doing' is about 'doing the truth', living out the faith we profess in all its implications for private and public life. Among many Catholics there is a renewed stress on this feature of faith particularly in situations of poverty and injustice. Yet it is a necessary quality of the faith of all Christians for whom the Gospel is a way of life. For many in the Church this aspect of 'doing' must go beyond the traditional form of giving alms and donations to those who are deprived. It should also look to and challenge the evils embodied in social systems that are the root cause of much poverty and injustice. 'Belonging' refers to the belief that 'the Church as community is the place where the reality of Jesus can be discovered'. New forms of this particular dimension can be found in the growing number of small Christian communities. In today's society these can meet the need of people to get away from the emptiness and anonymity of the secular city. Unfortunately, not all find this sense of community in parishes and the Church: 'the very bigness of the Church can be an obstacle to meeting the new needs that arise in a time of secularisation'. Many find strength in a variety of smaller groups where 'a cluster of new hungers can best be met'. These respond to a felt need for support, for companionship in questioning and searching, a need for sharing and for being challenged, a need for solidarity in active service of others, a need to voice an intelligent critique of the dehumanising forces around us. He says that in his experience blockages to faith especially among the young, have 'less to do with doctrinal difficulties than with the disappointment with the Church on the level of experience and community'.[42]

Gallagher is aware that when speaking of these four elements or aspect of our faith different theological views colour the understanding and the way of activating them in our life of faith. He and others talk of theologising 'from above' or 'from below'. This can be related to the propositional ('from above') and/or the personal, experiential ('from below') approach. Gallagher realises that tensions can arise from playing them off against each other or in attempting to hold them in some healthy and delicate balance. Much of this debate has been considered in the first part of this chapter and elsewhere. Like the Directory, Gallagher insists that each of the 'pillars' is important and that they are interrelated in any maturing faith.

---

[42] M. P. Gallagher, *Struggles of Faith*, p.78

> *Without 'doing' the other three are doomed to half-life. Belonging can become cosy. Listening can be escapist. Meaning can be merely 'in the head'. Likewise, 'doing' needs its three companions if it is to be saved from the fate of secular activism unrooted in religious strength'.* [43]

Two practical caveats

From all that has been said in the Directory and in the writings of others in the Church it is clear that all the dimensions are essential features of a maturing faith. None should be ignored or neglected. None should be overstressed to the detriment of the others. However, at certain stages of our faith journey, one or other of them may feature more prominently than the others in the way we live out our faith. The experience of their own Christian community and of celebration will play a large part in the faith development of children. Young people may be motivated by the call to serve and take part in activities organised by CAFOD, SVP or a HCPT group. Others may be more inspired by a reflective or charismatic prayer group or a theological discussion group. The elderly may be devoted to their daily Mass and devotions. Temperamentally we may be more inclined to one or other of the key features of faith. Personally we must take care that we value and have a place for each of the key dimensions in our faith and spiritual lives. We can, of course, be less mature in some of these aspects of faith than in others. We should be aware of that and seek to improve in each area. We must also take care not to assess another person's faith and Christian commitment entirely by reference to one or other of the dimensions as if it were the absolute criterion of assessing a person's faith. There are many levels of belonging and commitment. While we may judge other people, especially the young, on one particular feature such as knowledge of doctrine or attendance at Sunday Mass, we ourselves may be less mature in other aspects of the faith such as witness of life, prayer and service to others in need. They may give much more time and energy to the service of others or in taking part in other forms of reflection and prayer. We frequently use the terms 'prac-

---

[43] ibid, p.56.

tising' and 'non-practising' Catholics. We should remind ourselves that there is more to the 'practice' of the faith than attending Sunday Mass, central and important as that is as a feature of our faith.

My second caveat concerns the need to avoid the danger of placing these dimensions in more or less parallel lines and thus missing their essential interdependence and interrelationship. The Directory stresses that they are interdependent and develop together. They flow from and into each other. When we come to a fuller understanding of the great Christian doctrines we are we led into a sense of religious celebration and prayer and see practical implications and demands for our lives. The Directory speaks of this interrelationship.

> *Each great catechetical theme – catechesis of God the Father, for example – has a cognitive dimension as well as moral implications. It is interiorised in prayer and appropriated in witness. One task echoes the other: knowledge of the faith prepares for mission; the sacramental life gives strength for moral transformation.*[44]

To acknowledge God as Father opens us to prayerful respect and leads us to turn in service to our brothers and sisters, sons and daughters of the same Father. We should not simply learn certain formulas but we should come to an appreciation of their significance for our lives and our world, God's creation. This appreciation will flow into prayer and action. This is what the Directory implies when it states that 'content' embraces 'cognitive', 'existential' and 'behaviour' aspects and again when it speaks of developing content 'through the threefold dimension of word, memory and witness (doctrine, celebration and commitment in life'). Understood in this way, we come to see faith as holistic and addressed to the whole person. In our catechetical sessions or religious education lessons the dimensions should interrelate whether our starting point is a doctrine of the Church or reflection on some common, significant aspect of human experience. As we have seen in the previous chapter, the Directory gives an indication of how the doctrine of the Trinity might be unpacked by spelling out 'its vital implications for the lives of human beings'. Good

[44] GDC, n.87

teachers and catechists can also lead young people and adults through an exploration of significant experiences to an appreciation of Catholic doctrines and celebrations. I recall an example of this. A head of R.E. told me about his classes on the theme of conflicts and relationships in community with a year 10 group. The pupils began by exploring the various conflicts that they felt in themselves, with friends, with others in the school and within the family. After some time spent in discussing these issues, they asked if they could prepare and celebrate the liturgy for the sacrament of reconciliation. As in this case, if we begin with some experiential theme it should have cognitive dimensions in so far as it leads to a fuller appreciation of the particular human experience being explored and to a better understanding of some aspect of Christian belief and celebration. There is also a behavioural aspect in so far as those being addressed are challenged to consider their own actions and the quality of their relationships. A reflective and prayerful dimension can also be present. While we may begin with experience, our aim should be to enrich it and relate it to the Christian message of hope and meaning. In the case of R.E. lessons, pupils will then have a better understanding and deeper appreciation of what has been discussed even if they cannot fully commit themselves to the Christian faith. Others will have been helped by the acquisition of such understanding to deepen their Christian faith and commitment. I conclude with another quotation for the Directory.

> *Every dimension of faith, like the faith itself as a whole, must be rooted in human experience and not remain a mere adjunct to the human person. Knowledge of the faith is significant. It gives light to the whole of existence and dialogues with culture. In the liturgy, all personal life becomes a spiritual oblation. The morality of the Gospel assumes and evaluates human values. Prayer is open to all personal and social problems.*[45]

---

[45] ibid, n.87

Chapter Eleven

A variety of soil, a variety of approaches

Throughout her two-thousand–year history, the Church, continually prompted by the Holy Spirit, has accomplished the task of paying her obligation of evangelising 'both to Greeks and Barbarians, both to the wise and the foolish' (Romans 1:14) with an immense variety of experience in proclamation or catechesis.[1]

In situations requiring 'new evangelisation' ordinary catechesis is, at times, offered to young people and adults who need a period of prior proclamation and awakening in their adherence to Christ.[2]

In December of 1999 *The Tablet* published a special report on a poll undertaken by Opinion Research Business on religion in Britain. In a sense the poll results do not tell us anything that we did not know or at least suspect. They do, however, throw into relief the decline in organised religion since the 1950s The decline certainly has not slowed down but appears to have accelerated somewhat in the last decade of the century. In 1990, for example, a majority of Britons (58 per cent) claimed that they belonged to a particular religion. In 1999 when respondents were asked whether they regarded themselves as belonging to any particular religion only a minority (48 per cent) claimed that they did. In spite of the decline, a quarter of the population still claim that they attend church at least once a month and nearly half the population (48 per cent) claim to attend religious services at least once a year. Despite the decline in religious belief, many people say that they are 'spiritual' (27 per cent). A similar percentage of the population claim to be 'religious' (27 per cent). Those who undertook the poll conclude that 'this survey is not good news for organised religion in Britain as the millennium looms' especially after a decade dedicated to evangelisation and renewal.[3]

---

[1] GDC, n.164
[2] ibid, n.276
[3] Gordon Heald, 'Taking faith's temperature', The Tablet, 18th Dec. 1999, p.1729

In a leading article entitled 'Not faithless at the millennium' the writer comments on the findings of the survey. The article calls for more research into the quality of religious belief and how it moves over time. That is certainly necessary. It raises the question 'to what extent do changes in this area reflect a shift from habit or social custom when an active faith has become an unfashionable minority interest? Or is it a shift in language?' The article states that some will see a half-full glass as half-empty. For the latter there is plenty to arouse alarm and despondency. It would appear clear that 'the idea of religion, as associated with formal doctrine, church-going and strict morality, is in sharper decline than vaguer forms of religiosity'. While there is need for more research, there is still, according to the writer, food for thought on reflecting on the poll findings. What strategy should be put in place? The writer asks 'should the strategy be to try to turn the 'spiritual' into the 'religious' – in the terms in which these respondents understood the distinction?' It ends by arguing that 'any missionary endeavour has to start by understanding the culture, and respecting what is good in it'.[4] To some extent the poll findings and the comments back up what I shall discuss with regard to young people and the faith in a later chapter. I found the article and comments in *The Tablet* helpful because they once again highlight the wide diversity in the religious and spiritual situations among people in Britain today.

Have we strategies to meet the diversity of situations?

In our Catholic parishes and schools we make contact with families of irregular practice who are nonetheless not entirely without any interest in spiritual and religious matters. In discussing the faith of Christians the Directory recognises that a prime category requiring consideration is that of the 'many people who have been baptised but lead lives divorced from Christianity'.

> *This in fact constitutes a mass of 'non-practising Christians' even though in many hearts religious feeling has not been completely lost. Reawakening these to the faith is a real challenge for the Church'[5]*

---

4 'Not Faithless at the Millennium', The Tablet, 18th Dec. 1999, p.1703.
5 GDC, n.25

The *Tablet* articles and other writings, including the Directory, begin to raise questions about our strategies or approaches in the task of evangelisation and catechesis in such situations. When, in the local churches, we are faced with what the recent *General Directory for Catechesis* describes as 'the entire panorama of these religious situations' what specific strategies do we have? What particular approaches can and do we adopt in order to address the needs of the people in each of these different situations? How seriously are we convinced by the advice given in the Directory that at times we should adopt 'a missionary dimension rather than a strictly catechetical dimension'? Do we understand what is implied in 'a missionary dimension' as distinct from a 'strictly catechetical dimension'? How do we understand and attempt to translate into practice the call for 'new evangelisation'? How prepared are we to identify, recognise and address the needs of the diversity of situations that face us? Are we convinced by the words of the 1971 Directory that it is not a question of 'merely preserving traditional religious customs, but rather one of also fostering an appropriate re-evangelisation of people'? Even if we are convinced of this, do we know how to set about it? Unfortunately, I can only share the questions I cannot provide the answers. Nor can I say, as the person in the Television advert does, 'I know a man who can'.

I believe, however, that the latest Directory does have some useful directives and guidelines that can help us reflect further on the situation. The text makes us very much aware of different levels of interest in and commitment to the Christian faith among people today. These range from total disinterest through some attraction to Christ but without any firm commitment, to a willingness to learn more about Christ and his Gospel and to be part of the community and finally, to a commitment to lifelong discipleship. In our work as educators to and in the faith we meet people at each of these levels. It is no longer uncommon to find a mixture of all of these levels among people in our various catechetical and religious education groups. While we may be uncertain or frustrated when faced with this variety of situations and needs, it may be helpful if we pause for a moment and remember Jesus as catechist.

> *He made himself a catechist of the Kingdom of God for all cat-*
> *egories of persons, great and small, rich and poor, healthy and*
> *sick, near and far, Jews and pagans, men and women, right-*
> *eous and sinners, rulers and subjects, individuals and groups.*
> *He is available to all. He is interested in the needs of every per-*
> *son, body ad soul. He heals and forgives, corrects and encour-*
> *ages, with words and deeds.*[6]

The Directory, while identifying the levels of faith in people, hints at and makes some rather general suggestions about possible activities that might help address the different needs. As educators to and in the faith we shall have to consider the points made and seek to translate them into practice for our own particular situation. The Directory is very repetitive in this section and because of some of the language used, it does not make for easy reading. However, it does seem to me to have important implications for our work in educating to and in the faith.

The process of evangelisation

The first part of the Directory discusses catechesis within the Church's mission of evangelisation. Referring to the *Constitution on Divine Revelation* and Paul VI's exhortation on evangelisation, the Directory recalls that God reveals himself as one 'who desires to communicate himself, making the human person a participant in his divine nature. In this way God accomplishes his plan of love'. God communicates his plan through human events and words and he does so 'progressively and in stages'[7]. Evangelisation 'which transmits Revelation to the world, is also brought about in words and deeds'[8]. The Church, prompted by the Spirit, 'transmits Revelation through evangelisation; she announces the Good News of the salvific plan of the Father and in the sacraments, communicates his divine gifts'. The Church, we are reminded, 'exists in order to evangelise'. The Church does so through a complex interplay of various

---

[6] GDC, n.163
[7] ibid, nn.36-37
[8] ibid., n.39

aspects: 'proclamation, witness, teaching, sacraments, love of neighbour'. These aspects are 'the essential elements of evangelisation'.
However none of them can be identified with the process of evangelisation.[9] Just as God communicates his plan of love 'progressively and in
stages', so the Church 'always operates in slow stages'. At this point the
Directory makes reference to Vatican II's decree on the Church's missionary activity and outlines the key elements in the process or stages of
evangelisation as set out in the decree. These are in fact the key stages in
the catechumenate in the *Rite of the Christian Initiation of Adults*. The
decree presents a formalised overview of the personal journey to and in
the faith of adults and of the support that should be provided by the
Christian community.

- The presence of Christians who give witness to the Word and to
  people in their relationships of respect and love for people. In
  sharing with people, they arouse some interest in the Gospel and
  what it has to say about the meaning of human life.

- The proclamation of the Gospel and the call to conversion which
  for the person concerned is still only in its initial stages. The new
  convert sets out on a spiritual journey which involves a change of
  outlook and morals manifested in one's private life and in social
  implications.

- The admission of converts with liturgical rites into the
  catechumenate that is not only an exposition of dogmatic truths and
  norms of morality, but also a period of formation in the entire
  Christian life.

- The setting up and formation of the Christian community.[10]

In the context in which it is considered in the Directory this overview
brings out the fact that the personal journey to conversion and faith is of
its essence gradual and includes a number of definite progressive steps or
phases. Faith cannot be considered a matter of social custom but of a free
and deliberate choice. Nor is the choice for faith a sudden, once-for-all
decision but one of progressive development undertaken with the support
and help of the believing community. Faith encompasses the whole person, not just the head but also the heart. It is more than intellectual assent

[9] ibid. nn. 45-46
[10] ibid, n.47

to truths. It is a personal commitment to follow in the way of Jesus, to be a disciple, to be Church. Of course, people can slip back on the journey or abandon it all together. Speaking of people in a variety of contexts, the Directory constantly stresses the need for gradual, progressive stages in the journey to and in faith and urges us to acknowledge and respect each of them. In a footnote the text speaks of three clearly distinct phases or situations in the process which in a sense summarise the phases in this ongoing process. It mentions 'initial situations', 'gradual developments' and 'situations of maturity'.[11] The process of evangelisation therefore, should be structured in stages or essential moments around these situations in which the persons involved find themselves. We may be faced with persons who show little real interest in the faith and being Church. We may be dealing with adults who show some initial yet hesitant interest in the faith and the Church. They may, on the other hand, be willing and ready to undertake a deeper commitment and take part in an initial catechetical process of instruction and apprenticeship in the faith and Christian way of life. Others may have responded to the call to discipleship and seek an ongoing formation which will strengthen them in their Christian vocation in the Church and in the world. In addressing the needs of people in each of these situations the text enumerates three distinct yet overlapping activities and the type of persons to whom they are addressed.

- MISSIONARY ACTIVITY: directed at those who do not believe or those who live in religious indifference.

- INITIAL CATECHETICAL ACTIVITY: directed at those who have made some choice for the Gospel and those who wish to complete their initiation.

- ONGOING PASTORAL ACTIVITY: directed at Christians of mature faith.

However, here again it is stated that the process of conversion or maturing in the faith is not necessarily one of steady, continuous progress. At times it may be necessary to repeat one or return to an earlier stage depending on the spiritual growth of each person.[12]

---

[11] GDC, n.47, footnote 42
[12] GDC., n.49

Different functions of the ministry of the Word in this process

When speaking of the ministry of the Word in the context of evangelisation the text mentions several functions or forms of that ministry. This key ministry has been exercised in many varied ways since the apostolic times with 'accentuations or tones' suited to the 'situation of faith of each person or group of persons in their concrete situations'[13]. Once again, the same three main phases or stages are picked out with a few added.

- CALLING OR SUMMONING TO THE FAITH. This is realised through 'primary proclamation' addressed to those who do not believe, those who choose unbelief, those on the margins of Christian life and those of other religions. The religious awakening of children of Christian families is included in this form.

- INITIATION INTO THE FAITH. This is directed at those who have made the initial choice for faith and are now to be introduced 'into the life of faith, of the liturgy and the charity of the People of God'. This is achieved mainly through catechesis and the sacraments of initiation. Included in this form are those adults not yet baptised but preparing for baptism, adults already baptised who wish to return to the faith, those who wish to complete their initiation, and the catechesis of children and young. Christian education in the context of the family and religious instruction in schools are included in this 'initiatory function' of the ministry of the Word.

- CONTINUOUS EDUCATION IN THE FAITH. This is intended for those Christians who need constantly to nourish and deepen their faith throughout their lives. This takes place in a variety of forms 'systematic and occasional, individual and community, organised and spontaneous'.

- THE LITURGICAL FUNCTION. This is realised in the context of the celebration of the sacraments and other rites and celebrations of the Word. The homily has special importance in this context. Also included is the immediate preparation for the reception of the sacraments.

---

[13] ibid., n.50, note 61.

■ THE THEOLOGICAL FUNCTION. This is achieved through serious study of the faith in dialogue with other sciences and disciplines.

These are all recognised as important forms of the ministry of the Word. For pastoral reasons a particular form 'must assume more than one function'. Catechesis, for example, 'together with its initiatory forms, has frequently to discharge tasks of mission'. The same homily, depending on circumstances, can take on both the function of summoning some people to the faith and, at the same time, of deepening the faith of others.[14]

The process of conversion

The Directory goes on to speak of the process of conversion: 'the Christian faith is, above all, conversion to Jesus Christ, full adherence to his person and the decision to walk in his footsteps'. It is answering the call to be his disciple which 'demands a permanent commitment to think like him, to judge like him and to live as he lived'. In this way the believer joins the community of disciples and appropriates the faith of the Church.[15] Faith is saying 'yes' to Jesus Christ and involves a change in the way one lives one's life. Faith and conversion 'arise from the heart'.

> *By meeting Jesus Christ and by adhering to him the human being sees all his deepest aspirations completely fulfilled... Faith responds to that 'waiting', often unconscious and always limited in its knowledge of the truth about God, about man himself and about the destiny that awaits him. It is like pure water which refreshes the journey of man, wandering in search of his home'.[16]*

In this passage we have a rich description of the 'fides qua', that trusting faith by which a person says 'yes' to Jesus Christ and becomes a disciple. It goes without saying that such faith does not happen once and for all. As was the case with the first disciples, with Peter as a good example, it is a gradual process and has its ups and downs. Here and elsewhere in the text, the community is invited to undertake various activities that support

---

[14] GDC, nn. 51-52.
[15] ibid., n.53
[16] ibid, n.55

and encourage each person at key stages on his or her journey to and in the faith. This means that we have to appreciate the stage at which each person is, and provide support and encouragement suitable for them at that particular moment on the journey. Faith, we are reminded, is a gift to which a person, prompted by the Spirit, gives a full and free response. Mary is seen as the model of such faith. In this context too the text outlines a process of conversion that lasts the whole of life. Once again several important moments in the process are identified.

- ■ INTEREST IN THE GOSPEL. A person's interest is aroused after having heard something of Jesus and his Gospel but as yet there is no firm decision for discipleship. It is a period of searching, of a religious quest.

- ■ CONVERSION. After this period of searching the person may make a firm, yet still initial, option for faith in Jesus Christ and his way of life.

- ■ PROFESSION OF FAITH. There is now a greater desire for a more profound knowledge of Jesus Christ and his Gospel. At this point catechesis 'initiates the person in knowledge of faith and apprenticeship in the Christian life, thereby promoting a spiritual journey which brings about a progressive change in outlook and morals'. This, we are told, is achieved in sacrifices and challenges as well as in moments of joy.

- ■ JOURNEYING TOWARDS PERFECTION. The baptised now seek to continue to grow towards perfection – 'be perfect as your heavenly Father is perfect'. In this journey the Christian is 'moved by the Spirit, nourished by the sacraments, by prayer, and by the practice of charity, and assisted by multiple forms of ongoing education in the faith'.

The ministry of the Word is at the service of this process of full conversion from the first interest in and proclamation of the Gospel, through catechetical activity which sets the foundations and basic structure for conversion, to continuing education in the faith.[17]

---

[17] GDC, nn.56-57

Evangelisation in certain social, religious situations

At this point the Directory again states that evangelisation today takes place in a very diversified and changing scene. It distinguishes three basic situations each 'requiring particular and precise responses'. Firstly, there is the situation of those 'peoples, groups and socio-cultural contexts in which Christ and his Gospel are not known' or situations in which Christian communities are not mature enough 'to incarnate the faith in their own environment and proclaim it to other groups'. In such a situation missionary activity is called for especially towards young people and adults. It includes an invitation to conversion, a process that normally takes place within the catechumenate. Secondly, there are situations in which we are dealing with Christians who are fervent in their faith and who bear witness to the Gospel in lives of service. This situation calls for pastoral activity and catechesis that helps strengthen such faith. Thirdly, the Directory refers to 'an intermediate situation' where groups of the baptised have lost a living sense of the faith or no longer consider themselves members of the Church. Such situations require 'new evangelisation' and 'primary proclamation and basic catechesis are priorities'. The Directory reminds us that throughout the history of the Church such diversity has always existed. What gives it new significance today is the fact that 'increasingly different situations oftentimes coexist'.

> *The boundaries between pastoral care of the faithful, new evangelisation and specific missionary activity are not clearly definable, and it is unthinkable to create barriers between them or to put them into watertight compartments. In fact, each of them influences, stimulates and assists the others.*[18]

However carefully we make theoretical distinctions between the various aspects of catechesis and the ministry of the Word, in pastoral practice they frequently have to merge together in the task of educating to and in the faith. The Directory stresses, as other documents have done, that the model for all catechesis is the baptismal catechumenate and that adult cat-

---

[18] GDC, n.59

echesis must be considered the chief form of catechesis and it should be a point of reference for the catechesis of other age groups.

Catechesis in the process of evangelisation

In the second chapter of this first part the Directory considers catechesis within the process of evangelisation. Catechesis is distinct from the missionary activity or first proclamation that is directed towards those who do not yet believe and those who live in religious indifference. Strictly speaking catechesis is subsequent upon such missionary activity in so far as it 'promotes and matures initial conversion, educates the convert in the faith and incorporates him into the Christian community'. Catechesis builds on some initial decision to undertake the journey of conversion and faith. This is not always present in adults who present themselves or children and the young who are presented by parents for catechesis in our parishes and schools. Accordingly 'in pastoral practice it is not always easy to define the boundaries of these activities'[19]. This calls for some sort of 'pre-catechumenate' or 'new evangelisation'. Reference is made to the section in *Catechesis in Our Time* where this issue is considered. Catechesis, as distinct from initial conversion, 'has the twofold objective of maturing initial faith and of educating the true disciple of Christ by means of a deeper and more systematic knowledge of the person and the message of Our Lord Jesus Christ'. Yet we must allow for the fact that initial evangelisation has not always taken place. Children who have been baptised as infants often 'come for catechesis in the parish without receiving any other initiation into the faith and still without any explicit personal attachment to Jesus Christ'. Parents sometimes bring children for baptism at a later age. Many teenagers and young people who have been baptised and who have received some systematic catechesis and the sacraments 'still remain hesitant for a long time about committing their whole lives to Jesus Christ, even though they do not try to avoid religious instruction in the name of their freedom'. Such children and young people are in our catechetical groups and in the classrooms of our Catholic schools. Finally, adults too face temptations 'to doubt or to abandon their faith, especially as a result of their unbelieving surroundings'.

[19] ibid., nn.61-62

> *This means that 'catechesis' must often concern itself not only with nourishing and teaching the faith but also with arousing it unceasingly with the help of grace, with opening the heart, with converting, and with preparing total adherence to Jesus Christ on the part of those who are still on the threshold of faith. This concern will in part decide the tone, the language and the method of catechesis.'[20]*

As priests, catechists and teachers we need to identify with care and honesty the situations of people – children, the young and adults – who present themselves on different occasions, whether for the sacraments of baptism, confirmation, first communion, marriage or in our schools. In the light of this, we need to work out together the 'tone, language and method' best suited for the people we address. We will then need the confidence to adapt resources and programmes to meet their particular needs. The *Catechism of the Catholic Church* encourages such 'indispensable adaptations' in order to meet the diverse circumstances that are determined by 'differences of culture, age, spiritual maturity and social and ecclesial conditions amongst all of those to whom it is addressed. Much careful attention should be given to them'[21]. We must also bear in mind, as the Directory states, that 'catechetical renewal should be based on prior missionary evangelisation'.[22] In this connection it is useful to recall what is said in another section of the Directory, part of which I quoted in the chapter on faith, doctrine and life.

> *In first evangelisation, proper to the pre-catechumenate or to pre-catechesis, the proclamation of the Gospel shall always be done in close connection with human nature and its aspirations, and will show how the Gospel fully satisfies the human heart'.[23]*

Walter Kasper makes a similar and relevant point. He expresses the opinion that 'theology and proclamation have to be missionary in the true sense of the word'. By that he means that they have 'to interpret the arti-

---

[20] CT, n.19
[21] CCC, n.24
[22] GDC, n.62
[23] ibid, n.117

cles of faith in such a way that they are comprehensible in actual human situations; so that they are a genuine challenge to people, and a demand that a decision should be made'. He forcefully declares that 'without this existential location they are without any living power'[24]. Cardinal Martini speaks of the evangelist as 'one who does not wait for people to come to him; he goes out to meet them; he moves towards them instead of being a tower of strength to which they have to come'. He says that the charism of the evangelist 'confers a certain capacity to enter into the souls of others, to discover their unexpressed needs, to move into situations apparently far removed from the sphere of the Gospel, to help others towards conversion by detecting the first stirrings of grace'[25]. Jesus in the Emmaus story is a model of such evangelisation. He walks with the downhearted disciples, listens to their concerns and dashed hopes. Having won their confidence and respect he is able to challenge them – 'you foolish men…' He then patiently instructs them about the true meaning and significance of his life and death in the light of their expressed fears and anxieties. They continue to deepen their understanding when he stays with them and breaks the bread. His walking the road with them and listening to them was the first and necessary step on their journey to and in faith. It is a step that we may rather impatiently wish to skip or hurry through. In this context it is worth revisiting the thoughts and writings of some of those involved in the anthropological, experiential phase of the catechetical movement. They were concerned with attending to the soil before or while planting the seed of the Word. They too spoke of a stage of 'pre-evangelisation' or 'pre-catechesis'.[26] A very recent report of the Bishops' Conference Working Party on Sacramental Initiation gives serious consideration to the real situations in which people are with regard to the sacraments. Each section of the report contains three main parts: 'looking at our situation', 'what God might be saying' and ''what might God be asking us to do'.[27] From a fairly quick glance at the report I find it to be one of the most down-to-earth, realistic approaches to the whole question of sacramental initiation. Some may be looking for more immediate and concrete solutions and answers, but it is necessary to give full pastoral consideration to the many issues involved.

---

[24] W. Kasper, op. cit., p.21
[25] C. M. Martini, Ministers of the Gospel, St. Paul Publ., 1983, p.11.
[26] see chapter four
[27] Working Party on Sacramental Initiation, On the Threshold, Matthew James, 2000

Catechesis as initiation into the faith and ongoing education in the faith

Taking up the concept of catechesis already expounded in previous documents, the Directory recognises catechesis as one of the essential moments in the rich, complex and dynamic reality that is evangelisation. It notes that there are activities that 'prepare for catechesis' and activities that 'derive from it'. The moment of catechesis 'is that which corresponds to the period in which conversion to Jesus Christ is formalised, and provides a basis for first adhering to him'. Catechesis in a variety of ways discharges 'the initiatory function' of the ministry of the Word in so far as it 'lays the foundation for the building of the faith'. This 'initiatory catechesis' is the necessary link between missionary activity which calls people to faith and the pastoral activity which continually nourishes the Christian community in faith[28]. The text lists some fundamental characteristics of catechesis in the initiation process

- Catechesis should encompass a comprehensive and systematic formation in the faith.

- Such comprehensive formation should include more than instruction; it is an apprenticeship of the entire Christian life; it implies education in the knowledge of the faith and in the life of faith.

- Catechesis should provide a basic and essential formation centred on the core of Christian experience, the most fundamental truths of the faith and the essential Gospel values.

- Catechesis should incorporate the convert into the community which lives, celebrates and bears witness to the faith[29].

Catechesis has the further task of providing ongoing education in the faith that goes beyond basic, initiatory catechesis. In order to encourage this process 'it is necessary to have a Christian community which welcomes the initiated, sustains them and forms them in the faith'. The Gospel and the Eucharist are the constant food for the journey of conversion and faith. This continuing formation in the faith should not only be directed at individual Christians but at the Christian community itself. Various forms of ongoing catechesis are mentioned.

---

[28] GDC., n.64
[29] ibid., nn.67-68

- The study of Scripture.

- The reading of events and the study of the social teaching of the Church.

- Liturgical catechesis, promoting a deeper understanding and experience of the liturgy and prayer.

- Occasional catechesis at special events in family, social and church life.

- Spiritual formation which encourages perseverance in prayer and in the duties of following Christ.

- A systematic deepening of the Christian message by means of theological reflection and study.[30]

In a later section when discussing forms of adult catechesis these and other points are again mentioned and further developed. The Directory at this point also considers the relationship between catechesis and religious instruction or education in the school context. I shall reflect on some of the issues involved in this discussion in a later chapter.

Companions on the pilgrimage of faith

Throughout this chapter I have followed the text of the Directory. I have done so because it seems to me helpful that we are reminded in this official way of the great diversity of need that we are called upon to address. The ideas of 'missionary activity' or some sort of 'pre-catechumenate' along with 'new evangelisation' are no longer concepts to be applied only in the so-called missionary countries. It is also helpful to be reminded in official documents that we must have the courage to make the necessary adaptations in a way that seeks to keep true to the great catechetical mission statement – 'fidelity to the Word of God and fidelity to the People of God'. The Directory does not provide immediate practical help in drawing up resources to meet each of these needs. Nor can any one resource meet all the needs of the people, young and adults, in the various groups with which we have to deal. We should ensure that we know people and find the confidence to provide suitable help for their

---

[30] GDC, n.71 see also n.176 in which particular forms of adult catechesis are considered.

journey. It is also helpful to see that official texts recognise the blurred boundaries and the lack of absolutely clear distinctions in practice between the various aspects of the pastoral task of educating to and in the faith. I also hope that reflection on the text will enable us to be more realistic in assessing resources that we can use and more realistic in our judgements of the success or failure of our various endeavours with different groups or individuals in our parishes and our schools.

Reflection on the Directory should help us appreciate just how rich true Christian faith is involving as it does the head and the heart, the whole person who freely accepts to follow Jesus Christ, to be his disciple with the other disciples who make up the Church. This is not an easy choice in today's world. Once the initial choice has been made, it is a gradual, life-long process that includes high and low moments, moments of greater or less fidelity. Throughout the journey we need the help and support of fellow pilgrims. We do not and cannot make the journey alone. If we wish to help others on their journey of faith, it is useful to recall some of the key moments on our own journey. If we are to walk with others, young people or adults, it can be helpful to remember some of the high points and low points, the moments of struggle, doubt and challenge and the times of excitement and joy, as well as the people who accompanied and supported us. I find the following passage from the Italian Bishops' 1970 document very helpful, it is one we can all meditate on as we reflect on our own personal journey of faith and as we seek to accompany others on their faith journey.

It is a journey which may involve simultaneously both the joys of encounter and the continuous demands of further searching; both sorrow for infidelity and the courage to start afresh; both the peace that comes from discovery and anxiety arising from the realisation that even more is involved; both the certainty of truth and the constant need for new light'.[31]

A second passage which seems to me to be very helpful and apt in this context is from Eamonn Conway's article 'Midwives to the Mystery'.

---

[31] TFNW, n.17

We do not have to be people with the answers. We do have to show that we have the courage to grapple with the eternal questions. This means that we also need the courage to share with others our questions and our doubts... We cannot walk the road for people. Nor will we be of much encouragement if we give the impression that we are miles ahead or have our faith journey completed years ago.[32]

These passages will resonate and ring true for many of us involved with the young and adults in parishes and with young people in our schools. I conclude these reflections with a quotation from Michael Paul Gallagher which also seems very apt: 'only with reverence for the natural pace of people's searching, can the Gospel be heard with new power, and the only lasting faith for today will be born from a free decision'.[33]

[32] E. Conway, 'Midwives to the Mystery', The Furrow, July/August 1994, p.420
[33] M. Gallagher, Struggles of Faith, p.83

Chapter Twelve

Adults and the young, pilgrims together on the road

The need for continuing growth in faith and in the appreciation of its significance at different stages of life is a fundamental one, which is grounded in the imperatives of different stages in a person's development.[1]

Adults are asked in a special way to commit themselves to the catechetical service and, in a broader sense, the pastoral care of their brothers and sisters, both the little ones and grown-ups, always keeping in mind the different situations, problems and difficulties with which they are confronted.[2]

Since Vatican II there have been some fairly dramatic shifts in emphases in our understanding of the mission of educating people to and in the faith. Chief among these is the shift from an almost exclusive emphasis on the instruction of children in the context of schools to a much broader understanding of the coming to faith and growth in faith as a lifelong process that includes children, the young and adults of all ages. In fact, adult catechesis has been declared the priority. The process of conversion to discipleship continues throughout life. This has been a constant theme in all recent writings on catechetical matters. John Paul II in *Catechesis in Our Time* points out that the concern for lifelong catechesis was 'one of the most constant concerns of the Synod Fathers.' He goes on to say that if catechesis is to be effective, it must be ongoing and permanent because 'it would be quite useless if it stopped short just at the threshold of maturity since catechesis, admittedly in a different form, is no less necessary for adults'[3]. The bishops of England and Wales, in the aftermath of the National Pastoral Congress held in Liverpool in 1980,

[1] A Report to the Bishops of England and Wales, Signposts and Homecomings, St. Paul Publ., 1981, p.125
[2] International Council for Catechesis, Adult Catechesis in the Christian Community, St. Paul Publ., 1990, n.23.
[3] CT, n.43

gave a description of catechesis that, while mentioning other important aspects, stressed the ongoing nature of the process of growth in faith.

Catechesis is a work of education and formation in Christian living; it is a gradual, many-sided process of growth in faith. It is lifelong because our potential is never fully realised and we can always explore further the reality of God and his love for us. It is a community process because we grow through our relationships with others.[4]

A life-long process of growth and development

Such an understanding of the process of educating in the faith follows from the description of the journey of faith given in the passage from *Teaching the Faith the New Way* with which I concluded the last chapter. It follows from the understanding of faith as the response to the call to discipleship. It is a lifelong journey with many twists and turns on the road as we move on from the teen years, through young, middle and late adulthood. The Directory distinguishes phases in the process of conversion to discipleship from the time of expressing an interest in the Gospel and the Church right through to the phase of mature personal choice to follow the way of Jesus in the community of the Church. These phases are not necessarily age related. Teenagers and young people in their twenties can be very committed to the Christian way of life much more so than many older adults. However, they are committed as teenagers and young adults. Life's journey will lead them into new situations and bring new experiences. Our faith needs to be constantly renewed and enriched through these new experiences, some joyful, some painful. Different challenges and opportunities present themselves at each stage of life and these can have an effect on the way we come to understand and live our Christian faith. In some cases, for a variety of reasons, our faith may be impoverished and threatened in these new situations. This may lead to a temporary or total abandonment of the faith. On the other hand, some

[4] Bishops of England and Wales, The Easter People (EP), St Paul Publ., 1980, n.126

experiences and circumstances in life may lead to a renewed interest in and commitment to the Christian faith. For example the experience of being a parent may be the reason why a young father or mother begins to show renewed interest in religion and the Church. The experience of separation or divorce may be a situation that causes others to turn away from the Church and the faith. The Directory says that people can be 'prey to all kinds of changes and crises, sometimes profound'. As a consequence, 'the faith of adults must be continually enlightened, developed and protected' so that they 'may acquire Christian wisdom which gives sense, unity and hope to the many experiences of personal, social and spiritual life'[5].

It is for these reasons that in the text of *The Easter People* the bishops stated that 'the continuing Christian education and formation of adult members of the Church must become a priority in our Church's educational labours'. They pledged themselves to accept 'the pastoral implications of the decision, including the allocation of personnel and resources that may be necessary'[6]. The report on the educative task of the Catholic community, *Signposts and Homecomings,* develops the argument that Christian formation is a continuing process and that there is a clear need for adult religious education. I shall consider some of the points raised in this text. Kevin Nichols in *Cornerstone* frequently emphasises the importance of work with adults although, in my opinion, he does not give it sufficient coverage despite his statement that 'perhaps the most important development in the next decade will be the religious education of adults'[7]. Nevertheless, all these writings clearly affirm the ongoing nature of the process of educating to and in the faith and they particularly stress the need for adult catechesis. As Piveteau and Dillon pointed out in the late 1970s 'by these ringing declarations our efforts and concerns are now beckoned, not to say wrenched, away from habitual emphases, to a wholly novel perspective and practice'[8]. Many people in the Church are of the opinion that the practice has not entirely caught up with the theory. There has been a good deal of rhetoric concerning lifelong education in the faith and of the importance of adult catechesis. Yet over the last ten or twenty

---

5 GDC, n.173
6 EP, n.145
7 K. Nichols, Cornerstone, St Paul Publ., 1978, p.47.
8 D. J. Piveteau & J. T. Dillon, Resurgence in Religious Instruction, R. E. Press, University of Notre Dame 1977, p.229

years there have been developments in this regard. Diocesan catechetical and religious education centres now have a person or team whose specific brief is to set in motion and coordinate this aspect of the work. A number of parishes have programmes geared to the variety of needs of adults and are constantly on the look out for resources and materials that will enable them to meet the demands of ongoing education in the faith. A recent paper of the Committee of Catechesis and Adult Christian Education speaks of the achievements made in adult catechesis since Vatican II. It also sets out some challenges and concerns.

> *Despite the many valuable developments and initiatives in adult formation in recent years, the work remains underfunded, under-resourced and undervalued relative to the priority given to it in the teaching of the Church.*[9]

The interrelationship of faith and human development

In previous chapters I considered the relationship between faith, doctrine and life in general terms and I looked at the stages in the conversion process. Here I wish to look more specifically at our Christian faith in relation to the changing contexts of people's lives as they develop and mature. In chapter nine I reflected on faith, on the way that a person makes sense of his or her existence. Faith can be understood as 'having an orientation in the world, a perspective from which to experience the world and interpret these experiences'.[10] Faith is seen as a way of understanding and interpreting the universe and one's place in it that, in turn and of necessity, calls forth some response in the way one lives one's life and relates to other people. It is generally in times of crisis, change or decision that individuals or groups consider more seriously and articulate more precisely the faith by which they live. For Rahner the Christian faith tradition is not simply a matter of formal obedience to propositions but is

[9] 'Priority of Adult Formation', in Briefing vol. 29 n.8, 11th August 1999, p.11.
[10] D. Capps, Life-Cycle Theory and Pastoral Care, Fortress Press, Philadelphia, 1983, p.79.

a way of addressing the great, inescapable questions of existence in the light of the Christ event. For Schillebeeckx, as we have seen, the Christian faith tradition can only be truly appropriated and developed in a personal way when it is experienced as 'the liberating answer to the real questions that we ask'. Christian faith, in such a view, is essentially related to the experiences and phases of our human development because these colour and shape our aspirations and our questions and, consequently, our way of understanding and living our faith. As educators to and in the faith, therefore, besides having a knowledge and understanding of the tradition – doctrines, sacraments, moral codes and Scripture, we must also have an understanding of and sensitivity to the needs and experiences of individuals in the various stages of their human development. This is necessary if we are to enable them to deepen their Christian faith at crucial moments in their personal development. The report *Signposts and Homecomings* underlines this point.

> To educate in a sacred tradition cannot consist in merely imparting information. It involves an interaction between statement and interpretation, between the understanding of faith itself and the appropriate ways of bringing it to bear on the changing human problems; both the understanding and the application, moreover, need to develop in response to changing situations and also to the individual's personal development through the ever changing states of human existence.[11]

The report speaks of a process of continuing reappraisal and continual conversion because 'the Word of God can be grasped only in so far as it is translated into the familiar context of daily life'. It also notes that 'the context changes and the individual changes through the course of life'. This fact underscores the need for continual growth in faith and 'in the appreciation of its significance at different stages'. The report then refers to the 'idea that there are stages in the development of faith analogous to the stages which have been distinguished in the development of conceptual thinking and moral development'.[12] The 1971 Directory makes the same point: 'the life of faith passes through various stages, just as does a

[11] Signposts and Homecomings, p.125
[12] ibid., pp.125-126

man's existence while he is attaining maturity and taking on the duties of his life'. It declares that 'the acceptance of this faith, and its explanation and application to life are different according to whether there is a question of the very young, children, adolescents, young adults or adults'. It is for this reason that the task of educating to and in the faith is one that lasts throughout the whole of a person's life.[13]

Focus on the needs of people at their particular stage on the journey

Exeler in his essay *Faith and Education* argues against what he calls a narrow textbook kind of catechesis which 'fails to encourage people effectively towards real humanity' and which, in his view, has proved to have had 'a predominantly domesticating effect'. This, he says, can be caused by an excessive preoccupation with 'churchy' matters: when 'catechists are satisfied if catechism and Bible are learned', when 'people are considered believers on the basis of this sort of knowledge' and when they 'keep the externals of regulations and perform particular rites and customs'. While such a concern with knowledge and practice are not unimportant, an over concern with them may well 'cover up the very thing which they should express – that life with God which is real life only as long as it penetrates into every area of human existence'. Catechists, he urges, should be 'in the service of faith and of freeing the human person for his or her possibilities'. They should be more aware of 'the interrelation of maturing experience of life and the actual structure of faith'. This is demanded, he says, because the maturing process continues throughout life and passes through 'a mass of crises and continually necessitates new advances'. The catechist should develop a keen sense of what is distinctive about each stage of maturing 'so as to be able to accompany people according to their particular situation'. He speaks of the need to take seriously the 'preconditions' of faith, by which he refers to the way individuals see and feel about themselves and others and the world from within a particular experiential situation. These preconditions, he thinks, are skipped over far too lightly. He mentions the case of

---

13 GCD, n.30

a young person who has so little experience of being trusted that he or she is unable to trust anyone else and is also incapable of reaching real faith in a loving God. He gives as another example a person who, because he is embittered, because he sees little to be thankful for, is not, on the basis of this precondition, ready to celebrate Eucharist. However important Eucharist is in the theological conception of Christian life, Exeler is of the opinion that a catechist cannot simply announce the message or proceed to instruct such a person in the understanding of Eucharist without any sensitivity to his or her actual experiences at that particular time. For Exeler, these examples 'show how the maturing processes of the basic structures of human existence and of faith are connected and work together'. A child cannot be defined as a small adult; a child's faith cannot be considered a miniature edition of an adult's faith. At the same time it would be futile for an adult to try to keep his or her faith in a childish state through all the other stages of life.

This is linked with the fact that faith is not a quickly memorised summary of truths but a new kind of existence in which a person is brought into relation with God and into the movement of God's people in the march of history... The particular shape of a person's faith at a given time has its own characteristics, its particular way of working at a specific age, and its relativity. Faith, too, has to proceed by means of experience of life and of a deeper knowledge of oneself and of the world. [14]

Scott, like Exeler, states that the Church's educational activity is a process that spans the time between birth and death. The Church, he says, must ask itself what it has to offer people on this developmental journey. This demands knowledge of the stages of the journey and an appreciation of the resources the Church can make available to facilitate such a journey. The Church carries a reservoir of wisdom, a treasure of tradition that can assist human development and enable people to negotiate the various stages of human life. In literature dealing with human development throughout life, these are often referred to as life passages. Instruction, sacrament and ritual can help in this task. Scott stresses, however, that an

---

14 A. Exeler, 'Faith and Education', The Voice of the Hidden Waterfall, K. Nichols (ed.), St .Paul Publ., 1980, pp.51-60

essential feature of the content or the curriculum for adult education in the faith is what he terms 'the ecological context of people's lives – the stuff of their daily experience'. If the Christian vision is to empower people's lives, catechists need to be receptive to 'the existentially important questions and crises in people's lives'. Only in this way will people be enabled to interpret the religious significance of their lives and celebrate the meaning of life's passages: 'hidden in the challenges of our human life-passages are the agenda for the Church's religious education'.[15] It is only in this way, he suggests, that the Church can reclaim its 'root humanism' and 'the incarnational principle'. It is precisely in this way that the Church is seen to speak not only for itself or to be preoccupied with its own survival, but to be concerned with enabling Christians to mature and develop as persons enriched and enlightened by its wisdom and tradition.[16] The points that these writers are stressing can be seen as practical attempts to translate what is said in other terms in the recent Directory. The Directory states that catechesis seeks 'to promote a progressive and coherent synthesis between full adherence of the person to God (fides qua) and the content of the Christian message (fides quae)' and 'to help the person discern the vocation to which the Lord calls him or her'.[17]

Adult education in the faith as a priority

The fourth part of the 1997 Directory is entitled 'Those to be Catechised' and begins by again reminding us that catechesis is meant for all types and categories of people and that attention must be focused on the 'diverse life situations of people'. In addressing these different situations catechists will employ many different approaches and adapt the Christian message and the methods of educating in faith to meet these different needs. Adaptation must keep in mind the needs of the whole person and what the text describes as 'the interior world of the person, the truth of being human'. Adaptation can be considered proper and suitable 'the more the questions, aspirations and interior needs of the per-

---

[15] K. Scott, 'The Local Church as an Ecology of Human Development', Religious Education, 76, 2, 1981, pp.158-160
[16] ibid., p.144
[17] GDC, n.144

son are considered' because 'faith contributes to the development of the person.[18] The Directory does not give a great deal of space to the section on 'catechesis according to age'. However, unlike the 1971 Directory and most other documents, it begins by considering adults rather than beginning with infancy and working through childhood, adolescence and ending with adulthood. That seems to me to be very significant. It certainly gives a visible sign of taking seriously the recent constant stress on adult evangelisation and catechesis as a pastoral priority in the Church.

Attempting to define an adult is complex and probably not all that helpful. We are all unique. When we speak of adults we speak of people in a wide age range who have many different experiences in life and who are at different phases of interest in and commitment to the Christian faith.[19]. Writers on human development distinguish in broad terms the rather obvious key life stages of young adulthood, the middle years and late adulthood. Not all theorists agree about the number or duration of these life stages. This is not the place to study in any depth the theories of adult development and adult education. It is certainly helpful if those who undertake adult catechesis have some awareness and understanding of what educational theory says about the characteristics and nature of adult education. Within each of the various stages of adulthood educationalists talk of 'developmental tasks', that is a series of age related tasks that normally occur during a particular stage of life. For example, selecting a mate, starting a family can be considered an appropriate task in young adulthood. Dealing with possible increased responsibility at work or with unemployment, with older children, on the one hand, and ageing parents on the other are features of the lives of many people in the middle years of adulthood. Adjusting to decreasing physical strength and health and to retirement and reduced income can be considered factors of life in late adulthood. The maturing adult has to deal successfully with these tasks. In his theory of adult education Knowles is of the opinion that such tasks provide the chief stimuli or motivation for learning: 'people become ready to learn something when they experience a need to learn it in order to cope more satisfyingly with real life tasks or problems'[20]. These tasks

---

[18] ibid., nn163-171
[19] see J. Gallagher, Guidelines, Collins, 1986, p.28
[20] M. Knowles, 'An Adult Educator's Reflections on Faith Development in the Adult Life Style', K. Stokes (ed), Faith and the Adult Life Cycle, Sadlier, 1982, p.67

are clearly related to a multiplicity of social roles: child, parent, spouse, worker and the like. The assumption of specific roles at various points in life, in the opinion of Gooden, 'demands preparation, readiness, commitment and adaptation'[21]. This has evident implications for catechesis, for example, in marriage preparation, in preparation for parental responsibility at times of baptism, first communion, confirmation, and other stages in the development of the young, in taking up ministries, at time of retirement and so on. 'Crisis' is another key concept of developmental theorists. Because the word 'crisis' seems to speak of the dramatic and traumatic, some theorists prefer other terms such as 'seasons', 'passages', 'transformations' However, in general terms, crisis refers to a time when individuals experience significant changes – physical, psychological, social. These must be faced if individuals are to mature and develop as persons: 'crises, be they marriage or divorce, a birth or a death, being hired or fired, are catalysts by which people grow'[22]. Some crises are event related, such as the death of a loved one, the loss of a job, the diagnosis of an illness. Others are related to the ageing process and they occur in the life of everyone in the middle and later years.[23] The 1971 Directory speaks of adult life crises that Christians must successfully pass through. Although these crises are less obvious than those experienced by adolescents, 'they are not to be considered less dangerous or less profound; in these times the adult's faith must be constantly illumined, developed and fortified.' The Directory mentions several reasons for declaring adult catechesis to be a priority in the pastoral activity of the Church.

- ■ Adults have a greater experience of life and are constantly trying to cope with the joys and sorrows that are part and parcel of human life. They are faced with the questions, hope and fears that come with these experiences. They need help to reflect on them in the light of the Christian faith.

- ■ Adults have many roles and responsibilities to fulfil in a variety of spheres – family, professional, civic, social. They look for help in fulfilling these tasks as part of their Christian vocation in life.

---

[21] W. Gooden, 'Response and Comments from an Adult Development Perspective' K. Stokes (ed), ibid., p.95
[22] ibid., p.44
[23] See J. Gallagher, Guidelines, pp.26-26

- They are faced with crises, with the problems and demands of change that are not always easy to accept.

- Adults play a key role in the development of children as persons and as Christians. It is through enriching contact with the adult Christian community that the faith is communicated to children and the young.[24]

Different tasks and forms of catechesis for adults

Adults fit into a variety of categories when we consider their relation to the Christian faith. As we saw in the last chapter, some will need some form of pre-catechesis, some will be ready for initial and basic catechesis, others will profit from ongoing education in an already maturing faith. The 1997 Directory more or less repeats what was said in the 1971 Directory with regard to the different forms of adult catechesis. The catechumenate or Christian initiation is a key form for many in the Church both for those preparing for baptism and for those seeking to renew their baptismal commitment. Catechesis is called for on the occasion of the principal events of life such as marriage, baptism of children and the times of the celebration of other sacraments, at times of illness or bereavement. As the text says 'these are times when people are moved more strongly than ever to seek the true meaning of life'. People need the help of catechesis on the occasions of change in their circumstances of life. It mentions as examples entering military service and emigration. More relevant situations might be the move to secondary school, leaving school, redundancy, moving house and leaving one parish and becoming part of another. Prayers with the sick and their relatives, prayers in the homes of bereaved families are features of the ministry of the Word and of educating people to and in the faith. Those present will benefit in different ways from the presence and help of the community represented by the priest and others in the parish. Some service with symbols and prayers might provide the help that is needed for those concerned.

---

24 GCD, nn.92-94

> *These changes can indeed increase one's spiritual goals, but they can disturb the spirit and snatch away hope. The Christian community has a duty to supply those who experience them with necessary help in fraternal love. The Word of God, which in these circumstances is sometimes more readily accepted, ought to be a light and an aid to them.[25]*

For some adults a programme that enables them to deepen their understanding of the Church's faith and introduces them to theological reflection will meet a felt need. They may be preparing to take up a particular form of lay apostolate and look for help in acquiring the necessary understanding and skills. Some may be keen to be introduced more fully into a prayerful appreciation the Scriptures or to the study some contemporary moral questions. The documents also stress the need for catechesis to assist people in the performance of their various roles and duties. Adults should be helped towards a spirituality suitable for lay people in a pluralistic, secularised world. Catechesis should foster an ecumenical attitude and dimension and help enable adults to share their faith with others, especially the young.[26] Special mention is made of those 'whose need for the consolation of the Christian community is all the greater because of the intensity of their isolation and suffering'. These include 'the disabled, the elderly, the sick, and all who find themselves on the fringes of society (refugees, immigrants, nomads, prisoners)'. The possibility of their involvement in the community 'is often underestimated and unappreciated'. In our catechetical activity we should 'show special concern for those living in irregular situations'.[27] All of these catechetical activities should be considered in the pastoral plans of dioceses and parishes. It goes without saying that in some parishes, particularly where local people may lack the confidence to take up such tasks, it will prove very difficult to address all these needs. Still, efforts should be made to encourage and enable members of the community to take up some of these tasks. It may come as a surprise to them and others that they are good with some people in certain situations.

---

25 GCD, n.96
26 GCD, nn.96-97; GDC, nn.175-176; International Council for Catechesis, op. cit., nn.34-53
27 International Council for Catechesis, op. cit. n.55

Problems and tasks enlightened by the faith

John Elias is of the opinion that 'the journey of faith is a dimension of the human journey' and he suggests that for too long the starting point for adult religious education has been doctrines, moral laws and the ritual practices of religion. These, of course, cannot be ignored and at times the study of these will meet the expressed need of individuals and groups. However, he stresses that there can be another starting point: 'the challenge is to begin where people experience themselves to be and to shed light on their problems and tasks both from religious sources and other sources'.[28] In this context I find a passage from Vatican II on the priestly ministry relevant. It can be applied not only to priests but also to all involved in educating to and in the faith.

Very little good will be achieved by ceremonies, however, beautiful, or societies, however flourishing, if they do not direct towards training people to reach Christian maturity. To encourage this maturity priests will help people solve their problems and determine the will of God in the great and small crises of life.[29]

This relates to the goal and methods of adult catechesis. The document from the International Council for Catechesis on adult catechesis strongly reminds us that we must be 'acutely sensitive to men and women in so far as they are adults'. Adults bring with them a wide variety of experiences. They have learnt a great deal either consciously or unconsciously over the years. They are, therefore, resources to be tapped and not mere passive recipients of information and teaching. They have much to contribute and need to be encouraged to do so. They are to be respected for the responsibilities and roles that they fulfil. They look for help in dealing with immediate questions, problems and tasks. They will be less interested in theoretical knowledge that seems abstract and unrelated to their lives. They do not learn simply by being told or informed about doctrines or other issues. At this level they learn more from sharing and

---

[28] J. L. Elias, The Foundations and Practice of Adult Religious Education, R. E. Krieger Publ., Malabu, Florida. 1982, p.92
[29] Vatican II, Decree on the Ministry and Life of Priests, n.6, Flannery (ed.)

reflecting together. This dimension of a community that welcomes, encourages and supports them is absolutely essential in the process of helping adults, and indeed young people, grow in their personal Christian faith.

> *One of the most valid criteria in the process of adult catechesis, but one which is often overlooked, is the involvement of the community which welcomes and sustains adults. Adults do not grow in faith primarily by learning concepts, but by sharing the life of the Christian community, of which adults are members who both give to and receive from the community.*[30]

The atmosphere of the place in which a group meets should be welcoming, the setting should be comfortable and help put people at their ease. Tea and biscuits help less formal discussion and enable people to get to know each other. It is very difficult to take part in discussion and reflection when the seating arrangements are not conducive to this – when people are seated row by row, looking at each other's back. These are by no means trivial considerations, they are vital if we understand catechesis in the way the bishops do in *The Easter People*. They describe it as 'process of education and formation in Christian living' that is gradual, many-sided, lifelong and 'a community process because we grow through our relationships with others'. It is a process of learning to be disciples together within the community of the Church. Most adult programmes or resources give helpful advice on these matters.

Family and community catechesis

The education of children and the young to and in the faith takes place, or should take place, first and foremost in the home, in the family, backed up by the support of the local Christian community. The bishops in their proposals issued at the end of the Synod on the family categorically stated that 'God made parents the first educators of their children and the right cannot be taken away from them[31]'. John Paul II in *Catechesis in Our Time* says that 'family catechesis precedes, accompanies and enriches all other forms of catechesis' Because of this 'we can-

---

[30] International Council for Catechesis, op. cit., n.28
[31] 'Synod Propositions (3)', The Tablet, 14th February 1981, n.29.

not make too great an effort to prepare parents to be catechists of their own children'.[32] Parents are due and have a great need of the support of the community in fulfilling this task. Many lack confidence in their ability to help their children develop as Christians; they are unsure of what in practice that means. They find it difficult to cope with their growing children when they question religious teaching and values and show little interest in or commitment to the tradition and Catholic way of life. We need to affirm parents, to support them in their task of living and sharing their faith with their children. We need to help them understand how best they can do this. This is a task that the parents and the community took upon themselves at the baptism of the child. In the introduction to the rite of baptism of children we are reminded that 'children cannot profess a personal faith'. They are baptised 'in the faith of the Church' which is proclaimed for them 'by their parents and godparents, who represent both the local Church and the whole society of saints and believers'. At the baptism of children it is the adults, especially the parents and godparents, who profess their faith. They are reminded that, in asking for baptism for their child, they are taking on the responsibility 'of training them in the practice of the faith'. When they indicate that they have understood this responsibility, the minister names the child and announces 'the Christian community welcomes you with great joy'.

This leaves us with the question whether children should be baptised if there is little sign of belief and commitment in parents and godparents. There would seem to be a variety of pastoral approaches in different parishes. Some parishes demand from the parents some definite signs of faith and belief and a clear undertaking that they will fulfil their promise of educating the child to and in the faith. If these are missing, baptism may be delayed or refused. After some period of preparation and reflection with the parents, other parishes are content with some signs of goodwill recognising that parents themselves are in need of encouragement and help towards faith and belief. For all it should be an opportunity for evangelisation or catechesis. For some parents it will be an occasion of further maturing in their faith. For those who may be largely nonpractising Catholics it may be a chance to reawaken religious feelings that are not entirely lost. Some priests and catechists see in the desire to have the

---

[32] CT, n.68

child baptised a love for the child that should be blessed, encouraged and supported. Theological and pastoral arguments can be made for different approaches and practices. The Directory urges pastoral concern for the 'diverse life situations of people' which should move catechists 'to employ many different approaches to meet them and adapt the Christian message and pedagogy of faith to different needs'. The pastoral tone of the Directory is clearly in evidence when it states that 'such adaptation must be understood as a maternal action of the Church, who recognises people as the field of God, not to be condemned but cultivated in hope.[33] The hope would be that a welcoming, supportive community might invite people to faith. Condemnation may well close people off from the Church for good. In the introduction to the rite of baptism the Church forcefully reminds us that 'the local community has an important part to play in the baptism of children and adults'. In the case of children we are told that 'before and after the celebration of the sacrament the child has a right to the love and help of the community'. This can be done through various supports offered to parents in the parish particularly, though not exclusively, at the time of sacramental preparation. As I have already noted, the recent working party report *On The Threshold* has some very useful reflections on this matter. The good Catholic school should be considered an important feature of the love and help offered by the community.

More through witness than teaching

Parents educate their children in faith mainly through 'the witness of their lives, a witness that is often without words'[34]. They share their lives and their faith mainly in an 'atmosphere of respect, trust and love' which they seek to create in their homes'[35]. The Directory affirms this by stressing that family catechesis 'is a Christian education more witnessed to than taught, more occasional than systematic, more ongoing than structured into periods'. It also highlights the growing importance of the role of grandparents: 'their wisdom and sense of the religious is often at times decisive in creating a true Christian climate'[36.] Perhaps we do not help hard-pressed parents appreciate that their attempts to create this atmos-

---

[33] GCD, n.169   [34] ibid., n.68
[35] 1981 Synod on the Family, bishops' proposal 26
[36] GDC n.255

phere in their homes is in a very real way living out what lies behind our belief in the Trinity. Perhaps we do not help them appreciate enough that their love and trust for their children are, for the children, the first, and therefore a very profound, experience of the love and trust of God.

> *By being the people they are – strong or weak in faith, affectionate or distant, lax or firm, patient or inconsistent – parents convey attitudes to their families often quite unconsciously but nonetheless strongly and perhaps ineradicably. It is a fundamental principle, therefore, that the experience a child has of God in his or her own home is bound to be formative.*[37]

When speaking of the family we must take care not to think of it in rather bland, pious terms. It is too easy either to idealise or to be overcritical of the family. The ideal rarely exists. In families people exist who, 'in a variety of circumstances and to a greater or less degree, try to share their life and love, to relate to and feel responsible for each other'.[38] To live in a close, loving relationship is something we greatly desire, it is nonetheless costly and demanding. All families, some more than others, have their ups and downs. Yet it goes without saying that a healthy family life is vital for the full human growth and development of children. It is equally important for the life of faith. Very young children sense and absorb the atmosphere around them whether it be one of love, trust and respect or one where these human qualities are missing or at least to some extent lacking. Their early experiences of family relationships form the basis of their sense of self worth or lack of it. They form the basis of faith understood in the broad sense which, as Maurice Wiles, and others, puts it, 'implies an attitude of ultimate confidence about the world'. These early experiences also lay the foundations for Christian faith in the loving plan of God for each of us. Besides these more implicit experiences of faith and beliefs, the family should introduce appropriate occasions for family celebration and prayer in which children can actively participate making use of family events, the liturgical seasons and the rich symbols of our Christian tradition. Older children are keen and anxious to participate more actively in the community, they wish to feel that they belong. This is the time when many, boys and girls, may be interested in serving at the

---

[37] Signposts and Homecomings, p.100
[38] J. Gallgher, op., cit., p.42

altar or in other activities in the parish. This should be encouraged in the parishes because it is an essential step in deepening their experience of being Church. During this period the faith of children is very much that of the family and the other significant adults in their lives – grandparents, close relatives, teachers and others.

Christian formation and the growing child

Those baptised as children 'must be later formed in the faith in which they were baptised'. We are told that 'Christian formation, which is their due, seeks to lead them gradually to learn God's plan in Christ, so that they may ultimately accept for themselves the faith in which they have been baptised'[39.] Faith, as we have seen, is a gift of God and, at the same time, a free human response to God's plan in Christ. Catechesis in the family, as in any setting, has no in-built success mechanism. It always runs the risk of failure at least in the sense that the young may choose not to take up the practice of our Catholic tradition. Yet even in such circumstances parents need not necessarily consider that they have failed. Nor should we cause them to feel that they have failed. Many influences affect young people's decision. However, when parents continue to love and accept their children, though saddened by their personal decisions and way of life, they show something of the goodness of the 'prodigal father' in the parable.[40] The 1997 Directory speaks quite forcefully of the stage of pre-adolescence: 'sufficient account is not taken of the difficulties of the needs and of the human and spiritual resources of pre-adolescents'. It even goes so far as to declare them 'a negated age group'.

> *Very often at this time the pre-adolescent, in receiving the sacrament of Confirmation, formally concludes the process of Christian initiation but from that moment virtually abandons completely the practice of the faith. This is a matter of serious concern which requires specific pastoral care, based on the formative resources of the journey of initiation itself.*[41]

---

[39] Introduction to the Rite of Baptism of Children, n.3
[40] see J. Gallagher, 'Catechesis and the Family', Celebration and Challenge, St.Paul Publ., (Homebrush NSW), pp.118-129
[41] GDC, n.181

We are all aware that children seem to grow and develop faster than they did some time ago. Through the rapid progress in communications they are more informed, even if they do not have the necessary experience to cope with and properly discern what is good or bad in what they see and hear through the media. At the stage of late primary school they are already beginning to ask questions and express opinions about standards and values upheld by parents and other adults. Later still in the teen years, even those brought up in a committed and practising home and who themselves have been active in Church life, will enter what has been termed the stage of 'searching faith'. Baptised in infancy they could not profess a personal faith, now is the time when they need to work out for themselves the faith by which they can live. This is the time when any inherited faith must become, however hesitantly, 'my faith'. This searching period can last over a good number of years. To many it may appear negatively as a period of doubt and rejection. Yet for many young people it is a time of profound religious questioning and searching that is part of the necessary transition from the acceptance of the faith of those close to them to the choice of faith that is more personal. It is often not an easy time either for parents or for adolescents. Yet it is a time when the young are in need of companionship of those who are older, a companionship that is compassionate, understanding and challenging but not patronising or over judgemental.

It is for this reason that the Christian community must give very special attention to parents. By means of personal contact, meetings, courses and also adult catechesis directed toward parents, the Christian community must help them assume their responsibility – which is particularly delicate today – of educating their children in the faith.[42]

---

[42] ibid, n.227

Partnership in educating to and in the faith

In this context it is useful to call to mind that the Church calls for a strong partnership between various agencies and settings involved in educating children and the young to and in the faith. These include the home, the parish and the school and other agencies or settings such as youth clubs and youth associations. John Paul II points out that they share a common task but each has distinct roles with 'very specific responsibilities'.[43] It is important that we appreciate each of these roles if those involved are to work together in mutual harmony for the good of all. For example, it is not a question of handing over to parents the task of the school or parish catechists. The stress on family catechesis is not to deny the school its rightful task within the pastoral mission of the Church, nor is it asking parents to be professional teachers. A good number of years ago now, when I was speaking on this subject one particular teacher was clearly annoyed and threatened by such ideas. At the coffee break she accused me of being a fifth columnist dropped behind the lines by the bishops. I was naturally somewhat puzzled by this. She explained that, in her view, I was there to prepare teachers for the closure of Catholic schools. Nothing could be further from the truth. However, teachers and catechists do have to remember that parents are the first educators of their children. It is the task of teachers and catechists to help parents with their professional skills and vocational dedication. The notion and practice of partnership is now more fully accepted though it is not without its difficulties and misunderstandings in some places. Canon Law states that schools are to be considered of great importance 'since they are the principal means of helping parents to fulfil their role in education'. This calls for 'the closest cooperation between parents and the teachers to whom they entrust their children to be educated'.[44] One of the main aims of the *National Project of Catechesis and Religious Education, Living and Sharing Our Faith,* was to further and foster partnership between home, parish and school by providing resources that would help each in their specific task.[45]

---

[43] CT, n.16
[44] The Code of Canon Law, Collins, 1983, Can.796
[45] see J. Gallagher, 'Living and Sharing our Faith: a National Project', Priests and People, Aug.-Sept.,1991

The time when children are preparing for the sacraments of initiation provides opportunities for this working together in partnership. These should not be the only occasions when this partnership takes place. What is offered in the parish should be an experience of community catechesis and not just the instruction of children in classrooms outside schools by one or two parish catechists. In some parishes a group of older parishioners of different ages, including teenagers, are part of the catechist team. This approach provides not only instruction in an understanding of the sacraments, it also enables the children to experience Church as a community of believers. Sacramental programmes are, I believe, impoverished if they concentrate exclusively on the instruction of children in understanding and celebrating the sacramental moment or event in isolation. They can be opportunities for helping children and parents grow in faith together. The time of sacramental preparation can be for some parents a motivating moment when they are more ready to take part in a reflective learning experience that will help them come to a greater appreciation of their developing task with growing children. Not all, of course, will be so motivated. We should not make unrealistic demands on the time and energy of busy parents who face many pressures in trying to make ends meet and attending to the needs of different members of the family. What we offer should not only be seen as yet another duty imposed on them but a chance to reflect on and share with others the joys and burdens of parenthood and the chance to develop as parents, persons and Christians. In this regard I found the work of Wim Saris, a Dutch Salesian, very helpful and practical.[46]. I worked with others in using and adapting his resource material in several parishes some years ago. I recall one session held in an area of Liverpool when the topic for reflection and discussion was 'Children: gift or burden?' A woman present exclaimed that it was the first time that anything 'holy' had recognised that children might be burdens, not just wonderful gifts from God. She proceeded to wax eloquent on kids as burdens. When she was asked if she would prefer to be without them, she was equally eloquent about the joys they had brought her. At the end of another session one lady said that she had thoroughly enjoyed it because it was 'about me, not the Church!' Of course it was about both, about her place in the Church as a parent. The trouble was, she had little appreciation of her own place and importance in the mission of the Church with her chil-

---

46 W. Saris, Together We Communicate, Collins, 1982; Living the Faith Together, Collins, 1985

dren. I conclude this chapter with a quotation that speaks of this appreciation of the 'ordinary' in our lives, especially the lives of parents.

In their struggle to live life to its fullest, to be generous and self giving, to grow in their original faith about life's goodness and worth, people are already responding to God. Often they do not recognise much of their ordinary daily activity as such a response. Sadly, neither do we, and so we fail to affirm and support their faith. If belief and Church practice are to have any relevance to daily life there is need to help people to recognise God present and active in their daily experience. It is this life which the sacraments ultimately celebrate.[47]

Family and community catechesis should concern itself with these topics of life and relate them to the great Christian themes and celebrations. In this way the adults support each other in their faith journey and enable each other to take up the task of educating the young to and in the faith. On this road adults and the young are pilgrims together.

---

[47] E. Conway, 'Midwives to the Mystery' The Furrow, July/August 1994, p.419.

Chapter Thirteen

The Faith and young people today

In general, it is observed that the first victims of the spiritual and cultural crisis gripping the world are the young. It is also true that any commitment to the betterment of society finds its hopes in them[1]

Today faith will be more searching than sure, more personal than institutional, more complex than simple, more a victory won in the teeth of defeat than an easy assumption of certitude[2]

As a Salesian of Don Bosco I am reminded in our Constitutions that 'evangelising and catechising are the fundamental characteristics of our mission'. As I mentioned in the preface, in our twenty-third General Chapter held in 1990 some two hundred Salesians from around the world gathered in Rome for a period of two months. After the formal business of elections was completed, we considered the question of how we could best carry out our mission of evangelising and catechesing young people today. We reflected on how we might best communicate the faith to them, on how we might best accompany them in their approach to and growth in the faith. After prolonged deliberations, the document we produced was entitled *Educating Young People to the Faith*. The title is interesting. Catechesis is frequently described in official documents as a process of 'educating *in* the faith'. We were conscious that many are not yet ready for education in the faith; it is more a matter of educating to the faith. Having considered the great variety of contexts and situations in which Salesians work, we drew up a list of the different categories of relationships that young people have with the Church. The chapter document very forcefully states that 'young people who have no contact with the Church form the largest category'; 'young people who are fully committed form a small minority, but their presence is a real sign of hope'. It was recognised that the reasons for the alienation of so many young people are varied and are manifested in different ways. The Chapter text goes on to state:

---

[1] GDC, n.181
[2] M. P. Gallagher, Help My Unbelief, Veritas, 1983, p.123.

The challenge posed by young people who remain at a distance from the world of faith is the most universal factor emerging from all the analyses that have been made. It can apply even to those who have passed through the first stages of Christian initiation. Many young people with freedom of choice allow their lives to be confined within a secularist vision, which seems attractive to them. The large number of young people who remain far from the Church present a great challenge to the Salesian communities.[3]

This is now a common phenomenon among adults and young people and is a challenge faced in homes, parishes and schools in Britain today. The great variety of interest in and response to the faith among Catholics, young and not so young, is a major pastoral concern and challenge for the Church today. The 1997 *General Directory for Catechesis* is aware of the fact that 'local churches are obliged to address the entire panorama of these religious situations'. The text quotes a reflection of John Paul II in the encyclical *Redemptoris Missio*. The Pope acknowledges that 'entire groups of the baptised have lost a living sense of the faith, or even no longer consider themselves as members of the Church and live a life far removed from Christ and his Gospel'. In this situation the Pope calls for 'a new evangelisation'.[4] Priests, parents, catechists and teachers are aware that with very many people who attend our schools or parish cate-chetical programmes we are engaged in a process of educating to the faith rather than, or as well as, educating in the faith. Many are not yet ready for a catechetical programme because they lack the basic religious back-ground to which the Christian message can be related or because the reli-gious and Christian dimension of their lives has become dulled by other influences that have a more immediate and appealing attraction. Christian doctrines can appear almost as some foreign language. In this situation we are faced with daunting questions: how best can we fulfil the task of sharing our faith with them? How can we courageously and sensitively seek to help others come to and grow in faith? This calls for more reflec-tion on faith: faith as gift and faith as a free human response to the invi-tation to discipleship. We need to bear in mind that the world and Church

---

3, 23rd General Chapter of the Salesians of Don Bosco, Educating Young people to the Faith, Editrice S.D.B., Rome, nn.76-77
4 GDC n.59

of today are very different from those in which our Christian faith matured. We need to look at the help and support that the believing community can and should provide in these circumstances. We need also to appreciate and allow for the fact that individuals must have space and time enough to make their own personal decision.

We believe; how can we help others believe?

As parents, priests, teachers and catechists, we profess a common faith and may wonder why it seems so difficult for many young people and others, even members of our own family, to profess these beliefs and be active within the Church community. Every Sunday as we celebrate Eucharist we stand and pray together:

We believe in one God, the Father, the Almighty...
We believe in one Lord, Jesus Christ...
We believe in the Holy Spirit, the Lord, the giver of life...
We believe in one holy, catholic and apostolic Church...

This is our faith, this is the faith of the Church down through the centuries, this is the core of what we and Christians throughout the world believe. We are conscious of the fact that many, even those with whom we share our life and love, are not present with us at the Eucharist, do not join us in our common profession of faith. Many parents who care deeply about their children and who try to live and share their faith are saddened and pained by the apparent lack of Christian belief and practice in their children: 'my daughter is living with her boyfriend'; 'my son no longer comes to Mass'. Too often we hear the sad lament 'where did we go wrong?' Priests, parents and parishioners who each Sunday profess their common faith are often saddened and bewildered by the absence of so many young people: 'we believe, why can't they?' Some go so far as to question the value of our Catholic schools: 'why such lack of knowledge and practice of the faith after all these years in Catholic schools? Some ask the question 'are we getting our money's worth?' Many blame the teachers and the R.E. resources. In their turn, teachers may blame parents:

'some children arrive at primary school and cannot make the sign of the cross'. Priests and catechists can frequently be frustrated in their efforts to run successful sacramental and other catechetical programmes: 'we believe and sincerely wish to share our faith and beliefs; why do so many appear to lack interest, not to be ready for or open to our Christian faith and beliefs?'

We believe. How can we share our faith and our beliefs with others, especially our own children as they grow up? Unfortunately, there is no short, simple, direct answer to that poignant question. Like it or not, we are dealing with complex issues involved in the understanding of each individual human being and of the society and world in which we and they live. For today's young people the Church is only one stall in a large market place and for many of them it does not seem an attractive one. The Church stall certainly faces some stiff competition from other agencies. We must bear in mind that faith is ultimately a free and personal response. Ruth Duckworth points out that 'many people will have mediated it (faith) to me and helped me grow; but in the last instance I cannot live by any person's faith but my own'[5]. It is important to bear in mind what the theologian, Walter Kasper says of this particular feature of faith: 'faith is a fully and wholly human act in spite of all the indebtedness and bestowal of grace. It is a person who believes and not the Holy Spirit in a person'[6]. There are many factors and other attractions that influence and compete for the attention of each individual person. Much as I would like to offer one, there is no absolute guarantee that others will share our faith and beliefs; not even committed, practising, understanding, caring parents; not a vibrant welcoming parish with well prepared liturgies; not the most inspiring of teachers nor orthodox, sound R.E. resources. These can all help and play a crucial role in assisting the person to make his or her own response and choice for faith. However, they cannot by themselves guarantee that any individual will join us in our common profession of faith. The 1971 Directory reminds us that we are 'responsible for choosing and creating suitable conditions which are necessary for the Christian message to be sought, accepted, and more profoundly investigated'. It goes on to state that that is where our task ends because 'adherence on the part of those being taught is the fruit of grace and freedom' and does not

---

5 R. Duckworth,'What is at issue in R.E. Today', The Sower, 262, 1, 1974, p.3.
6 W. Kasper, An Introduction to Christian Faith, p.21.

ultimately depend on what we might do[7]. This may be a sobering and even disquieting thought. We know that we cannot make others believe but we would like to find some panacea which would somehow ensure that they would in fact freely believe along with us. Unfortunately, there is no such panacea. We can, however, do a great deal to help. To do so we must seek to understand and appreciate each person in his or her searching and questioning and, like Jesus in the Emmaus story, relate our beliefs to their questions, doubts, struggles and aspirations. We must, at the same time, be aware of and appreciate the positive and the negative factors in the culture and society that have an effect on their questioning and searching.

Helping them believe in today's world and Church

It is too simplistic simply to blame certain people or aspects of Church life– parents, priests, teachers, catechists, modern catechetics, R.E. resources – for the apparent or real lack of belief and practice especially among many of today's young people. It is also facile and of little use simply to bemoan the times in which we live as if there were some golden age when faith and beliefs were shared with clarity and ease without any of our present day hassle. It has never been that simple at any time in the Church's history. As a Salesian of Don Bosco our Constitutions present me with a challenge in this regard.

> *Inspired by the optimistic humanism of St. Francis of Sales, the Salesian believes in people's natural and supernatural resources without losing sight of their weakness. He also makes his own what is good in the world and does not bewail his own times; he accepts all that is good, especially if it appeals to the young.[8]*

In the recent synod of European bishops many interventions spoke of a crisis of faith in Europe, a sense of the absence of God, the 'apostasy' of

[7] GCD, n.71
[8] Salesian Constitutions 17

Europe. Some analyses of the situation in Europe were sombre and verging on the pessimistic. At the same time many bishops warned against any sense of despair. There were clear signs of hope in the fact that many more people were searching for a deeper meaning to their lives and were more open to the transcendent. I have already made reference in the preface to the message that the bishops addressed to the Church in Europe. It is a message of hope. They quote John Paul II's speech at the opening of the synod: 'do not give way to discouragement, to ways of thinking and living which have no future, for we place our sure hope in the Word of God'. The bishops urge us 'to proclaim the gospel of hope, to celebrate the gospel of hope and to serve the gospel of hope'. Such hope is 'no dream or utopia. It is real because Jesus is Emmanuel, God–with-us.'[9] However we judge the present situation in the Church and especially young people in the Church, we are challenged to renew our belief that God is with us, that the Spirit is alive in today's Church as much as in the Church of past ages. It is in the here and now that we are called to be Church. While many in the Church are daunted and disturbed, others are enthused and excited by the call to be the Church in Europe today while not ignoring the serious problems and issues that have to be faced.

The call for 'new evangelisation'

There is nowadays a certain ambivalence in religious matters: on the one hand, there is a general apathy and indifference towards Christian faith and belief; on the other hand, there is a new searching and hunger for the spiritual dimension of life. In his book *Help My Unbelief* Michael Paul Gallagher describes an occasion when he was giving advice to a student who had came to talk to him abut some problem or worry. In attempting to help the student he began by saying 'when I was your age…' to which the student replied 'but, Father, you were never my age'. Taken aback, Gallagher began to realise that the student meant that he, the priest, was never nineteen in 1983. It is useful for parents, teachers, priests and catechists to bear in mind the obvious fact that we were never nineteen or twenty-three in the year 2000. This is, of course, true and has clear implications

---

9 'Gospel of Hope', Briefing vol.29 n.11, 10th November 1999, pp.22-27.

for the way we set about trying to understand the influences that effect the attitude of the young and others towards the Church and the faith today. Yet it is a fact that some of us too easily overlook. In judging and helping the young and others in matters of faith, we must bear in mind that we are at a different stage or season of our journey in faith. Nor can we assume that the attitude of today's teenagers and young adults towards faith will be the same as ours was at those particular ages. There are many reasons why this cannot be so. Quite simply the world and Church in which they are growing up and living in are different from the Church and world in which we grew up and lived in some ten, twenty, thirty, forty years ago. If we are to help them to faith and belief we must recognise this evident fact and not simply wish that things are different than they are. As I was writing this chapter I received a copy of *The Furrow* review. I was particularly interested in the text of an address by Anne Looney, a teacher of R.E. She delivered the address to the National Conference of Priests in Ireland. Discussing the question of being faithful as a Catholic in Ireland today, she rather strikingly expressed the same idea that I am trying to make.

> *We have to learn that the faith of our fathers is not good enough for our sons and daughters, not because there was anything wrong with it, but because it was the faith of our fathers and mothers and while it served them well and they served it well, their sons and daughters find it wanting in face of the Celtic Tiger.*[10]

In his book *Struggles of Faith* Michael Paul Gallagher is also aware of the new environment of faith in today's society in Ireland as elsewhere, that impacts on the young and their attitude to the Church and the Christian faith.

> *What had been a fairly unified world view becomes scattered, pluralist, unsure of its bearings. It all adds up to a post-rural rhythm of life with a resultant relativising of the traditional authorities in many spheres.*[11]

---

[10] A. Looney, 'On Being Faithful', The Furrow, Vol. 50, 12, Dec. 1999, p.658
[11] M. P. Gallagher, Struggles of Faith, Columba Press, 1990, p.52

As Looney points out in her paper, many of the changes which have taken place in the rest of European culture and society since the First World War have been concentrated into twenty years in Ireland. What she and Gallagher have to say about young people and the faith within the Irish context has been true for much longer in Britain.

We may be disturbed by such talk. We may call into question the veracity, even the orthodoxy of such talk. Yet both General Directories recognise this reality, however, unwelcome it may be to us. The 1971 Directory acknowledges that 'believers of our time are certainly not in all respects like believers of the past' and 'faith requires explanations and new forms of expression so that it may take root in all successive cultures'[12]. The text points out that scientific, technical, industrial and urban civilisation frequently divert the attention of people away 'from matters divine and makes their inner concerns with regard to religion more difficult'. A religious crisis can easily occur. Social communications are exerting an ever-wider influence among the Christians, especially young adults 'who suffer grave crises and are not infrequently driven to adopt ways of acting and thinking that are hostile to religion'[13]. With large numbers becoming indifferent to religion or having a faith that has little effective influence on their lives, the question is not one of 'merely preserving traditional religious customs, but rather one of also fostering an appropriate re-evangelisation of people'[14]. The 1997 Directory also acknowledges that Christians today, as in every age, are not immune from the influences of human situations, they too are affected by the climate of secularism and ethical relativism prevalent today. Such things 'call urgently on the sower to develop new evangelisation, especially in Churches of long-standing Christian tradition where secularism has made greater inroads'[15]. In the case of the young, rapid and tumultuous socio-cultural changes, increase in population, unemployment and the pressures of the consumerist society among other issues, have a profound effect.

---

[12] GCD n.2b
[13] ibid. n.5
[14] ibid. n.6
[15] GDC nn.24-27

> These all contribute to make of youth a world in waiting, not infrequently a world of disenchantment, of boredom, of angst and of marginalisation. Alienation from the Church, or at least diffidence in her regard, lurks in many as a fundamental attitude. Often this reflects lack of spiritual and moral support in the family and weaknesses in the catechesis which they have received. On the other hand, many of them are driven by a strong impetus to find meaning, solidarity, social commitment and even religious experience.[16]

In the context of evangelisation, the Directory goes on to stress 'missionary proclamation and catechesis, especially of the young and adults' as a priority. It suggests that, at times, we should adopt with young people 'a missionary dimension rather than a strictly catechetical dimension'.[17] I have already examined what the Directory says about these features and stages of evangelisation. These are features of our task that we can easily overlook as we make assumptions about the readiness of people for catechetical instruction in the doctrines of the faith. Work may be needed to prepare the soil for the planting of the seed.

Young people and the faith

I find the document *The Religious Dimension of Education in a Catholic School* very helpful when considering young people in relation to 'the faith'. While the document speaks of the context of a Catholic school, the points that it makes are also relevant to the situation in homes and parishes as well as to young people beyond school age. It is not entirely irrelevant to the situation of many young adults in the parishes and of young parents involved in sacramental programmes. In the next chapters I shall look more specifically at the school context. The document acknowledges that we proclaim the Gospel message in a vastly changed environment and that young people are faced with new issues and questions. The first part of the document gives an overview of the religious dimension in the lives of young people today and talks of some of the key characteristics

---

[16] ibid, n.182
[17] ibid. n.185

of young people. It recognises that 'for many young people, a critical look at the world they are living in leads to crucial questions on the religious plane' and states that 'large numbers of them sincerely want to know how to deepen their faith and live a meaningful life'.[18] Later, when considering the nature of religious instruction in the classroom, the text expresses no surprise that the young people bring into the classroom what they see and hear in the world around them, especially from the mass media. As a consequence 'perhaps some have become indifferent or insensitive'. Teachers are urged 'to accept pupils as they are, helping them to see that doubt and indifference are common phenomena, and that the reasons for this are readily understandable'[19]. Some people may find it surprising that a document from a Vatican congregation accepts that doubt and indifference are common and that the reasons are readily understandable. I am not sure that we find it easy to understand the doubts and indifference of many of our younger contemporaries. It is especially hard for caring, committed parents. Rather than trying to understand the situation, many seem simply to lament it. Yet if we are to sow the seed of the Word with any hope of real and lasting success, we must pay attention to the soil in which we scatter it. That is precisely the advice given in the Vatican document. It is advice suited not only to teachers but also to all those who are engaged in the process of educating the young to and in the faith.

> *But they (teachers) will invite students in a friendly manner to seek and discover together the message of the Gospel, the source of joy and peace.*
> *The teachers' attitudes and behaviour should be those of one preparing the soil. They then add their own spiritual lives, and the prayers they offer for the students entrusted to them.[20]*

Parents and others may also find some help and comfort in this passage. In a later section more advice is given to teachers, and this can include parents, catechists and others. While they are 'teachers of the faith, like Christ, they must also be teachers of what it is to be human'. This

---

[18] Congregation for Catholic Education, The Religious Dimension of Education in a Catholic School, (RD), Catholic Truth Society, 1988, n.21
[19] ibid. n.71
[20] ibid. n.71

includes giving witness to such human qualities as 'affection, tact, under-standing, serenity of spirit, a balanced judgement, patience in listening to others, and prudence in the way they respond, and finally, availability for personal meetings and conversations'[21]. There is need for friendship and patience. Our Salesian constitutions urge us to imitate the patience of God in this respect. Meditation on the parable of the Prodigal can help achieve this 'serenity of spirit'. The Directory encourages us to accompany and support the young as they journey towards their personal choice for faith. The concept of 'preparing the soil' is a central theme of the 1997 Directory. One of its chief aims is to foster 'a greater consciousness of the necessity to keep in mind the field in which the seed is sown, and to do so with the perspective of faith and mercy'[22]. Yet as we, parents, priests, teachers, catechists, walk with them and seek to tend the soil in readiness for the seed, we need reassurance and support for ourselves. We need affirmation that what we do is the right thing for them and us. The 'sowers' also need to be cared for and supported. Too often, parents, teachers and others are made to feel a sense of guilt and carry the blame when the situation is complex rather than simple.

Categories of young people in relationship to the faith and Church

The Vatican document on the religious dimension of education, in my opinion, is rather optimistic when it says 'perhaps some have become indifferent and insensitive'. In the General Chapter we Salesians consid-ered the situation to be more drastic. This would appear to be borne out by the findings of a survey dealing with the attitude of young people of Rome with regard to the Church and the faith. The findings were report-ed in an article in the Italian newspaper *Avenire*. In a seminar held in the Lateran University in May 1992, 'Rome's youth, between faith and indif-ference', it was acknowledged that indifference to the faith characterised most of Rome's young Catholics. The figures speak for themselves: 60,000 of Rome's estimated 650,000 young people, i.e. less than 10 per cent, are reckoned to have any sort of regular contact with Sunday Mass

---

[21] ibid, n.96
[22] ibid, n.14

or parish associations. The fact that 90 per cent had such weak links with the Church did not mean that they were in no way religious. The conclusion drawn was that the Church structures did not seem to provide adequate answers for these 'children of secularisation' for whom God is 'superfluous and has no effect on their lives'[23]. This is not restricted to Rome, it is a worldwide phenomenon. Nearer home, we need only consider the figures reported in the *Catholic Times* in January 2000. In its leader article reference is made to the soon to be published R. E. resource for key stage 3 in Catholic secondary school, *Icons*. The article speaks of the 'stark reality' that teachers have to deal with: 'most pupils will have very little grounding in their faith at home and very few attend Mass'. The article goes on to say that a recent visit to a Catholic school threw up some depressing statistics: 'out of each of eight classes of 16 year olds visited, there was at best three practising Catholics out of 32, at worst none'. It concludes: 'the fact that most young Catholics no longer practice their faith is particularly worrying'[24]. There may be a somewhat too high expectation of what an R. E. resource can do in such circumstances. I shall return to this in the chapter on catechesis and R.E. in our schools. No doubt this situation is experienced to a greater or less extent in most western countries and cultures. It is now being felt in the new democracies of Eastern Europe in countries that had a strong Catholic identity despite communist persecution.

There is remarkable agreement between the conclusions of the Salesian 23rd General Chapter regarding young people's faith today, and those outlined by Michael Paul Gallagher when speaking of young Irish Catholics. Over all, the smallest, though a very significant group, are the young people who remain active and involved in various Church activities. They may be involved in liturgy, possibly through folk groups. They take part in social action and may help with children's catechesis or in some form of youth work. They are prayerful and take the opportunity to join others in shared reflection. Gallagher reckons that in Ireland these form about 10 per cent – not unlike the situation among Rome's young people. In Britain it will be much the same, though possibly slightly less. In the Salesian Chapter document the largest group worldwide consists of those who have no contact with the Church. Although their families are

---

23 Avenire, 20th May, 1992
24 'Lessons rethink set to provide morale booster', Catholic Times, January 30th 2000, p.8

basically religious, some have lost touch with the Church, as result of, what is in many places, a de-christianised environment. Others were born into families and social contexts whose values are unconnected with those of religion. In some places, young people who live in poverty and on the margins of society are unaware of the existence of Christian, or indeed of any religious values. If they do know them they do not see that they have any relevance to their own lives, which are taken over with the struggle to survive. Not all of these are to be found in the so-called 'underdeveloped' countries. In the Irish context, Gallagher thinks that about 10 per cent are embittered by and hostile to their Catholic upbringing. They are highly critical of the church as institution as they perceive it. He maintains that the large majority lies somewhere in the middle. His overview and that in the Salesian document see a number of different groups in this middle category. There are those who participate to some extent, those for whom Catholicism remains a spiritual home, a place of roots however shaky. Among these there are those who look for meaning and values in life, though they have little concern for much of the Church's teaching. They are often attracted and helped by special events – helping the handicapped or the elderly, working with HCPT (Handicapped Childrens' Pilgrimage Trust) groups in Lourdes, joining friends on reflective weekends or taking up some cause for justice and peace. Others 'practise' but do so more out of social custom. Many opt out quietly and gradually without anger, even without rows with parents. They just drift away and remain cultural Catholics[25]. This variety can be found in our schools and parishes among the young and not so young. The 1997 Directory stresses that this diversity of religious situation should be kept in mind. It also says that we should remember that 'the most successful catechesis is that which is given in the context of the wider pastoral care of young people, especially when it addresses the problems affecting their lives'[26]. I shall take this up again in the next chapter when discussing the pastoral and educational ministry in our schools.

---

[25] Educating Young People to the Faith, nn.64-74; Struggles of Faith, p.36
[26] GDC, n.184

Some characteristics of the young

The Vatican document on the religious dimension of education begins by considering young people in a changing world. It recalls that the second Vatican Council in the *Constitution on the Church in the Modern World* provided a realistic analysis of the religious condition in the world and paid explicit attention to the situation of the young.[27] In the years since the Council there have been further radical changes, not least in the youth scene. The document encourages research into the questions and needs of today's young in different cultures and contexts. While acknowledging that local situations create great diversity, the text sets out some of the characteristics that can be considered common among the young. Obviously what is said is by its very nature general and will not fit every situation; nonetheless, it can be helpful to reflect on the general issues raised in the document. The document speaks of an environment that is largely devoid of truly human relationships in the family and in society. For many this is true also of the Church. This felt lack of affection leads to a deep sense of loneliness. Many young people are, as a consequence, more depressed than in the past. They have a greater sense of insecurity and a lack of self-esteem and self worth. The text refers to an environment that is almost entirely based on money values and a consumerist way of life. This encourages a dull indifference to religious and spiritual issues. It is rooted in a pragmatism that is concerned only for the immediate present, on what I can get here and now. Many drift with the social tide or thinking of the moment.

Despite all modern progress, there are grave concerns and worries about the future. The fear of a nuclear disaster is a reality for many young people. There is the very real fear of unemployment, already and at times for long periods experienced by their elders. Many suffer the hurts of marriage breakdown and divorce. A greater number of young people are in single parent families. In many places they are the victims of dire poverty. Many find little sense or meaning in life and seek comfort in drugs, in the abuse of alcohol and sex, and look for other means of escape from the harsh realities that face them. Little wonder then that a certain instability normal in the young is more accentuated today: today's 'yes', may be tomorrow's 'no'. There is a generosity in the young that is rather vague,

---

[27] GS nn.1-10, especially n.7

often full of enthusiasms for popular causes but with little realistic focus or specific orientation. Reeling off the drugs-alcohol-sex-escapism list may seem melodramatic, but for many young people some of this, if not all of it, is their lived reality. It is good to see that a Vatican document takes notice of these realities and encourages us to do the same.[28] We cannot simply expect to share the faith with the young if we do not wish to share and understand their concerns and if we do not try to relate these concerns to the truths of our Christian faith. Nor can we view the world and Church from our own particular corner and expect everywhere else to be the same. There is a great diversity of contexts and situations. The Directory, as I noted earlier in the chapter, recognises that 'local churches are obliged to address the entire panorama of these religious situations'. This applies very much to our parishes and schools.

Uncover, purify and develop authentic values

Various documents, including the Salesian Chapter document, highlight some of the values that are seen to be of particular importance by the young. The young generally lay special value on the respect for the dignity of each individual person. People are of equal dignity whatever their gender, their creed or their colour. For the most part they seek an enriching relationship between people, relationships based on freedom, justice, tolerance, respect for those who are different. There is a concern and sensitivity for cultural and religious values, a sensitivity for the great issues of our world: the environment, third world debt, the problems of starvation and disease. There is a strong appeal for new relationships that will overcome a sense of isolation, sometimes to satisfy immediate needs, at other times in a search for lasting and stable relationships of trust and love. The 1997 Directory refers to such issues as the 'modern areopagi', points of authentic values. The term 'modern areopagi' is a reference to Paul's preaching on the hill in Athens, the Areopagus, when he looked for positive values in the culture of the Athenians. He eventually focused on the 'unknown god' of the Athenians in an attempt to help them understand the God of Jesus Christ. Among some of the values in today's youth culture the text enumerates communications, civil campaigns for peace,

---

[28] RD, nn.10-17

development and liberation of peoples, the protection of creation; the defence of human rights, especially of minorities, women and children; scientific research and international relationships[29]. The Directory urges us to follow the example of Paul by uncovering, purifying and developing such authentic values.

In his book *'Clashing Symbols'* Michael Paul Gallagher has a chapter on cultural discernment. Once again I find what he has to say to be both thought provoking and helpful. In the introduction and elsewhere I have already made reference to his striking phrase 'recognising smoke signals of hope arising from what may at first sight seem like a burnt out desert'. I wish to develop his ideas more fully here. Gallagher is of the opinion that at the end of the twentieth century the dominant feature among young people with regard to religion is apathy. There is much less anger and alienation because most young people have little contact with the Church. There is, however, in his view, 'a whole generation of baptised young adults whose formative experiences with religion and Church are so thin as to be almost nonexistent'[30]. As a consequence of this 'much discourse about evangelisation may assume the presence of preambles of attitudes or dispositions that can no longer be taken for granted but have to be created and awoken.[31] He suggests that in this situation 'the first task is a ministry of disposition, an awakening of the hungers to which the truth may eventually be seen as an answer'. He goes on to speak of the need for 'discernment'. This he describes as 'a specifically spiritual and Christian way of reading reality'. He examines the section in the Acts of the Apostles, chapter 17, where Paul addresses the Athenians. Paul's initial reaction to the Athens was one of understandable disgust – 'there his whole soul was revolted at the sight of a city given over to idolatry' (17:16). However, Paul undergoes a change of attitude and sees signs of 'genuine religious hungers' and identifies 'seeds of the gospel' among the Athenians. Making reference to the altar of the Unknown God, Paul declares 'the God whom I proclaim is in fact the one whom you already worship without knowing it' (17:23). Paul, says Gallagher, moves to a 'disposition of hope, rooted in the Spirit'. For Gallagher this is a way of discerning culture with 'consolation'.

---

[29] GDC, n.211
[30] M. P. Gallagher, Clashing Symbols, DLT, 1997, p.112
[31] ibid, p.114

> *Consolation does not mean rose tinted viewing. In fact it involves a double expectation: there will be conflict, ambiguity, and anti-values enthroned but there will also be signs of hope and real hunger, fruits of the Spirit. No situation is beyond redemption. Judge we must but in a spirit of discernment, even of aggressive discernment, never in a tone of dismissiveness... Consolation breaks the negative magnifying glass that can only see decadence or disaster. Discernment ultimately means sharing that conversion of disposition of St. Paul in Athens, and thus being able to recognise smoke signals of hope rising from what may at first seem like a burnt out desert'.[32]*

Messengers of hope: bless rather than bemoan

If we are to help others come to and develop in faith we must not only see and condemn the negative aspects in their life and culture. We must recognise and bless the good which, at a first or hasty glance, is often hidden, not always readily discernible in their lifestyle, their interests, their priorities and their questions. When faced with young adults who appear not to 'practise' or who do so only irregularly, we would do well to stop and weigh up the good that they do, the values they uphold. We should not only be ready to critisise and condemn; we should also appreciate and bless all that is good in them. Some years ago I was asked by a parish priest to preach at each of the parish Masses on the Sunday close to the feast of St John Bosco. The theme he gave me was 'bringing up your children in the faith'. A tall order, especially when it had to be done in the space of no more than ten minutes. Anyway, I did my best. After Mass a lady came into the sacristy. She informed me that she had intended to go home and exchange angry words with her twenty-year old son because he did not come to Mass. On reflection, after the homily, she said that she would go back and thank him because he drove her each week to Mass. She would, nonetheless, encourage him to join her. But that, of course, was his choice. This may seem a rather trivial example, but I hope it makes the point. Let us seek out what we can bless and affirm or, as the

---

[32] ibid, p.124.

Directory says, let us uncover, purify and develop the authentic values that are to be found in today's culture and the young.

Like Paul we should seek to recognise the smoke signals of hope that rise from what may indeed seem like a burntout desert. If we only see the present situation as a burntout desert there will be no room for dialogue and sharing, we will fail to be the people of hope that the bishops at the recent Synod invite us to be. They ask us to be a people who proclaim, celebrate and serve the 'gospel of hope', a hope that is 'no dream or utopia' but 'real, because Jesus is Emmanuel, God-with-us'. Damian Lundy's favourite quotation from Vatican II was the sentence from *The Church in the Modern World:* 'We can justly consider that the future lies in the hands of those who are strong enough to provide coming generations with reasons for living and hoping'[33]. If we wish to share our faith and attract people to our faith we must present it in such a way that it addresses the real questions, problems and aspirations of people today and, in the light of the Good News, provides them with reasons for living and hoping. However, the choice is ultimately theirs. I conclude this chapter with two quotations that have relavance to the young in relationship to the faith and Church today. The first is part of an interview given by Timothy Radcliffe, Master General of the Dominicans, to some sixth formers of Worth School.

What has Christianity got to offer young people?

I think, hope, above all else, hope. In most places in the world the challenge for young people is that they can feel sometimes caught by despair, wondering whether they have a future, where their lives are going to go. I have just come back from Columbia which is a very violent and difficult place. Meeting people around the country, whenever I say, 'What is the big challenge?', they would say, 'To believe it could ever be different, to believe it could ever change'. Now I think that is what Christianity offers you. You know that in the hands of God and in our hands, as his children, we can in fact make a world that is better.[34]

---

[33] GS, n.31
[34] 'Interview for Identity, Worth School', Doctrine and Life, March 1999, 49, 3, p.140

The second quotation is from Bishop David Konstant's homily at the memorial Mass for Damian Lundy. It aptly speaks of Damian's outstanding pastoral approach and skills in dealing with young people which, in my view, offer an example and model for all of us who seek to be companions on the road of life and faith with young people today.

> *My first memory of Damian is at Kintbury, that large, comfortable figure, completely at ease - guiding young people to discover, understand, be glad about, celebrate their faith and to begin to realise that their faith - inchoate, inarticulate, unformed - was part of the faith of the Church.*

> *Like a conductor with a scratch orchestra, he discovered new instruments, giving players confidence to try them out and to learn what they were capable of. The concert was always fresh, never polished, always worthwhile because, though rough music, it was genuine, true, creative, imaginative and hopeful.*[35]

[35] B. Conroy & G. Rummery, *For Our Life is but a Song*, McCrimmon Publishing, 2000, p.14

Chapter Fourteen

Catholic Schools: A pastoral and educational ministry

At great cost and sacrifice our forebears were inspired by the teaching of the Church to establish schools which enriched mankind and responded to the needs of time and place.[1]

It should be remembered that the most successful catechesis is that which is given in the context of the wider pastoral care of young people, especially when it addresses the problems affecting their lives.[2]

In this chapter I wish to share some reflections on our Catholic schools from the perspective of our Christian faith. I shall focus on our Christian faith and beliefs as central to our understanding of education, and on how our schools can provide a setting for the Church's evangelising and pastoral work with young people today. In the following chapter I shall consider the potential and limitations of our Catholic schools in the task of the faith development of the young today, together with the understanding of catechesis and religious education and their place in the curriculum. Much of what I have already said about faith, the dimensions of faith and the variety of levels of faith, especially among the young, must be borne in mind when reading these chapters.

In the last decades much has been written on the nature and purpose of Catholic schools in a time of almost endless change and constant development in government educational policy when, in the opinion of many, the distinctive values of Catholic schooling are under threat. We are faced with the challenge of upholding and defending our faith vision of life expressed in Gospel values as essential and relevant to our mission in education. In the competitive market culture that now influences much of official educational theory and practice those with responsibility for our schools face difficult dilemmas. They struggle to hold in some delicate

---

[1] Congregation for Catholic Education, The Catholic School, (CS) Catholic Information Office, 1977, n.65
[2] GDC, n.184

balance the need to survive in such a competitive atmosphere and, at the same time, to act on and give witness to the Christian principles that underpin our view of education. We also have to give serious considera- tion to what our schools can realistically achieve in educating today's young to and in the faith. This is demanded of us in a time of decline in commitment to the Christian faith, its beliefs and practices. Within in our schools there is the same variety of soil – different levels of faith and belief – that are set out in the Directory as we saw in a previous chapter. What approaches can and should schools take in these circumstances? The Pope encourages us to take up the task of 'new evangelisation'. He urges us to fulfil the 'grave duty' to 'offer religious training suited to the often widely varying religious situations of the pupils'[3]. Do we recog- nise and accept that there are 'widely varying religious situations' among our pupils that call for a variety of approaches and strategies? How can a school set about this task? How should we judge and assess their efforts in this regard?

A difficult and complex task

Some in the Church appear to fail to appreciate the complexity of the situation and simply criticise and condemn schools for failing to transmit and pass on the Catholic faith and beliefs to young people today. Others, particularly teachers, feel that they are doing a reasonably good job though sometimes without a great deal of affirmation or recognition of what they do in fact achieve. Much of what is done in our schools in the task of providing a broad and balanced education for our pupils, including faith development, should be judged from the perspective of a wider pastoral concern for the young and their needs in a complex, con- fusing world. This is, of course, an essential feature of proclaiming and living the Good News, of evangelisation, of educating the young to and in the faith. At times, however, we need to express appreciation for the great deal that is done in schools as part of the Church's pastoral service to the young and as an essential backdrop to their personal, moral, spiri- tual, religious and faith development. There is much that can be and is

3 CT, n.69

being done in schools that enables pupils to have a greater sense of self worth and to come to and grow in Christian faith, or at least to have a deeper knowledge and respect for Christian beliefs and values. This is a task that belongs to the whole school staff, not just the R.E. department and a chaplaincy team. At the same time, however, we cannot be complacent and assume that all is well with every Catholic school. Teachers and those with responsibility for our schools must constantly reconsider and assess what is being done to preserve and develop the distinguishing features of Catholic schools and to educate the young to and in the faith in the situations in which they find themselves today. We must recognise the demands of our time and place and work together to address them. In a Vatican document we are reminded that loyalty to the educational aims of the Catholic school calls for 'constant self-criticism and a return to basic principles, to the motives which inspire the Church's involvement in education.'

One must recognise that, more than ever before, a Catholic school's job is infinitely more difficult, more complex, since this is a time when Christianity demands to be clothed in new garments, when all manner of changes have been introduced in the Church and in secular life, and, particularly, when a pluralist mentality dominates and the Christian Gospel is increasingly pushed to the sidelines.[4]

Catholic schools, a rich part of our heritage

Throughout the world the Church has built schools as a key feature of Christian service to individuals, families and society. These schools exist in a great variety of situations and within many different educational systems. The model of Catholic schooling that we have in England in Wales is not the same everywhere in the Church. In India, for example, where the number of Catholics is only about one percent of the population, we Salesians and many others run schools in which the vast majority of staff and students are of other faiths such as Hindu, Sikh or Muslim.

---

[4] CS, nn.66-67

In many 'missionary' countries this is the case. Official documents recognise these schools as Catholic. We are told that, 'in the certainty that the Spirit is at work in every person', the Catholic school 'offers itself to all, those who are not Christian included, with all its distinctive aims and means, acknowledging, preserving and promoting the spiritual and moral qualities, which characterise different civilisations'[5]. The most recent document from Rome speaks of the public service offered by Catholic schools in countries where Christians are a minority or in developing countries. This text states that 'clearly and decidedly configured in the perspective of the Catholic faith… Catholic schools have always promoted civil progress and human development without discrimination of any kind'[6]. In Europe the history of the development of Catholic schools is different and has been very much focused on the needs of Catholic children and families. In some countries Catholic schools are an officially recognised part of the education provided by the state with a variety of financial arrangements. In other places Catholic schooling is totally independent from the state system and has to be entirely funded by the Catholic community. The history of how and why Catholics set up and developed schools is different in every country.

The Catholic community in England and Wales has in the past and continues today to put enormous effort in terms of finance and personnel into establishing and maintaining schools for Catholic children. As I quoted in the historical reflections, the bishops in 1852 preferred the establishment of good schools to every other work. They wished to provide adequate education for the poor and they wanted it for all. 'A place in a Catholic school for every Catholic child' was the declared aim of the bishops. Prior to the Second World War, Catholic education was very much a parochial affair. As Paul Hypher points out, the Catholic parish community 'strove to focus its catechetical, educational role and its caring apostolate to the family on the Catholic school'. The school sought to provide education for Catholic children who would otherwise receive no formal schooling and to safeguard their Catholic faith against the errors of other Christian denominations and the influence of secularism. Historically, the elementary schools catered for children from five years of age until the compul-

---

[5] ibid., n.85
[6] Congregation for Catholic Education, 'The Catholic School on the Threshold of the New Millennium', (CSTTM), n. 16, in Briefing vol. 29 n. 3, 10th March, 1999, p.30.

sory school leaving age and were 'parish schools in the best sense of the word'. Situated near the church they were a living part of the daily life of the parish. They provided basic education and were agents of social concern for the poor and needy in the parish.[7]

Facing new challenges

Changes and developments in educational policy of different governments have lessened this direct parish control of our schools. Our Catholic maintained schools are closely associated with the national system of education in which Church schools enjoy particular rights as voluntary schools sponsored by the Church. The bishops and their educational agencies keep a careful eye on the situation to ensure that such rights are not eroded by any new legislation. In their message issued after the National Pastoral Congress in 1980 the bishops reaffirmed their belief in the value of Catholic schools. In their message they stated 'whatever new educational priorities may emerge we must neither belittle the contribution which schools have made in the past nor underestimate their potential for the Church now and in the future'.[8] Today our schools exist in different and constantly changing situations. Among factors that affect schools are population shifts, falling roles, urban redevelopment, decline in religious practice and commitment, the breakdown of family life, our multicultural and multi faith society.[9] We can add to this list the plethora of new legislation that continually bombards those involved in running our schools. Many teachers and school governors are frustrated by so many new initiatives that often seem ill conceived and at times threaten to undermine important aspects of our Catholic concept of education. For these reasons, which to a large extent lie beyond our control, many questions are being asked about the continued value and viability of our schools and about how we may best ensure that they continue their pastoral mission in this new historic situation. In the book *The Contemporary Catholic School* several papers highlight aspects of the

7 P.A. Hypher, 'Catholic Schools and Other Faiths', in The Contemporary Catholic School, T.Mc Loughlin, J. O'Keefe & B. O'Keefe (eds), Falmer Press, 1996, p.221.
8 The Easter People, n.134
9 See J. Gallagher, Our Schools and Our Faith, p.10

tensions and dilemmas that now face those with responsibility for our schools[10]. The bishops in *The Easter People* remind us that 'there are many questions which we need to ask about the Catholic school if it is to fulfil its role as a Gospel-inspired community'.

Our Christian faith and our concept of education

In the early 1980s Paul Hirst in an article 'Education, Catechesis and the Church School' argued that 'in education any faith the educator has is irrelevant to his goals'.[11] That may be so on Hirst's understanding of 'faith' and 'education'. It is certainly not a view that many Catholics would hold. As I have discussed faith in earlier chapters, it can hardly be considered irrelevant to our view of educating the human person. At its most basic, faith is the way we understand the meaning of human life, its significance, its dignity and purpose. For Christians, as the Catechism expresses it, faith is our response to God who reveals himself enlightening us as we search for the ultimate meaning of life. This has practical and direct implications for the way we understand and try to live our lives and how we set about helping others to understand and live theirs. I find the point made by Rodger when speaking about beliefs, about what a person 'believes in', to be helpful in this context.

> *The point is that what a person 'believes in' is what has some real purchase in terms of what he thinks and feels and does, how he judges and decides, what attitude he adopts, what course of action he considers worth pursuing. In these we show what we are committed to, what we really regard as important – which is to say, what we believe in.[12]*

[10] The Contemporary Catholic School, see especially G. Grace, 'Leadership in Catholic Schools'; R. Pring, 'Markets, Education and Catholic Schools'; T. H. Mc Loughlin 'The Distinctiveness of Catholic Education'

[11] P. H. Hirst, 'Education, Catechesis and the Church School', The British Journal of Religious Education, 3,3, 1981, p.89

[12] A. R. Rodger, Education and Faith in an Open Society, Handsel Press, 1982, p.14

In my view what Rodger says is very pertinent to the way we seek to run our schools and to organise the various aspects of life in our schools in the light of our Christian beliefs. Educators cannot take up a totally neutral stand that is somehow detached from their own personal views about what is of value in life. If somehow they try to do so, then such a concept of neutrality is what they happen to 'believe in'. Care must, of course, be taken to avoid any form of indoctrination or forcing of one's views on others. That concern, however, does not and cannot demand of us some neutral stand. Such a position is not possible. The recent document from the Congregation for Catholic Education talks of the dangers in 'a supposed neutrality'. It regrets the fact that 'there is a tendency to forget that education presupposes and involves a definite concept of the human person and life'. To claim neutrality for schools 'signifies in practice, more often than not, banning all reference to religion from the cultural and educational field'[13]. This principle of a value laden education balanced with respect for persons and their freedom is clearly set out in the text *The Religious Dimension of Education in a Catholic School.*

> The religious freedom and personal conscience of individual students and their families must be respected, and this freedom is explicitly recognised by the Church. On the other hand, a Catholic school cannot relinquish its own freedom to proclaim the Gospel and to offer formation based on the values to be found in a Christian education; this is its right and duty. To proclaim or to offer is not to impose, however; the latter suggests a moral violence which is strictly forbidden both by the Gospel and by Church law.[14]

Some distinguishing characteristics

Over the years I have helped to facilitate many in-service days for whole school staffs dealing with the question of the nature and purpose of Catholic education and of the distinguishing features of the Catholic ethos of our schools. The question is asked 'What makes

[13] CSTTM, n.10
[14] RD, n.6

Catholic schools different from other schools?' 'What is distinctive about our schools?' Some seem less than satisfied with references to Christ and the Gospel, to the fact that we focus on the whole person. They say that these could be applied to Anglicans or to others who hold certain educational philosophies regarding the dignity of the person. That is of course true. However, I am personally delighted rather than perplexed by the fact that such is the case. I am not sure that we can detect any one single particular feature that absolutely distinguishes Catholic schools from every other type of school. It is more probably a combination of a variety of features. At the heart of our philosophy and practice of education must surely be our Christian faith vision concerning the significance of human life and the dignity of every person as created by God and redeemed by Christ. Within our Catholic tradition certain distinguishing features can be enumerated although they will be adapted to the particular needs of individual schools in different situations. Tom Groome, for example, lists five characteristics that he sees as 'distinguishing characteristics of Catholicism' that have an influence on our view of Catholic schooling. These distinct yet overlapping features of Catholicism can be called 'theological characteristics in that they are grounded in the Catholic understanding of God and human existence'. They are:

its positive anthropology of the person;
its sacramentality of life;
its communal emphasis regarding human and Christian existence;
its commitment to tradition as a source of its Story and Vision;
its appreciation of rationality and learning, epitomised in its
  commitment to education.

Groome goes on to mention three more 'pervading commitments that are particularly relevant to Catholic education':

the commitment to 'people's personhood' – an ontological concern;
the commitment to 'basic justice' – a sociological concern;
the commitment to 'catholicity' – a universal concern'.[15]

---

15 T. H. Groome, 'What Makes a School Catholic ?' in T.H. McLaughlin, J. O'Keefe and B. O'Keefe (eds) Contemporary Catholic School, Falmer Press 1996, p.108

In his opinion, 'the collage of these eight characteristics constitutes education that is Catholic'.

In the report *Signposts and Homecomings* the authors seek to 'keep in view some of the most fundamental aspects of Christian belief which must radically affect the approach to education'. They identify certain 'strands in the Christian educational ideal' and suggest four key elements which, if kept in balance, will ensure that the essential aspects are not overlooked. The four key elements are:

> a perspective centred on Christ as universal Saviour;
> a deep respect for the individuality of all human beings;
> the recognition that all men and women are the children of
> God and included in the scope of Christ's redemptive love;
> the promotion of a sense of mission arising from baptism and
> which empowers Christian pupils to continue and perpetuate
> the salvific work of Christ in the world.

The authors of the report are of the opinion that what is distinctive about Catholic education will be apparent, if a proper balance is preserved between these four elements.[16]

It is surely not out of place to suggest that the dimensions of the faith which I discussed earlier should be considered essential elements or features of Catholic schools. I think that some adaptation of the terms used by Michael Paul Gallagher could be useful in this regard.

■ MEANING. This will include opportunities to take up the search for the true significance and purpose of life. It will comprise encouraging pupils to reach beyond the limitations of present experience, knowledge or imaginings. It will include providing the opportunity to explore the great questions of life. Teachers, not only R.E. teachers, can help pupils consider them in the light of Christian beliefs in order to come to a deeper knowledge and understanding of the Christian faith in which 'the high calling and the deep misery which people experience find their final explanation'.

16 Signposts and Homecomings, pp.115-123

■ LISTENING. This can embrace the opportunities for time and space for reflection, for quiet, for prayer, for spiritual development. It includes liturgical and extra liturgical celebration, the display and use of symbols and other rituals, reflective away days and retreats.

■ DOING. This aspect looks to the moral and social development, which will include creating opportunities for the service of others in the school, the local community and the world beyond, encouraging social awareness, the care for people and our world as part of building God's Kingdom of justice, peace and love. Opportunities should be provided that allow pupils the chance to take on suitable responsibilities within the school and to have a voice in the running and evaluating of certain aspects of the life of the school. In this way they become active agents in their own education. Church documents stress the importance of this aspect of schooling.[17]

■ BELONGING. This will encompass a welcoming environment in which pupils, parents and staff will experience a sense of belonging, recognition and acceptance, an experience of Church. All involved in the school should strive to create a sense of community in which Christian values are not only taught but also experienced in the life of the school. While not every one in the school, pupils and staff, will be of the same community of faith, they should share in and feel responsible for the school community which is inspired and challenged by the Christian faith enshrined in Gospel values.

In this context it will be useful to look again at chapter ten where I discussed educating people to and in each of these dimensions of faith. It could be a useful exercise to spell out implications for the life of the school under the headings of these key dimensions of our Christian faith and to draw up some action plan to ensure that they are translated into reality in the daily life of the school. In doing so the different religious needs and levels of faith commitment of staff and pupils should be borne in mind. The responsibility for creating and maintaining this community environment rests with all those who are members of the school community. It cannot be left to the chaplain and the R.E. staff.

---

[17] Sacred Congregation for Catholic Education, Lay Catholics in Schools: Witnesses to Faith (LCS), CTS, 1982, nn18-19; J. Gallagher, Our Schools and Our Faith, p.39; RD, n.29

The recent Vatican document on the characteristics of Catholic schools

The document on Catholic education on the threshold of the new millennium stresses that it is an opportune time to 'devote careful attention to certain fundamental characteristics of the Catholic school which are of great importance'. It recalls the focus of the 1977 document *The Catholic School* which was on the 'nature and distinctive characteristics of a school which would present itself as Catholic'. It declares its present aim as one of offering 'a word of encouragement and hope' to all who those are engaged in Catholic schooling. Among the fundamental characteristics that it mentions are the following:

> *the Catholic school as a place of integral education of the human person through a clear educational project of which Christ is the foundation;*
> *its ecclesial and cultural identity;*
> *its mission of education as a work of love;*
> *its service to society;*
> *the traits which should characterise the educating community'.*[18]

The text briefly touches on aspects of these characteristics. It speaks of the contribution the school makes to 'the evangelising mission of the Church'. In this context the school is seen as a 'privileged environment'. The text gives special mention to the school's part in the pastoral care of people, especially of the less fortunate of pupils who experience difficulties of all sorts. Another characteristic of the Catholic school flows from this pastoral, evangelising mission: 'it is a school for all, with special attention to those who are weakest'[19]. It expresses appreciation for what it terms 'the unpretentious yet caring and sensitive help' offered to parents and families. One of the chief aims of the Catholic school 'should be contact and dialogue with the pupils' families'. Parents' associations should be promoted. Such collaboration fosters the 'personalised approach which is needed for an educational project to be efficacious'[20]. The document regrets the difficult financial restraints experienced in some countries

[18] CSTTM, n.4
[19] ibid., nn.5 & 15
[20] ibid., nn.5 & 20

which affect the recruitment and stability of teachers and may lead to the exclusion of pupils who cannot afford to pay. The text decries such 'selection according to means which deprives the Catholic school of one of its distinguishing features, which is to be a school for all'[21].

Great stress is placed on 'the centrality of the human person': 'the person of each individual human being, in his or her material and spiritual needs, is at the heart of Christ's teaching'. It is precisely because of this that the text declares 'the promotion of the human person is the goal of the Catholic school'[22]. It recognises also that the school is 'a place of ecclesial experience', it can provide an experience of Church. As in other documents, the possibility of a 'synthesis between culture and faith' is seen as 'one of the most significant elements' of a Catholic school. Knowledge set in the context of faith, it states, 'becomes wisdom and life vision': 'the various school subjects do not present only knowledge to be attained, but also values to be acquired and truths to be discovered'[23]. The importance of a community dimension is underlined, one that is marked by healthy and caring relationships and collaboration between all involved: students, parents, teachers, governors and non teaching staff. In the Catholic school such a community dimension is 'not a merely sociological category; it has a theological foundation as well'[24]. The document closes by citing a passage from the Pope in his encyclical *Redemptor Hominis* where he states that the human person 'is the primary and fundamental way for the Church, the way traced out by Christ himself'. Such a way cannot, therefore, be foreign to those who evangelise. As a consequence, the text concludes that 'it follows that the work of the school is irreplaceable and the investment of human and material resources in the school becomes a prophetic choice'[25].

People as our focus, Christ as our model

I sometimes begin an in-service day with a picture of a young person with a large question mark and surrounded by symbols depicting, among other influences, home, parish, school, leisure time, employment and unemployment. My point is that our focus as educators is on the person, the young person growing up in a bewildering and baffling world. I

---

[21] ibid., n.7   [22] ibid., n.9
[23] ibid., n14   [24] ibid., n.19   [25] ibid., n.21

often follow that with the Vatican II text, one which I have cited else-where, that says that 'the future lies in the hands of those who are strong enough to provide coming generations with reasons for living and hop-ing'. That is an essential part of our task as educators – 'to provide rea-sons for living and hoping'. The text of another Vatican document on schools is also relevant when it declares that the teacher is not simply a professional person who systematically transmits a body of knowledge in the context of a school. The teacher is 'an educator', 'one who helps form human persons'[26]. This is a constant theme in all Church documents on education. This can be summed up in a quotation from *The Catholic School*.

> The purpose of instruction at school is education: the develop-ment of persons from within, freeing them from that condi-tioning which prevents them from becoming fully integrated human beings. Its educational programme is intentionally directed to the growth of the whole person.[27]

In this task we are enlightened by the Christian vision of the person, of life and its meaning. Other schools will undertake this task but with a dif-ferent motivation and interpretation of life and its significance. The doc-ument *The Religious Dimension of Education in a Catholic School* acknowledges that 'the Catholic school is like any other school in the complex of events that make up the life of the school'. As a civic institu-tion, a Catholic school shares many of the aims, methods and character-istics of other schools. We cannot opt out of the demands of the national curriculum, of responsible management of finances and of the assessment of teachers and pupils according to national standards. We may well be critical of certain aspects of these features of educational policy, but we cannot simply ignore them if we wish to remain within the dual system. However, the Vatican text goes on to declare that 'there is one essential difference: it draws its inspiration form the Gospel in which it is root-ed'[28]. The Vatican document recognises that it is not always easy to bring these two aspects into harmony. It is a task that requires constant atten-

[26] LCS, n.16
[27] CS, n.29
[28] RD, n.47

tion. Education in the context of a Catholic school is not simply secular education plus Catholic R.E., liturgy and other Catholic practices and devotions. The faith or religious dimension permeates all aspects of school life: management, organisation and structures, the curriculum, discipline, the system of reward and punishments, the relationships between all involved in the school, appreciation and welcoming of parents and an openness to the wider community[29]. There is another passage from a Church document that I find helpful and it is one that appeals to teachers when I use it in-service work.

> *A Catholic school: its characteristics are rooted and grounded in the Christian concept of life centred on Jesus Christ: He is the one who ennobles people, gives meaning to human life, is the Model which a Catholic school offers its pupils.*[30]

We could do well to reflect and meditate on this and other passages. Christ is the one who ennobles people. Surely that is at the heart of all our efforts in educating children, the young and adults. To seek to 'ennoble' people as Jesus did is a tremendous mission and vocation and it is one that is open to teachers and all involved in education in whatever form. One of my favourite passages is the one in *The Catholic School* where it speaks of the school deriving its energy from a constant reference to the Gospel so that it creates a setting in which 'pupils experience their own dignity as persons before they know its definition'.[31] In this way the school 'is faithful to the claims of people and of God'. Here, in another form and in relation to the educational and pastoral mission of our schools, we have the constant theme in educating people to and in the faith – the double fidelity to God and to people in their particular situation. If the school sets out to enable pupils to experience their dignity as persons, I am convinced that something of God's love will touch their lives and enhance their self worth. If we create such a setting in which our pupils can grow as persons, then they may be more ready and able to come to an understanding of the dignity and worth of each person as expressed in our Christian faith and beliefs.[32]

[29] see Evaluating the Distinctive Nature of a Catholic School (3rd edition), Catholic Education Services., 1994.   [30] CS, n.35   [31] CS, n.55
[32] See J. Gallagher, 'The Catholic School and Religious Education: Meeting a Variety of Needs', in The Contemporary Catholic School, p.295-296

A broad pastoral care that serves many needs

Within our schools pupils come from a great variety of experiences and backgrounds and with different social, emotional, spiritual and religious needs. In this regard the second of the quotations with which I opened this chapter seems to me to be very relevant and worthy of note. Our endeavours to educate children and the young to and in the faith should be within the context of 'the wider pastoral care of the young, especially when it addresses the problems affecting their lives'. There is a section in a C.E.S. publication on spiritual and moral development which paints a picture of this variety of needs that teachers can identify as existing in their schools. I set the passage out in a series of bullets to highlight the various backgrounds and needs mentioned.

- Many in our schools come from secure, happy homes, and are well supported by their parish community. For them, the shared values of home, parish and school create an environment of trust and openness.

- Some of our pupils bring to school experiences which have seriously damaged their capacity or readiness to develop a sense of worth or the value of life and the world around them.

- Many of them are deeply marked by distrust, if not hatred, of themselves and of others. They are already cynical about anything which appears to be good or wholesome, and highly skilled at hiding their vulnerability and sensitivity.[33]

That may be disturbing reading but teachers are aware that this is a picture of the reality they face in their classrooms. The Vatican text concludes that 'there can be little doubt, therefore, of the importance of the environment we create for our pupils if they are ever to move out of the imprisonment of such experiences'.

The latest Vatican document issued at the end of the millennium paints a similar picture. The school, it says, is 'undoubtedly a sensitive meeting-point for the problems which besiege this restless end of the millennium.'

---

[33] Spiritual and Moral Development Across the Curriculum, published by the CES, 1995.n.35

> *The Catholic school is thus confronted with children and young people who experience the difficulties of the present time. Pupils who shun effort, are incapable of self-sacrifice and perseverance and who lack authentic models to guide them, often even in their own families. In an increasing number of instances they are not only indifferent and non practising, but also totally lacking in religious or moral formation.*[34]

In their general attitude towards their pupils and in their personal relationships with them, teachers can affirm and encourage those who are already supported in their families; they can attempt to heal and make whole the fragile and broken and touch the lives of the marginalised and disadvantaged. Michael Paul Gallagher reminds us that 'when self worth is wounded, a whole language of faith – human and religious – may stutter and fall silent…unreadiness for revelation can have roots in this area of a person's life'[35]. For a number in our schools a welcoming, caring atmosphere and the encouragement of teachers can lead to a greater faith in themselves and others and in God as the one who loves all people. For others pupils the help of teachers provides further support and companionship in the journey of life and faith. In undertaking this mission those with responsibility for our schools have Jesus as Model.

Called to serve new forms of poverty

The most recent document from the Congregation for Catholic Education recalls that in the past the Church established various types of educational institutes in response to the needs of the socially and economically disadvantaged. A number of outstanding men and women in the Church sought to meet the needs of children and young people left to their own devices and deprived of any form of schooling. The text mentions the work of the Ursuline sisters for poor girls in the fifteenth century, the work for boys by St Joseph Calasanz in Rome, by de la Salle in France and by Don Bosco in Turin. These great saints took up the chal-

---

[34] CSTTM, n.6
[35] M.P.Gallagher, Free to Believe, D.L.T., 1987, p.94

lenge of serving the needs of young people in the face of 'situations of incomprehension, mistrust and lack of material resources'. The document suggests that today we are called to address 'new forms of poverty' among children and the young.

Young people can be found again among those who have lost all sense of meaning in life and lack any type of inspiring ideal, those to whom no values are proposed and who do not know the beauty of faith, who come from families which are broken and incapable of love, often living in situations of material and spiritual poverty, slaves to the new idols of a society, which, not infrequently promises them only a future of unemployment and marginalisation. To these new poor the Catholic school now turns in a spirit of love.[36]

While this may seem somewhat dramatic, it does describe a good number of the pupils who are to be found in many of our Catholic schools in England and Wales. It is in this context that we are called to serve the new forms of poverty and to face the challenge of 'new evangelisation'. At the turn of the twenty-first century the Church document reiterates the exhortation of the second Vatican Council in which the bishops entreat Catholics 'to spare no sacrifice in helping Catholic schools achieve their aim'. In doing so they are encouraged 'to show special concern for the needs of those who are poor in the goods of the world or who are deprived of the assistance and affection of a family or who are strangers to the gift of faith'.[37] Yet it is precisely in trying to continue that mission that schools today are faced with serious dilemmas. Gerald Grace puts the point well and succinctly when he says that 'a competitive market culture in schooling is making it much more difficult to be in the service of the poor, the troublesome, the alienated and the powerless'[38]. These are hardly the points that we set out in the school prospectus or highlight in the colourful brochures that advertise what schools can offer pupils and families. They are, unfortunately, not good selling points that parents might find attractive when deciding what is the best school for their children.

---

[36] CSTTM, n.
[37] Vatican II, Christian Education, n.9 Abbott
[38] G. Grace, 'The Future of the Catholic School: An English Perspective', From Ideal To Action, J. M. Feheney, (ed), Veritas, 1998, p.195

The need to 'sell' the school and the call to serve those in need raise a number of questions that are far from simple or easy to resolve on such delicate issues as admission policies and procedures for and practice of suspensions and expulsions. They can be the cause of quite heated debate and very real tension among those involved in facing the issues. These are issues on which Headteachers and Governors frequently seek guidance. Some guidance can be found in a number of publications from the Catholic Education Service and others.

Facing the dilemmas and issues

Unfortunately, I cannot offer any clear-cut or quick solution to these problems that so many of those who have the responsibility for our schools have to face all too often. I am aware that any pastoral, theological reflections may offer some inspiration but certainly not an immediate practical solution to individual cases. We should not underestimate this wider pastoral care that our schools can and do offer to children and young people caught up in these 'new forms of poverty'. This is an important dimension of a living Christian faith within the Church community. It should not be judged merely as some sociological feature or considered less important than doctrinal instruction. It may well be the necessary 'missionary' activity that enables pupils to be more open to more directly catechetical activity. I often consider a good Catholic school to be the long arm of the Church, along the lines of the advert for Heineken lager, touching those parts that often the parish church cannot and does not reach. This is truly 'missionary' and 'evangelising' in the broad sense of which Paul VI spoke when developing the theme in his exhortation *Evangelisation in the Modern World.*

Some recent correspondence in *The Tablet* touched on the issue of the admission policies of Catholic schools. It has to be borne in mind that in some places our schools are oversubscribed and not all Catholics can find a place in local Catholic schools. This is certainly the case in parts of London. Elsewhere there are falling numbers of Catholics and there is an intake of a percentage of pupils who are of other Christian churches or other faiths. Situations vary greatly. A priest for north London considers the admission policies in some schools to be 'too demanding and exclusive' in so far as they go beyond the 'excellent guidelines of the bishops'. The bishops asked only that a child be a baptised Catholic. Schools often impose other conditions: that the child was baptised in the first years of life, serves at the altar or takes part in parish music groups and such like. He dislikes the fact that priests are frequently asked to provide details of family practice. The Director of Schools Administration in the Westminster archdiocese asked 'should it be the 'best' Catholics who get in or the one who is impoverished in the faith and needs extra support?' He mentioned that schools often do not admit children to a Catholic secondary school if they have not attended a Catholic primary school. This, he points out, is not always the fault of the parents since many are over subscribed. He considers proximity to the school as a decisive criterion for the admission of baptised Catholics. Another priest wrote that 'Children have rights too and have no say in their upbringing. We should act with understanding, mission and compassion'. He considered the use of Mass going as the criterion for entry into a Catholic school as 'too facile'[39].

With regard to the 'lapsed', I recall a bishop once saying that in baptism they made promises which they may not have kept fully. However, we, the Church community, also made promises to help and support both the child and the parents. We should keep our promise. Our schools offer one way of our attempting to keep our promises. There are different views among Catholics when considering these issues. It is a factor, frequently mentioned in this debate, that those who attend Sunday Mass are the ones who contribute to the parish collections out of which comes the levy for the Church's part in the financial upkeep of our schools. As I said, theological, pastoral reflections are helpful and necessary though they do not provide the immediate, practical solutions that Headteachers and Governors may be looking for. That does not mean that they should be ignored. It is essential that we give thought to the theological aspects that underpin the vision we bring to the consideration of such issues. If we fail to do so, we fail to take up the task set by the bishops in *The Easter People:* we need to ask many questions about the Catholic school if it is to fulfil its role as a Gospel-inspired community. As Catholics we may ask different types of questions arising from different theological perspectives.

---

[39] 'Home News: Catholic schools exclude too many, priest says', The Tablet , 4th March 2000, pp.327-328

Teaching: a pastoral and creative ministry

I conclude with one brief final thought. We frequently lament the fact that the publication of 'league tables' for schools can be crude and incomplete, if not incorrect, criteria for assessing and judging what makes a good school. There is, I think, also the danger of 'Catholic league tables' which can assess and judge a Catholic school almost entirely on the criteria of 'knowledge and practice of the faith'. I have no wish to belittle or downgrade the importance of sound knowledge of the Christian faith and beliefs as well as joining the community for the celebration of Sunday Mass. The problem for me arises when they are considered the absolute criteria for judging the school's success as a Catholic school. As with any league table mentality, there is the danger of ignoring the complexity of situations and of failing to take account of the people involved and their starting point. Unless we know where pupils started from, how can we gauge how far they may have travelled and in what ways teachers and pupils may have succeeded? Reflection on Jesus as teacher, evangelist, catechist may provide a truer appreciation of 'success'. He touched many people's lives. Not all of them showed him gratitude. When invited by him, not all stayed or followed him closely. Yet all were the richer for his presence and his touch. We can perhaps be over anxious about 'results', about 'getting our money's worth' out of the enterprise – evangelised, catechised, practising young people in numbers. We should be equally anxious, even more anxious, about the quality of our evangelising presence, touch and attitude as we serve the diversity of need among pupils and families in our schools. We should not undervalue the powerful potential of our schools in this regard. At the same time, we must constantly inspire and challenge them to recognise and fulfil this tremendous vocation.[40] The recent Vatican document which wishes to convey to teachers 'a word of encouragement and hope' spells out, almost poetically, the worth and dignity of the teaching ministry and profession.

> *Teaching has an extraordinary moral depth and is one of the most excellent and creative human activities, for the teacher does not write on inanimate material, but on the very spirits of human beings. The personal relationships between the teacher and the students, therefore, assume an enormous importance and are not limited by simply giving and taking.[41]*

[40] J. Gallagher in The Contemporary Catholic School, pp.295-297
[41] CSTTM, n.19

Chapter Fifteen

Educating to and in the Faith in our schools: Catechesis Religious Education

There is a close connection, and at the same time a clear distinction, between religious instruction and catechesis, or handing on the Gospel message[1].

Faith formation is a task proper to the ecclesia rather than to the classroom. But for an ever increasing number of students, the Catholic school may be the only ecclesia they ever encounter.[2]

In the historical reflections, I quoted a passage from the first synod of Westminster (1852) in which the bishops exhorted Catholics to give priority to the building of schools even over the building of Churches. As they then put it, 'it is the good school that secures the virtuous and edifying congregation'. Today that is clearly not the case, at least not in the sense that most of the pupils in our Catholic schools are among the congregation at the Sunday Mass in the parishes. Different groups in the Church put forward different reasons for this situation. People apportion blame to particular groups and a variety of circumstances. Faced with this situation, questions are now being asked about the value of Catholic schools from the point of view of their potential, or lack of potential, in the task of educating children and young people to and in the faith. Can schools educate to and in the faith? Are they trying to do so? How do we measure their success or failure in this regard? Expectations about what the school can and should achieve vary. When reflecting on these issues, much of what has been said in previous chapters concerning Christian faith and people, especially the young, must be kept in mind.

---

[1] RD n.68
[2] A. Looney, 'Teaching Religion to Young People Today', From Ideal to Action, J.M.Feheney, Veritas, 1998 p.81

Our Catholic schools and Church attendance: a paradox

I was recently given a copy of the official newspaper of the diocese of Wrexham in which there was the obituary notice of the former catechetical adviser, Sr Bernadette Foley, a good friend and for some time a colleague. Another article caught my attention. It talked of the paradox of the apparent success of Catholic schools nationally and the falling attendance, especially of young people, in our parishes. While Church attendance was falling, there was increased demand for places in Catholic schools. It would appear that the vast majority of our Catholic schools are succeeding as schools. League table measures continually show that Church schools in general, and Catholic schools in particular, are consistently taking high places. It was noted that this was particularly true of Catholic schools in less affluent areas. They are succeeding beyond expectations even though they may not appear at the top of the league tables. They are demonstrably providing a good academic education. It is said that our schools offer a good education in so far as they are distinctive in their religious provision and in the ethos or climate of the school. Strong emphasis is placed on good pastoral care for pupils. Reflecting on this situation, the writer poses the question:

> *Does the absence of the Church gathered in the pews arise as a result of some failure of the Church gathered round the school desk?*[3]

The writer does not lay the blame for the falling Church attendance directly or entirely on the school but calls for a greater sense of partnership by all concerned, not just parents and teachers, but others in the parishes. The article concludes by suggesting that if there was greater partnership and shared concern and activity between all the partners in the task of educating the young to and in the faith, then perhaps the paradox of attendance might be answered. This would seem to endorse the point made by the bishops in *The Easter People:* the school cannot be expected to do what of its very nature it cannot do alone – produce the fully committed member of the Church'[4].

[3] Wrexham People, February 2000.
[4] The Easter People, p.136

Not everyone would let the schools off so lightly as can be seen from a rather sad letter written to *The Tablet* by a priest in an inner city parish. In his letter the priest maintains that while inner city schools may have made remarkable achievements in the struggle for educational excellence, 'there is serious cause for concern over their effectiveness in handing on faith – the prime purpose for which they are constituted'. Having himself been a teacher and a priest in an inner city parish for more than a decade, he is of the opinion that 'despite a committed staff and excellent school with significant achievement in the league tables, from a Catholic standpoint we have failed'. He comes to this conclusion largely based on the fact that at the Sunday Masses 'there is hardly a young person in sight – on average out of 180 in school less than 12 are at Mass'. He is certainly correct when he sees his situation as typical of the inner city, and indeed other places. This is backed by some of the facts discussed in the chapter on young people and the faith today and the variety of soil considered in chapter eleven. The final words of the priest in his letter are understandably sad and discouraging, though, I feel, open to fuller discussion: 'we seem to have created a magnificent structure empty of meaning which gives reason neither for complacency nor hope'[5].

Limitations and potential of school – a pastoral challenge

Quite clearly there is no reason for complacency. There are serious issues here that call for further discussion and pastoral planning and evaluation. While the sense of discouragement is deeply felt, surely the situation calls for some serious pastoral rethinking before we can declare that such school structures are empty of meaning and that there is no reason for hope. As we saw in the last chapter, the most recent Vatican document on Catholic schools recognises the school as 'undoubtedly a sensitive meeting point for the problems' of today. Yet its message is one of 'hope and encouragement' and at the same time of challenge: 'to these new forms of poverty the Catholic school now turns in a spirit of love'. Among these new poor whom we are called to serve it specifically men-

---

5 'Our failing school' letter to The Tablet 13th May 1997, p.707.

tions 'those to whom no values are proposed and who do not know the beauty of faith, who come from families which are broken and incapable of love, often living in situations of material and spiritual poverty'. When we have spent our energies on such pupils, we may still wonder what real 'success' we have achieved in educating to and in the faith. The reflection in the document *The Catholic School* may be of some help in this context.

> *Catholic schools are often accused of not knowing how to form convinced, articulate Christians ready to take their place in social and political life. Every educational enterprise, however, involves the risk of failure and one must not be too discouraged by apparent or even real failures, since there are very many formative influences on young people and results often have to be calculated on a long-term basis'.*

When faced with such a situation and with other concerns, the question is raised whether the Church should perhaps give up her mission in Catholic schools and 'direct her energy to a more direct work of evangelisation' considered to be of higher priority or more suited to 'her spiritual mission'. The text gives a very clear answer and one that has to be considered in our thinking about and evaluation of our schools in the various situations in which they are called to be part of the Church's pastoral mission. It is one that is forcefully reiterated in the recent Vatican document.

> *Such a solution would not only be contrary to the directives of the Vatican Council, but would be opposed to the Church's mission and to what is expected of her by Christian people.*[6]

There is certainly no place for complacency. There is, rather, the need for much more patient, prayerful and heartfelt shared reflection and discussion on what is a worrying and complex issue. New needs and new situations may well be calling for new pastoral strategies, even a variety of strategies designed to meet specific needs of individual people and of particular locations in which our schools are called to serve. In such considerations we cannot ignore some of the inherent limitations of a school in

---

[6] CS nn.22 & 23

faith formation of the young. Chief among these is the matter of the time available: 'catechesis takes place within a community living out its faith at a level of space and time not available to a school – a whole life time'[7]. The time spent in school over the years is in fact only a small yet important part of a person's life span. The bishops' statement on R.E. begins by reminding us of this fact which has clear implications for what can be done in schools.

> *Discipleship in the Gospel is lifelong, a journey of faith coming to complete fulfilment only in the presence of God in heaven. The entire life of the disciple is marked by learning and growth. Lifelong growth in faith is a characteristic of Catholic life. An understanding of the educative task of the Church must start from this perspective and increasingly opportunities for lifelong learning need to be developed for every member of the Church.[8]*

The statement then goes on to stress the key role of parents: 'By their example and in their participation in the Mass and other sacraments, the foundations of lifelong faith and discipleship in their children are laid'. In this task parents need support from the parish community. As we have seen, even children of caring practising parents do not always commit themselves to the Christian faith and beliefs and many of those who attend our schools do not come from committed, practising families. This too has implications for what the school can achieve.

> *The religious formation offered by the school is inevitably influenced by the home background, and so it depends greatly on whether the home is co-operative or non co-operative... It needs to be recognised that the school is a relatively secondary influence in the religious search of young people. In terms of contact time, this is obvious (and in terms of such measurement the school may be more central than the parish).[9]*

---

7 RD n.68
8 'Religious Education in Catholic Schools', n. 1, Briefing vol. 30 n. 6, 14th June 2000, p. 21.
9 M. P. Gallagher, Help My Unbelief, Veritas, 1983, p.88

'Religious education': a term used in different senses

We are still left with the question about what our schools can and should do about faith education and formation of the pupils within the time and space available to them. Attention is frequently focused on religious education in the school. However, we need to be clear about what we mean by 'religious education'. In a number of recent texts from the bishops' conference 'religious education' is understood in two senses which are distinct yet complementary.

- Firstly, they speak of it in the broad sense of the beliefs and values which inspire and unify all aspects of school life, beliefs and values which the school seeks to communicate.

- Secondly, they speak of it in a narrower sense of R.E. seen as an area of the curriculum, a subject to be taught and evaluated in the same way as other subjects on the school timetable.

This use of the term in these two different senses can, I think, cause some confusion in so far as some seem to assume that R.E. as an area of the curriculum can and should achieve all the expectations of religious education understood in the broader sense. Religious education understood in this broad sense is the concern of all those who have responsibility in and for the school.

Religious education is very much a journey of formation involving every member of the school community, together with a pupil's family and parish community. It is in this context that the three elements of religious education, catechesis and evangelisation, coexist, providing mutual support and reinforcement.[10]

R.E. as a curriculum area to be taught is a key feature of Catholic schools but it is distinct from religious education understood in the broader use of the term. Those who teach R. E. together with other teachers and Governors play a vital part in creating the ethos and climate in the school that ensures that our Christian beliefs and values inspire and unify all

---

[10] R.E.: Curriculum Directory for Catholic Schools, p.10

aspects of the life of the school. However R.E. teachers and the chaplaincy team do not carry the whole burden of ensuring that religious education in this broad sense is realised in the school. They share this task with everyone else in the school. It goes without saying that R.E. as a subject on the timetable should have pride of place in Catholic schools. However, it is useful to recall the warning given in the Vatican document: 'religious instruction can become empty words falling on deaf ears, because the authentically Christian witness which reinforces it is absent from the school climate'[11]. Personally, I find it more helpful and less open to confusion to use the term employed in the Vatican document –'the religious dimension of education' rather than 'religious education' when referring to 'the foundation of the entire educational process'in our schools. It seems to me that this can help avoid any unnecessary confusion and unrealistic or too high expectations of R.E. as a subject taught in the classroom and puts the onus quite properly on all involved in the life of the school.

A major concern of those who responded to the questionnaire on the expectations R.E. in the classroom was the relationship between evangelisation, catechesis and religious education. The precis of the responses speaks of this relationship by referring to the diversity in religious interest and commitment of the pupils.

R.E. is seen as both education to and in the faith. 'Schools are concerned with education and cannot make assumptions about the faith commitment of its pupils'. What is offered will be received by some as education, by some as catechesis and by some as evangelisation.[12]

It is interesting to note that here and in the *Curriculum Directory* religious education is described as 'education to and in the faith'. By expressing it in this way, these recent documents take on board the fact that there is a wide range of interest in and commitment to the Christian way of life. It is in this context that an understanding about the relationship of evangelisation, catechesis and religious education is seen to be necessary and important. At the same time it is useful and necessary to bear in mind

11 RD n.104
12 'Expectations of R.E. in Catholic Schools', in Briefing vol. 30 n. 2, 16th February 2000, p. 6.

what the 1997 Directory says about the boundaries not being very clear-ly definable and to recall the warning to avoid putting them 'into water-tight compartments'. In pastoral practice these distinctions cannot be made in the abstract, i.e. apart from the people being addressed, or, to put it in the terms of the Directory, apart from the soil in which the seed is to be planted. It is the people whom we address who ultimately affect the outcome. For these pastoral reasons our activities can and do frequently 'assume more than one function'[13].

The Catholic school: in what sense 'a catechetical community'?

In their news release after their Low Week meeting the bishops issued a statement on R.E. in Catholic Schools. This was the culmination of the consultation process on the subject. They state that 'a Catholic school seeks to be a catechetical community in which the content and the life of faith is shared'. In a time when there is discussion about the distinct yet complementary nature of catechesis and R.E., some may wonder what is meant by the school as 'a catechetical community'. The bishops describe a Catholic school as a 'catechetical community' in so far as it seeks to pro-mote the wellbeing and freedom of every person, made in the image and likeness of God. It is this faith vision that 'shapes the daily life of a Catholic school as a community in which faith is expressed and shared through every aspect of its activity'. It is expressed and shared through the various dimensions of faith: prayer, sacramental celebrations, works of charity and through striving for justice in all it does. The school is a com-munity inspired and challenged by our Christian faith vision and that faith is proclaimed and celebrated in a number of ways while always respecting the conscience and freedom of each individual. The phrase of Paul VI in *Evangelisation in the Modern World* springs to mind and seems apt in this context. He refers to the 'respectful presentation of Christ and his Kingdom' as the right and duty of those called to evangelise.[14]

The bishops recognise the different levels of faith among pupils and the consequent different results of our 'respectful presentation of Christ and his Kingdom'.

---

13 GDC n.52
14 EMW n.30

> *We recognise that in a Catholic school the witness of its life is, for some, a first announcing of the Gospel, or even a prepara-tion for that announcement. In these ways, the meaning of life, as understood in the Catholic faith, is explored and experienced by all taking part in the life of the school, whether they are bap-tised Catholics or not, practising their faith in their own parish-es or not. This vision of the Catholic school lies at the heart of the firm expectation that Catholic parents send their children to Catholic schools, if at all possible. The partnership between home, parish and school is the best setting for the formation of maturing Catholic young people.[15]*

This takes account of what is said in the *General Directory for Catechesis* concerning the different pastoral activities that are part of the overall evangelising and catechesing mission of the Church. The Directory speaks of 'missionary activity', 'initial catechetical activity' and 'on-going pastoral activity'. These activities are undertaken in response to the needs and readiness of those who are addressed. The several forms and functions of these ministries have their place in schools. I think it worth-while listing again some of these for consideration in pastoral planning by all concerned with faith and religious education in the school context:

- Calling or summoning to the faith.
- Initiation into the faith.
- Continuous education in the faith
- Liturgical celebration.
- Theological reflection and study.[16]

It seems to me that schools, in the same way as parishes, have to be more realistically aware of the needs and readiness of pupils with regard to the faith. They should seek to set up pastoral strategies in the light of these. Pope John Paul II, as I have pointed out earlier, urges schools to take up the 'grave duty': 'to offer religious training suited to the often widely varying situations of the pupils'[17]. The same exhortation is made in the document *Lay Catholics in Schools.*

---

[15] Bishops Statement on R. E. in Catholic Schools, n.3, p.21
[16] See chapter 11, p.5
[17] CT n.69

> *Students will surely have many different levels of faith response; the Christian vision of existence must be presented in such a way that it meets all of these levels, ranging from the most elementary evangelisation all the way to communion in the same faith. And whatever the situation, the presentation must always be in the nature of gift: though offered insistently and urgently, it cannot be imposed.* [18]

In stressing that we take cognizance of the different levels of interest in and response to the faith among pupils it is not a question of advocating that we look to the 'lowest common denominator'. Rather it is a call to attend to all the pupils with their variety of religious needs. Bulckens speaks of 'differentiation' when planning and evaluating the faith and religious education of pupils.[19] We do this in other aspects of the curriculum in response to the needs, ability and readiness of each individual. Why should we not do the same with regard to faith and religion? Pupils who have the experience and background of practice and commitment can and should be encouraged to grow in the various dimensions of Christian faith. At the same time care, attention and respect must be given to those who have little experience of the Catholic way of life, to those who appear apathetic and disinterested and to those who show little or no commitment. In line with Church documents, 'the greatest respect' will be shown to those pupils who are not Catholic. This will include an attitude 'not only of respect, but also welcoming, and open to dialogue – motivated by a universal Christian love'.[20] Increasingly in some of our schools in particular parts of the country, we are faced with the delicate issue of dealing with children of other faiths. A consultation paper prepared for the Bishops' Conference looks at the issue from theological, pastoral and educational viewpoints.[21] All of this calls for careful pastoral planning and realistic evaluation of what can and is being achieved with individuals and groups in the school.

A mixture of these types of pupils will be present in R.E. lessons. I am not suggesting that these different groups of pupils should be put into dif-

---

[18] LCS n.28

[19] J. Bulckens, 'L'Enseignment de la Religion en Flandre', L'Enseignement de la Religion Catholique, J. Bulckens & H. Lombaerts (eds), Leuven Uniiversity Press, 1993, p.159

[20] LCS nn.42 &55

[21] Bishops' Conference of England and Wales, Catholic Schools and Other Faiths, Mathew James, 1997.

ferent classes for R.E. in some sort of selection process. I am rather advocating that we recognise that, in taking account of this situation, R.E. lessons are to be planned and evaluated on educational criteria as set out in recent documents and the statement of the bishops. As the bishops point out, there will be different levels of response at the level of faith which are distinct from but not opposed to or entirely separate from the educational aims of R.E. as an area of the curriculum. R.E. teachers, others in the school and the parishes must be helped to appreciate this fact. It does not mean that we are uninterested in the faith development of pupils. That is an essential aspect of the responsibility of the school within its recognisable limitations and potential. Various people with a variety of roles in the life of the school will need to work together in a partnership in which the roles of each with regard to the faith and religious development of pupils are clarified. Those who undertake these roles, particularly senior management, the chaplaincy team and the R.E. department, should be respected and supported by all other staff in the school. It is a question of 'we are all in this together'. Some will have key roles in planning and ensuring that the religious dimension of all educational activities within the school and the opportunities for the faith and religious development of pupils are appreciated and promoted by all in the school. In this sense the school is a 'catechetical community' in which 'the meaning of life, as understood in the Catholic faith, is explored and experienced by all'. However, we must also accept and respect the fact that, for a great variety of reasons, not all will in the end be strictly speaking 'catechised'.

The catechesis and/or religious education debate

Over the past twenty-five years there has been considerable discussion about the relationship and distinction between catechesis and religious education. Gerard Rummery was among the first in Britain to explore the distinction in his book *Catechesis and Religious Education in a Pluralist Society,* published in 1975. Bulckens suggests that the distinction was made officially for the first time by the bishops of West Germany in a synod held in 1974. They distinguished catechesis undertaken in the parish community from the teaching of religion in the schools. Great stress was placed on the demand for parish catechesis to

296 Soil for the Seed

complement and support the religious instruction in schools.[22] In many European countries the issue was being discussed and at times hotly debated. Already in 1982 mention of the distinction is made in the document *Lay Catholics in School*. While it acknowledges that 'education in faith is part of the finality of a Catholic school', it also states that 'the teaching of the Catholic religion, distinct from and at the same time complementary to catechesis properly so called, ought to form a part of the curriculum of every school'.[23] The clearest and fullest official exposition of the distinct yet complementary nature of the two concepts is set out in the document *The Religious Dimension of Education in a Catholic School* which I shall examine shortly.

In the 1960s there was wide debate concerning the nature and purpose of religious education in county schools. At that time there was talk of a 'minor revolution' brought about by the social and cultural changes which took place in Britain in the postwar years and by the developments in the philosophy of education and developmental psychology. The teaching of Christianity, it was argued, should no longer be given a privileged status in county schools. In a technological and secular Britain many pupils did not belong in any committed sense to the Christian churches. Britain was a multicultural and multi faith society. In this changed cultural context it was considered to be necessary that pupils should have a knowledge and appreciation of the nature and significance of religion as well as a sensitivity to and understanding of people of various religious faiths they were likely to encounter in many parts of Britain. The task of the school in relation to religious teaching was no longer seen to be identical with that of the churches. The teaching of religion in school should be justified on educational not theological grounds. It was deemed to be educationally and morally unjustifiable to uphold and teach only the tenets of Christianity in county schools or to seek to convert and initiate pupils into the Christian faith.[24] The phenomenological approach exercised considerable influence.

---

22 Bulckens op. cit., p.165; A. Bauer, 'Teaching Religion in Germany: an Historical Overview', Religious Education and the Future, D.A. Lane (ed), The Columba Press 1986, p.17
23 LCS nn.43&56
24 See The Fourth R, report of the Commission of R.E. in Schools, National Society & SPCK, 1970; M. Grimmit, What Can I Do in R.E.?, Mayhew McCrimmon, 1973; M. F. Mathews, Revolution in Religious Education, Religious Education Press, 1969.

This approach sees the aim of religious education as the pro-motion of understanding. It uses the tools of scholarship in order to enter into an empathetic experience of the faith of individuals and groups. It does not seek to promote any one religious viewpoint but to recognise that the study of religion must transcend the merely informative.[25]

The approach did not advocate a cold, detached study of religion but rather a sympathetic understanding of the life and thought of persons deeply committed to religious and non religious traditions. Many critics of the approach wondered whether this was really possible to the extent advocated by its supporters. Much was written on the subject of religious education in county schools. Kevin Nichols gives an assessment of this approach from a Catholic perspective in several texts [26].

The issue in Catholic schools

Among Catholics in England and Wales there was also discussion and debate about catechesis and religious education. Many were influenced by the general developments in religious education and an increasing number undertook studies in the universities in which these debates were conducted. Others were very much opposed to such influences in Catholic thinking. Many began to make the distinction between catechesis as an activity proper to the Church community, and religious education as a professional task of the teacher in the classroom. It was the responsibility of the catechist to initiate those who freely express an interest into the way of life of the Catholic community and to develop Christian faith. It was the job of the teacher to enable pupils to appreciate religion as a feature of human life and culture. In Catholic schools more time and attention would be given to the exploration of the Catholic tradition while also seeking to enable pupils to have and understanding of other traditions. It was the teacher's task to conduct such an exploration with a view to promoting reflective, critical understanding and apprecia-

---

[25] Schools' Council, Religious Education in Secondary Schools, Evans/Methuen, 1971, p.21
[26] K. Nichols, Cornerstone, St Paul Publ., 1978, pp.17-19; 'Religion as a Classroom Subject', Orientations, St. Paul Publ., 1979, pp.42-46.

tion of the Catholic and other traditions. It was argued by some that it was no longer possible to assume that 'the classroom of the Catholic secondary school is an extension of the local church and that teachers of religious education were catechetical assistants to parish priests'.[27]

When considering the issues involved in the catechesis/R.E. debate, Catholics generally distinguished three aspects:

- the ethos, climate or atmosphere of the school inspired by the Christian faith vision;
- the voluntary catechetical activities which should take place in a school;
- the teaching of religion as a classroom subject.

It was acknowledged that the Christian understanding of human life should influence the overall ethos and organisation of the school. Patrick Purnell developed this view and posed a number of challenging questions concerning the way Gospel values should be translated into the every day life of the school.[28] It was a recognised feature of the task of the school to provide opportunities for worship, prayer, retreat experiences, social and community service and membership of groups such as prayer groups or justice and peace groups. Pupils should be aware that these opportunities were on offer and they should be invited to make use of them. However, such activity should always be voluntary.

The debate about the suitability of catechesis in the classroom, as part of the aim and purpose of R.E., was more contentious. Many considered that it was unrealistic to assume Christian faith in many pupils and, since some initial openness to faith is required for catechesis, they were of the opinion that R.E. lessons could not be catechesis for many pupils. Some also argued that since catechesis should be freely undertaken, a compulsory religious education lesson was hardly the place where catechesis could properly take place. The report *Signposts and Homecomings* acknowledged that a relatively large number of pupils were apathetic, did not practise, and some were even hostile.[29] Purnell listed several significant factors which, in his opinion, made it clear that catechesis under-

---

[27] G. Turner, 'Catechesis and Theological Education', The Tablet, 30th August 1980, p.851

[28] A. P. Purnell, Our Faith Story, Collins, 1985, pp.128-130

[29] Signposts and Homecomings, p.14

stood as 'a dialogue between believers' was less appropriate in the class-rooms of Catholic schools in the mid 1980s.[30] Others, while accepting that all forms of indoctrination should be avoided, argued that Catholic schools were founded and funded to foster in the young an acceptance of Catholic teaching and a commitment to the Catholic way of life. There were misunderstandings as each group attempted to explain exactly in what way a Catholic school could undertake a catechetical ministry and the professional educational task of teaching religion. There was much open debate in the Catholic press. A strictly catechetical approach in the classroom was seen by many to be inappropriate. The reason for this was not only because the pupils were living in a pluralist, multi faith society, but also because among the pupils there was a wide ranging involvement in the Catholic tradition – from the purely nominal to the deeply com-mitted. In these circumstances some seemed to call for a broad, almost comparative study of religion in which the Catholic tradition would have a special place. Others who tried to work out the distinction in practice maintained that, while making no assumptions about the faith of pupils, the Catholic tradition would be properly studied.

Catholic doctrines and practices, the gamut of moral stances available to Catholics, the attitudes and tension, the joys and the incomprehensions of the Catholic tradition will be dealt with in as developmental and structured a way as ever they were in the catechetical method.[31]

For many that was not guarantee enough that pupils would be taught the Catholic beliefs and be encouraged to commit themselves to the Christian way of life.

From time to time the debate focused on diocesan and national R.E. resources for schools. An example of this is the various reactions to *Weaving the Web*, the R.E. resource prepared for pupils in key stage three, the first three years of secondary school. Over the years the Catholic press has published a good deal of articles and correspondence on the subject. Strongly differing views have been expressed. A criticism made by some

---

[30] A. Purnell, op. cit., p.75; pp.123-125
[31] D. A. Jackson, 'Catechesis and Religious Education', The Tablet, 22nd Nov. 1980, p.1155

was that it seemed more of a general R.E. programme rather than one written from within a Catholic perspective. In its study of other faiths some saw a danger of relativism. In this view it lacked catechetical intent and was too heavily experiential rather than doctrinal. Others argued that it was, in fact, a systematic programme in which pupils were enabled gradually and in a developmental way to explore and reflect on their own experience and key dimensions of the Catholic tradition which related to these experiences. Each year a feature of one other world religion was considered. This, it was claimed, hardly constituted a comparative study of religion. Supporters of the resource pointed out that it took aboard the variety of backgrounds and religious experiences of the pupils. Backed by the responses of many teachers, they claimed that it did provide catechesis for those who were already nurtured in the Catholic tradition and for those who were open to journeying in faith. Many of the different aspects of the catechesis/R.E. debate can be found in the arguments put forward by those for or against *Weaving the Web* as a R.E. resource for Catholic schools.[32]

Attempting to clarify the concepts: Church documents

The document *The Religious Dimension of Education in a Catholic School* in part four discusses the 'nature of religious instruction'. We are reminded that the mission of the Church is to evangelise and that the school is one of the agencies or places where evangelisation of the young can take place. The catechetical opportunities offered in a school should not be neglected. The quality of religious instruction is a key feature of Catholic schools. Yet sometimes, it is acknowledged, there is an uncertainty, a difference of opinion about the 'underlying principles governing the religious formation' possible in a school and 'the concrete approach to be taken in religious instruction'. The school is a civic institution with aims and characteristics the same as in other schools. At the same time it is a community 'whose educational goals are rooted in Christ

---

32 R. Lohan & M. McClure, Weaving the Web, Collins 1988; see D. Lundy & J. Gallagher, 'Weaving the Web: Problem or Opportunity?'; J. Redford, 'Where do we go from here?, The Tablet 22nd Feb., 1992; Editorial comment 'Within the Household of Faith', The Month, Dec. 1991, pp.510-512

and his Gospel'. There can be tensions in attempting to balance these features of a Catholic school. The document then states that 'there is a close connection, and at the same time a clear distinction between catechesis and religious instruction'. This is described as a 'sensitive area of pastoral activity'. Although I have touched on aspects of this issue elsewhere, I think it useful simply to list without comment the points made in the text under each of the terms.

Catechesis

- This is a pastoral activity that properly takes place within a believing community, the local church.
- It is a process that takes place gradually throughout the whole of life.
- It presupposes that the Christian message is received as a 'salvific reality', from within a perspective of faith, on the part of those addressed. In this regard it is 'unlike religious instruction' which does not presuppose such a faith dimension in the pupil.
- The aim of catechesis is maturity: spiritual, liturgical, sacramental and apostolic.

Religious instruction

- Its aim is knowledge: it tries to 'convey a sense of the nature of Christianity, and how Christians are trying to live their lives'.
- It should be integrated into the aims and objectives of the school.
- It can help strengthen the faith of believing students.
- Its distinctive characteristic is to be respected by those with responsibility in the school.
- It should have its place in the weekly timetable.
- It should have its own syllabus, approved by those in authority.
- It should seek appropriate interdisciplinary links.
- It should make use of the best educational methods available.
- It can be a subject for examination.
- It should be coordinated with catechesis offered in parishes, the family and youth associations.

- It is 'not easy to devise a course syllabus for religious instruction classes which will present the Christian faith systematically and in a way suited to the young people today'.

- In the light of the Catechism 'adaptations will be necessary' which will conform to the 'requirements of education authorities' and 'respond to the situations that depend on local circumstances of time and place'.[33]

The *General Directory for Catechesis* re-echoes what has been said and adds a few important stresses as well as remarking on the possible outcome of religious instruction for different students. Again, I consider it useful simply to list these for consideration.

Religious instruction

- Religious instruction is a scholastic discipline with the same systematic demands and the same rigour as other disciplines.

- It should present the Christian message and the Christian event with the same seriousness and the same depth with which other disciplines present their knowledge.

- It should engage in a necessary interdisciplinary dialogue in this way the Christian message influences pupils' understanding of important aspects of life.

- In the context of a Catholic school religious instruction is part of and completed by other forms of ministry of the Word (catechesis, homilies, liturgical celebration…).

- It will assist students who are believers to understand better the Christian message, by relating it to the great existential concerns common to all religions and to every human being, to the various visions of life particularly evident in culture and to those major moral questions which confront humanity.

- It will help those who are searching or who have doubts to find the possibility of what exactly faith in Jesus Christ is, what responses the Church makes to their questions, and gives them the opportunity to examine their own choice more deeply.

[33] RD nn.66-73

- It will assume the character of 'a missionary proclamation of the Gospel' for those who do not believe and may help toward a decision for faith.

- In certain circumstances it will have a more ecumenical character and a more interreligious awareness.[34]

RE: catechetics or academics?

I borrow the title for this section from an article with that title by Frank Hurl in *The Furrow*. His is just one of the articles which reflects on the new State approved syllabus for Religious Education which has recently been published for the post primary sector in Irish schools. Several writers defend the introduction of the new syllabus which approaches the subject 'from an explicitly educational point of view, rather than a catechetical or denominational one'. The same issues and questions appear to be being raised as in Britain and elsewhere. Hurl speaks of possible 'schizophrenia' in teachers 'who don't know whether they are to be catechists or facilitators of this new academic study'[35]. No doubt some teachers and others in England and Wales may feel something of the same as they try to come to terms with the stress placed on R.E. by the bishops as 'primarily educational'. Its primary purpose, they say, is to draw pupils into a systematic study of the teaching of the Church, the saving mystery which the Church proclaims. The emphasis is on 'as systematic study' the characteristics of which the bishops spells out:

> *Excellence in religious education, then, will be characterised by a clarity of succinct religious learning objectives and of key content, by appropriate methodologies, rigour, richness of resources, achievement of identified outcomes and accurate methods of assessment. Classroom R.E. will be a challenging educational engagement between the pupil, the teacher and the authentic subject material.[36]*

---

34 GDC nn.73-76
35 F. Hurl, 'Religious Education: Catechetics or Academics?', The Furrow, May 2000, p.279
36 'Religious Education in Catholic Schools', n.7, in Briefing vol. 30 n. 6, 14th June 2000, p. 22.

Such a comprehensive and systematic study of the Church's teachings, the basis for them and the relationship between faith and life will be done in a manner that encourages investigation and reflection, develops appropriate skills and attitudes, and promotes free, informed response to God's call in everyday life. The bishops reiterate the words of the Curriculum Directory.

> *The outcome of religious education 'is religiously literate young people who have knowledge, understanding and skill – appropriate to their age and capacity – to think spiritually, ethically and theologically, and who are aware of the demands of religious commitment in everyday life'.[37]*

The criteria by which R.E. is to be judged are educational. Some teachers and others in the Catholic community may not be at home with such language when speaking of R.E. A number may still consider that R.E. should be approached differently from other subjects on the curriculum. I have actually heard it referred to as 'the holy lesson'. They may question how they can or should assess a child or young person's faith or religious practice since, in their view, this is part of R.E. in Catholic schools. As Anne Holton says when speaking about the new Irish syllabus 'we cannot and dare not pass judgement on faith – that prerogative belongs to God alone'. Teachers examine knowledge, understanding, insight and skills. However, this is not incompatible with 'faith formation' since there is no 'dichotomy between formation and information'.[38] Patrick Devitt makes a similar point. In collaboration with all the school staff the R.E. teacher shares in the catechetical mission of the school. The R.E. teacher, however, also makes a unique contribution to pupils' faith development within the religion lessons by offering pupils 'what is not readily available elsewhere, namely, a challenging educational encounter with religion'. He speaks of R.E. teachers having, on the one hand, a 'direct aim' – knowledge and understanding, and, on the other hand, an 'indirect aim' – to help mature the faith of those open to it.[39] Some may find that helpful. Others may still be somewhat baffled by the distinctions being made.

---

[37] ibid. n5
[38] A. Holton, 'Religious Education: An Examination Subject', The Furrow, May 2000, p.288
[39] P. M. Devitt, 'The Challenge of Religious Education', The Furrow, March 2000, p.157

In an attempt to help clarify the distinctions I offer the following analogy. Those preparing for the priesthood spend a number of years in a seminary. There are many facets to their formation which will look to a holistic human and spiritual development Many people with a variety of expertise and skills will be involved in the training process. All of them play their part in the formation of the person preparing to take up the ministry of priesthood. Together they are all responsible for the candidate's overall formation. Individually they have responsibility for a particular sector. The theology lecturer is part of this wider team. However, his specific task is to introduce students into some aspect of the discipline that is theology. Theological knowledge is a central part of the overall training for the mission of priesthood and for personal faith development. In his teaching, the lecturer concentrates on the student's acquisition of theological knowledge of the subject area and he will eventually judge each student on his understanding of the theological concepts. In the role of lecturer he is not at that time expected to evaluate the student's readiness for the priestly ministry or his growth in Christian faith, though his evaluation of the student's knowledge and understanding is not completely unrelated to these aspects of the person's development. In a sense, as Devitt suggests, there is a 'direct aim' and an 'indirect aim' involved. It may be helpful to consider the specific role of the R.E. teacher in much the same way. All in the school have a part to play in the faith, the religious, spiritual and moral development of pupils. Those in the R.E. department have a specific role within that overall task. It is not their sole responsibility. They are key members of the team, not the only players.

A systematic study embracing Christian beliefs and the search for meaning

Among the points listed from the documents quoted in previous paragraphs, several spoke of the difficulty of devising a syllabus or resource for R.E. that would 'present the Christian faith systematically and in a way suited to the young today'. It is recognised that it is no easy task to produce resources that faithfully relate the Christian message to 'the great existential concerns common to all religions and to every human being'. Religious Education resources and programmes must help teachers provide a systematic study that embraces faith, doctrine and life. The *Catechism of the Catholic Church* in the Pope's words, provides 'a sure and authentic reference text for teaching Catholic doctrine'. In the light of the Catechism the Bishops' Curriculum Directory 'describes the content of curriculum religious education for Catholic Schools'. It 'is not a syllabus for use in the classroom' but a guide which expresses 'the opportunities for study, investigation and reflection offered to pupils and the knowledge and understanding which should be acquired by them'[40]. The bishops list three principal aims of R.E. in Catholic schools:

- knowledge and understanding of the Catholic faith and life;
- knowledge and understanding of the response of faith to the ultimate questions about human life, its origin and purpose;
- the skills required to engage in examination of and reflection upon religious belief and practice.

This calls for a proper and delicate balance between a systematic study of the faith, of Christian beliefs and their relationship with the great human questions about life and its significance. The 1971 General Catechetical Directory stressed the importance of this especially when teaching adolescents. What it says of catechesis is also relevant to the teaching of religion in our classrooms.

The principal task of catechesis in adolescence will be to further a genuinely Christian understanding of life. It must shed the light of the Christian message on the realities which have greater impact on the adolescent, such as the meaning of bodily existence, love and the family, work and leisure, justice and peace and so on.[41]

In Catechesis in Our Time, the Pope sets out some key features or essential conditions of any sound catechetical literature. Again, what is said has relevance for R.E.

- They must be linked with the real life of the generation to which they are addressed, showing acquaintance with its anxieties and questionings, struggles and hopes.

---

[40] RE: Curriculum Directory for Catholic Schools, p. 6.
[41] GCD nn.83-84

- They must speak a language comprehensible to the generation in question.

- They must make a point of giving the whole message of Christ and his Church without neglecting or distorting anything, and in expounding it they will follow a line and structure that highlights what is essential.

- They must really aim to give to those who use them a better knowledge of the mysteries of Christ, aimed at true conversion and a life more in conformity with God's will.[42]

As we have seen, true conversion and a life lived in conformity with God's will may well be an indirect aim of R.E. teachers, their primary aim is the educational aim of leading to 'a better knowledge'. For those pupils open to the faith, this knowledge will help them lead better and more informed Christian lives. For others who may not commit themselves to the Christian faith, they will be better informed about the way Christians understand the meaning and significance of human life in the light of their faith. Some may be encouraged to show a greater interest in the Christian faith and may look more critically at their own views about life and its meaning.

In 1974 the West German Catholic Synod discussed the question of teaching religion in school. The final text states that teachers should realistically assess their teaching by considering the following aims:

- pupils, on leaving school should not look upon religion as something superfluous or useless;

- they should be able to appreciate religion as an activity which enriches human beings;

- they should respect the convictions of others;

- in the context of religious pluralism, they should be able to confront the questions and problems of life;

- they should be more capable and willing to examine their own religious attitude and come to some personal decision in accordance with their own conscience;

- they should be stimulated to look seriously at the reality of faith.[43]

---

[42] CT, n.49
[43] See Italian translation Scuola e insegnamento della religione , publ. Elle Di Ci, Leumann, Turin, 1977, p.33

In the light of recent developments and the publication of the Catechism, we would add and specifically stress the aim proposed by our bishops: 'knowledge and understanding of the Catholic faith and life'. However, the points made by the German Synod are worthy of consideration. The synod text acknowledged that their aims might look rather modest when compared with more traditional expectations. It declared such aims to be realistic and achievable. It suggested that a more guarded and prudent evaluation of what can be done in the classrooms of Catholic schools might lessen the burden on both teachers and pupils and would reduce the risk of disillusionment at the outcome of religious teaching especially in secondary schools. The recent documents from the Bishops' conference should encourage, affirm and assist R.E. teachers in their attempts to offer pupils 'a challenging educational encounter with religion'. They should also help teachers and other concerned persons to understand and appreciate better the precise task of the R.E. department within the Catholic school as a 'catechetical community' in the light of the bishops' directives.

Chapter 16

On the road to Emmaus or Jerusalem?

Jesus came up and walked by their side; but something prevented them from recognising him. He said to them 'What matters are you discussing as you walk along?' They stopped short, their faces downcast (Luke 24:15)

May the world of our time, which is searching, sometimes with anguish, sometimes with hope, be enabled to receive the Good News - not from evangelisers who are dejected, discouraged, impatient or anxious, but from ministers of the Gospel whose lives glow with fervour.[1]

In most reflections on evangelisation and catechesis some reference is made to the Emmaus story. It has almost become the charter for those involved in educating people to and in the faith. The approach and attitude of Jesus towards the two disciples who are leaving Jerusalem with their hopes dashed is seen as a model of the understanding, compassionate evangelist and catechist. In his retreat to the priests of the archdiocese of Milan, Cardinal Martini spoke of several focal points in the Gospel of Luke which throw light on the figure of the evangelist. One I have already mentioned in the preface, that of 'Jesus the failed evangelist' rejected by the people of Nazareth. Another is the story of the two disciples on the road to Emmaus which is unique to the Gospel of Luke. Cardinal Martini says that Luke 'has elaborated it with a view of showing Jesus as a master of evangelisation'[2]. He also sees the dispirited disciples as representing other disciples of Jesus in times of crisis and disillusionment. I wish to reflect on Luke's story from these two specific aspects. Firstly, as is done in most reflections, I shall focus on Jesus as the model evangelist, catechist. Secondly, I shall focus on the two disciples as examples of many who are frustrated and discouraged in the mission of evangelisation and catechesis.

---

[1] Paul VI, Evangelisation in the Modern World, n.80
[2] C.M. Martini, op. cit. p.13

Focus on Jesus the evangelist

It is, as I have said, almost commonplace to meditate on Jesus' approach and attitude towards the two disciples when considering the mission of evangelisation and catechesis. It was thirty years ago that I decided to look at the story more carefully in the light of my own experience as a teacher of religious education in a secondary school in Bootle. At that time I was very disturbed and taken aback to discover that pupils of a Catholic school on completing their time at school had torn up pages of the Bible outside the school gates. I wondered whether it was boyish exuberance in bad taste or whether it was some sort of comment on what and how they had been taught. I could only guess. Possibly it was a bit of both. It may even have been a more general comment on the school itself and not just on the teaching of religious education. Whatever the reasons, the incident upset and disturbed me. Some time later, over the Easter period, I went to our Salesian retreat centre in Bollington with the intention of spending some days walking in the country and in preparing lessons for the next term. On the Wednesday of Easter Week I joined in the celebration of the Eucharist with a group who were on retreat. The Gospel for Easter Wednesday is the Emmaus story. The priest who preached suggested that most people seemed to highlight the point where the disciples recognised Jesus in the breaking of the bread and to stress the central importance of the Eucharist. He focused on the section where Jesus explained the scriptures to them and he highlighted the words of the disciples: 'did not our hearts burn within us as he talked to us on the road and explained the scripture to us?' He preached eloquently on the importance of scripture study and reflection. I could hardly disagree, but my mind wandered to those torn up bibles and to the fact that the hearts of those youngsters did not appear to burn within them as scripture was explained to them. In the light of this, I decided to study the story more carefully and prayerfully.

What struck me in a new and forceful way was the first section of the story in which we are told that Jesus came up to them, walked by their side, asked them what was worrying them and began to listen to what they had to say. It seemed to me that perhaps we tended to skip over this as some sort of preamble to the main points of the story which were generally seen to be his explaining scripture and breaking the bread. On reflection, I began to appreciate more fully that this section was not simply a way in to the story, but was a key feature. Before expounding scripture or providing answers to unheard questions, Jesus meets and befriends the two downcast disciples. He is aware that something is troubling them and wants them to share it with him. He becomes a companion on the road and talks to them; he is present with them and listens to them. On reflection, it seemed to me that we impoverish Luke's message if we focus entirely on the features of his explaining scripture and breaking the bread and overlook the first part or relegate it to a way of introducing the story and its message. We have here an example of the process of evangelisation used by Jesus, a model of the mission that bishops and all of us are urged to undertake in presenting the Christian message 'in a manner corresponding to the difficulties and problems by which people are most burdened and troubled'[3]. Luke's account gives an example of the patient teaching of Jesus and of the gradual journey of the two disciples towards true understanding and eventual commitment when they return to Jerusalem to tell the Good News to the other disciples. It is a gradual, progressive journey to and in faith in Jesus as Saviour

I began to consider Luke's story in relation to the situation of the youngsters who ripped up the bible and I began to wonder how they had been introduced to the riches of scripture. Was the study of the Gospels seen as the study of some ancient books which had little or no relevance to their lives, to their own questions or aspirations? I acknowledge that it is not so easy to achieve this when under pressure of preparing for exams with a group of teenagers who have varying interest in and motivation for the subject. Nonetheless, the gospel themes can and should be related to some of the great human concerns and questions. To fail to do so is to fail to portray them as the presentation of what Christians believe to be the Good News about God and his plan for our human lives. In his explanation, Jesus related the scriptures to the questions and doubts of the two disciples on the road and showed how the events of his suffering and death were part of the loving plan of God for Israel. The idea of a suffering Messiah was not how they conceived the saving plan of Yahweh for his people. They had entertained other ideas and hopes – 'our hope had been...'. Jesus listened and understood their fears and doubts; he addressed them and challenged them after wining their trust and confi-

---

[3] Vatican II, Pastoral Office of Bishops, n.13 (Tr. Flannery)

dence. On further reflection I began to appreciate connections between the message of Luke and much of what was said in the *General Catechetical Directory* and in the text of our Salesian special General Chapter - both published in 1971 in the wake of Vatican II. A passage from the Salesian Chapter text seemed particularly relevant.

> *For the Church sacred scripture is the key for interpreting our human history, for finding once again the true plan of God, and for discovering the real meaning of our world. Each generation setting out from its own experience of life and suffering, its own areas of sensitivity, its own aspirations and its own problems, has searched the gospel and has found there what was original, relevant and new.*[4]

Here we have in Luke's gospel account an outstanding example of how to fulfil the great ideal: fidelity to the Word, fidelity to people. Jesus' walking and taking with the disciples, his befriending them and listening to them was an essential aspect of preparing them for a fuller and richer understanding of the Good News that would transform their lives, making them not only disciples but apostles and witnesses to others. Luke's account gives a picture of a holistic process of evangelisation and catechesis, of a journey in which each step or stage is important and essentially interconnected. As we seek to open up to people the riches of scripture and to lead them to the breaking and sharing of the bread, the Eucharist, we must be attentive to their experiences of life. We are companions with them on the road. As fellow human beings we share their hopes, fears and aspirations while believing that it is 'through and in Christ', that 'light is thrown on the mystery of suffering and death which, apart form his Gospel, overwhelms us'[5].

Points highlighted in commentaries

All those who comment on the Luke's account recognise several significant moments or steps in the way Jesus brings the two to understanding and commitment as disciples and witnesses to the Good News.

[4] 20th General Chapter of the Salesians of Don Bosco, Rome 1971, n.285
[5] Vatican II, The Church in the Modern World, n.22 (Tr. Flannery)

Michael Paul Gallagher sees it as a precursor of the rediscovered stages of the Rite of Christian Initiation of Adults: pre-catechumenate, catechumenate, illumination and mystagogia. It is possible to the see a model for approaching the various situations and activities involved in the process of evangelisation set out in the 1997 Directory: 'initial situations' calling for 'missionary activity', 'gradual developments' helped by 'initial catechetical activity', and 'situations of maturity' made possible by 'ongoing pastoral activity'. Gallagher speaks of the Emmaus story as a model of walking with unbelievers: 'the two disciples were unbelievers in the sense that they were leaving the community behind'. For Gallagher the Emmaus story is 'perhaps the strongest Gospel foundation for slowness in bringing people to the Eucharist'. He warns against 'the temptation, when confronted with the typical unbeliever or half-believer, to opt for short cuts of sacramentalising at all costs'. At best, he thinks, this will lead only to 'token or short-lived conformism rather than any genuine steps to conversion'. The model set out in the Luke's story is a 'model of faith counselling', a practical model with six steps:

- walking genuinely with those who search;
- listening with reverence to their stories;
- being ready to offer a deeper vision through scripture of what they have experienced;
- respecting their freedom either to go further on the road of faith or to wait till the time is more ripe;
- letting the sacraments be the crown of a careful human journey of searching and honesty of dialogue;
- firing them with a mission to return to others to share what they have discovered.[6]

Cardinal Martini recognises a 'powerful symbolism' in the words that speak of Jesus drawing near and walking with them. Jesus takes the initiate. The cardinal reflects that 'once again it is Yahweh, the God of mercy, who draws near to man in his confusion'. Jesus walks with them at their own pace, he does not force the pace or the issues. He does not rush in with answers, ready-made pious thoughts or condemnation. He becomes a discreet, unobtrusive travelling companion. He employs a

---

6 M. P. Gallagher, Struggles of Faith, p.64; see his full commentary pp.63-65

'progressive method of questioning' that enables the disciples to bring out their problem gradually, helping them to clarify their own thoughts. When Jesus asks them what troubles them he gets a rather curt, brusque response accusing him of being the only one who is ignorant of what had been happening in Jerusalem over the last few days. Jesus patiently accepts the discourtesy and takes up the thread of the conversion once again. They tell their story and relate the facts without seeing or appreciating their significance: 'it is related as something quite incomprehensible, something which should not have happened, and which is a tragedy for all who had set their hopes on him'. In a sense 'they are reciting the Kerygma, saying the words of the Creed, the very words used to proclaim Jesus of Nazareth', but they fail to see the saving significance of it all. Jesus then jolts, challenges and admonishes them and proceeds gently to explain matters to them by opening to them the passages of scripture that throw light on their experience and their questions. They then begin to see the significance and deeper meaning of the events that they had experienced. Having finished his explanation, Jesus makes as if to go on but they invite him to stay and have supper with them. The invitation comes from them. They recognise him in the breaking of bread, 'a sign familiar to them' and one 'by which Luke certainly intends to indicate all the future manifestations of Jesus in his Church in the Breaking of Bread'. The cardinal goes on to talk of 'the most striking characteristic of the whole series of Jesus' revelations of himself to them':

> They do not say: Jesus spoke well, he explained it well, he was a good preacher, he set us on the right path, but they said: he kindled our hearts, he revealed himself as the friend who is able to liberate our embittered hearts, embittered because, from our point of view, God's plans seemed totally unacceptable.[7]

In all of this, Martini finds Jesus to be the model evangelist and teacher who 'uses his gifts as exegete and catechist to provide the explanation the two disciples were looking for'.

Timothy Radcliffe, Master General of the Dominicans, made a reference to the Emmaus story in his intervention at the recent synod of European

---

[7] C. M. Martini, op. cit., p. 28; see his full commentary pp.21-29.

Bishops. His intervention dealt with the crisis of authority today. The crisis of authority in the Church is, in his view, a symptom of a wider crisis of authority in our European culture where it is felt that any external authority which tells us what to believe or do is suspect. He warns that we cannot respond to that fear just by asserting the authority of the Church ever more strongly because people may either resist or take no notice. He asks what are we to do? He finds in the story of the journey to Emmaus 'a few clues'. The disciples flee from Jerusalem. They have heard the witness of the women but they are not convinced. This, he says, is sometimes our experience in Europe: 'we proclaim our faith with all confidence, as we must, but our witness will often not have authority'. Faced with the blindness of the two disciples, Jesus explains the scriptures. In Radcliffe's words 'he struggles with their minds' and 'we in the Church must appeal to the minds of men and women, showing them in the gospel the meaning of their experience'. But this will not suffice because 'our society is marked by a crisis in reason too'. In the Emmaus story Jesus walks with the disciples and accepts their hospitality. This is a model, an example for us.

> *To have convincing authority the Church must share the journey of people, enter their fears, be touched by their disappointments, their questions, their failures and doubts. Often we speak about people: about women, about the poor and the immigrants; about the divorced, those who have abortions, about prisoners, people with AIDS, homosexuals, drug addicts. But our words for Christ will have no real authority unless we, in a sense, give authority to their experience, enter their homes, receive their hospitality, learn their language, eat their bread, accept from them what they have to offer.*[8]

Radcliffe advises that, like the women in the Gospel, we must confidently proclaim our faith. That does not simply mean 'asserting our faith ever more strongly, hammering away'. That may well prove counterproductive and confirm some people's fears about the nature of authority in the Church.

---

[8] T. Radcliffe, 'Overcoming the Crisis of Authority Today', *Doctrine and Life*, 49, 3, Nov. 1999, p.514

> *We show that the Word we proclaim does not just stand over and against us. It is more intimate to our being than any word we could speak; it made us and it enters the darkest places of the human heart, and offers us all a home. Then we will be able to speak of the absolute claim of Christ with authority'.*[9]

These writers and many others have found in the story of the disciples on the road to Emmaus much fruitful thought which both encourages and challenges all of us who take up the task of educating people to and in the faith.

Focus on the dispirited disciples

Up to this point my focus has been on Jesus 'the master of evangelisation'. We have identified the two disciples with those people, young and adults, to whom we address our catechetical efforts. We identify them with unbelievers, half-believers, the alienated, with those disillusioned with the Church and religious beliefs and practices. In this context we come to appreciate the masterly way in which Jesus relates to them, then gradually and gently leads them towards understanding and commitment. We can also focus on the disciples as representing other followers of Jesus, ourselves, who at times are dispirited, disillusioned and who experience the questions, anxieties, even doubts, that come in time of crisis. They may represent us at various points on our life's journey, of our faith journey, or at moments in our work as educators.

Cardinal Martini points out that the two disciples were 'two of the privileged group; they are not two casual disciples'. They have been with Jesus and the other disciples for some time; they have seen all that he did and heard all that he taught. Nonetheless, despite all that, at this moment 'they are going through a time of crisis which is one of the normal trials of the evangelist and they are going through it by way of example to the whole community'[10]. Like the other disciples, Peter in particular, they could not recognise the Christ, the Messiah, in the suffering and crucified

---

[9] ibid. p.515
[10] C. M. Martini op. cit., p.21

Jesus. We recall Peter's declaration 'you are the Christ, the Son of the living God'. But he could not identify his idea of the Christ with the one who foretold that he would go to Jerusalem where he would suffer cruelly and die on a cross. It was because of this that Peter, who had at first been praised by Jesus, later earned the rebuke 'Get behind me Satan! You are an obstacle in my path, because the way you think is not God's way but man's'. (Mark 16:23) As Cardinal Martini puts it, they had taken on 'only half the kerygma'.

In most translations we read that the two disciples were 'discussing together', 'talking together about all that had happened'. Martini makes a very interesting point. Such translations are, he maintains, weak, not entirely accurate. They were not simply discussing or talking together; they were in fact 'arguing', going over things in a heated discussion. (The Greek verb used is 'syzetein'. It is the same verb as is used in the Acts of the Apostles 15:7 where we are told that in the council of Jerusalem the disciples argued heatedly about the question of circumcision for the Gentile converts.)

The abandonment of the kerygma has brought them no joy...
It was an experience which ended badly. They still feel this
experience bitterly; so they discuss and argue as to whose fault
it was, they blame their own lack of prudence. As always hap-
pens when things go wrong and people look for someone to
blame, someone will point out that he has made a mistake in
order to dispel the sense of bitterness and discontent.[11]

In the light of some of the critical moments in the historical developments of catechesis and religious education, I find this a feature of the story worth reflecting on, as does Martini. He describes how these two had decided to walk together away from Jerusalem, probably in order to return to their former pursuits, yet, despite the fact there was a certain friendship between them, there were also divisions, disagreements. He relates this to the experience of many priests and we could include others such as parents, catechists, and teachers..

---

[11] ibid. p.22

> *We ourselves can think of all the times when we – who have invested a lot of energy in evangelisation, in fact have staked our whole lives on it – can recall how upset we get when something goes wrong and even if we perhaps try to rise above it and put it out of our minds, in fact our hearts remain bitter and guilty because we feel we have failed in the very things we believed in most.*

The cardinal says that we should not be ashamed of such vulnerability. This only shows that we are not unaware or indifferent.

> *The failure to achieve what we set out to do, the disappointment of our hopes, these do harm and tend to create unhappiness, quarrels, even mutual accusations and various divisions which result from them. All these things show that the work of evangelisation, instead of bringing peace, has brought us disquiet, fatigue, uneasiness; this should give rise to fresh questions.*

Reflection on what the cardinal has to say may be of some help and encouragement and enable us to have better understanding and appreciation of the strongly held views of different individuals and groups within the Church when considering the delicate task of educating to and in the faith. It might help even if it does not take away some of the hurt, even pain and anger, that can be felt in such times of disagreement and division.

Pilgrims' hope

At the heart of our Christian faith is the belief that God comes to us in our humanity, in Jesus the Christ and in his gift of the Spirit. Such belief is the source of our hope. This is what the bishops at the European synod proclaimed again for our time.

> *We want to reassure you that the hope of which Jesus the Lord is the very source is no dream or utopia. Hope is real because Jesus is Emmanuel, God-with-us. He is risen and is forever alive in his Church working for the salvation of mankind and society. Our hope is sure: its signs are concrete, visible and in some ways tangible, because the creator Spirit, which the crucified and risen Lord has left as his first gift to believers, is always present.*[12]

---

[12] 'Gospel of Hope, n.3, in Briefing vol. 29 n.11, 10th Nov. 1999, p.22-27.

Emmanuel, our God, is with us, his gift of the Spirit is for our time also. It is reasonably easy to recite such beliefs in doctrinal statements or to sing of them in hymns and carols. To let them impact on our lives and on how we judge and make sense of the Church and society, however messy they may appear, is much more difficult to realise. In the first article of our Salesian constitutions there is a phrase which I find it useful to recall when faced with these situations: 'from this active presence of the Holy Spirit we draw strength for our fidelity and support for our hope'.

In an article in *The Furrow,* Bishop Donal Murray develops the theme of pilgrimage which is a theme taken up by John Paul II in *Tertio Millenio Adveniente.* It is a theme closely linked with the theme of hope. The bishop points out that today's pilgrimages are for the most part package tours: all pre-booked, the itinerary planned and set out for us, with guides and couriers ready to deal with any emergencies. Such was not the case in medieval pilgrimages to Compostela, Jerusalem or Rome. Pilgrims struggled along dusty roads which they had never traveled before. Bishop Murray considers such an experience to be familiar enough in Church life today.

> *As Christians in Ireland at the end of the millennium, we may well have occasional doubts as to whether we are on the right road and an uneasy apprehension about what might be around the next bend. And to make it worse, because we never expected the road to be like this, we lack some of the patience of the medieval pilgrim. Many people feel irate or lost and think that surely somebody should have organised things better.*[13]

The medieval pilgrims had a powerful sense of their destination. The dream of finally reaching the holy places kept their spirits up throughout the weary journey. Bishop Murray maintains that it is important for us to renew our hope in the circumstances of our time, when faced with tragedies, wars, injustice, and when feeling depressed by scandals in the Church, the decline in practice and the fall in vocations. He refers to a section of the Pope's letter concerning the new millennium where he speaks of 'a river that flows through human history from the event which

---

[13] D. Murray, 'A Great Pilgrimage', The Furrow, Dec., 1998, p.660

took place in Nazareth and then in Bethlehem two thousand years ago'. The event of the incarnation is the source of our faith and our hope. However, Bishop Murray points out that we cannot predict the flow of the river and at times 'we are tempted to think we know the way things should proceed and therefore we get upset and despondent when our journey takes on an unforeseen turn'. In this context he sees relevance in the story of the depressed disciples as they walk away from Jerusalem.

To Emmaus or Jerusalem?

The two disciples walk away from Jerusalem. When questioneded by the stranger they stop short, their faces downcast, and begin to tell the story of their dashed hopes – 'that he would be the one to set Israel free'. He was the one who would set Israel free, but not in the way they expected or wished. The idea of the Suffering Servant, the notion of the cross, was not part of the plan as they conceived it. Their walking away from Jerusalem is in direct contrast to Jesus who, after foretelling his future passion and death, 'resolutely took the road to Jerusalem' (Luke 9:51). They turn their backs on the plan of God which was fulfilled in Jerusalem. They walk towards Emmaus disappointed with the intention of returning to their old familiar ways of doing things, failing to comprehend the surprising, unexpected ways of God. Eventually Jesus enables them to penetrate the meaning of this plan and to see God's hand in the history of Israel and the events of the passion and death of Jesus. They then turn round and take the road to Jerusalem, the same road but this time in the right direction. They tell their story of what happened on the road: how their hearts burned within them as he talked to them and explained the scriptures to them and how they recognised him in the breaking of bread.

Jim Sweeney, a Scottish Passionist, who attended the synod on religious life as a consultant to the bishops of Scotland, also makes reference to the Emmaus story when reflecting on the crisis in religious life today. What he says can be applied to other aspects of the Church's mission, not least to the task of educating to and in the faith. Sweeney speaks of the 'resurrection experience of God' as 'the disclosure of the divine presence in new, unexpected and surprising places – salvation broken open on a cross; lordship in rejection, powerlessness, abandonment'. The God we fear we may have lost is to be found in other realities and in places where we would not think to look.

> *The journey to Jerusalem begins when we integrate the scandal of the cross with our understanding of God, when we start to find the God of the Resurrection in the events and experiences we thought had meant the loss of Him.*[14]

It seems to me that we can easily relate the reflections of Martini, Murray and Sweeney to some of our concerns and disappointments, our own dashed hopes, as educators of today's adults and young people. We may wish that our efforts had more evident success in greater numbers of evangelised and catechised adults and young people. We would not wish to measure success only in numbers but more so in quality and depth of understanding of the Christian faith and commitment to the Christian way of life. In this we may be disappointed and even disillusioned. With discernment we may come to recognise something of God's presence in unexpected and surprising places and people, we may recognise some of the 'smoke signals of hope' in what at first sight might appear 'a burnt out desert'.

It has been my hope that these and the others reflections that I have shared throughout this book may be of some encouragement to all of us involved in this great mission in whatever role. If, like the two disciples, we find ourselves on the road to Emmaus, I would hope that we might find the courage, as Jesus did, and resolutely take the road to Jerusalem. I end by quoting once again the *General Directory for Catechesis* which has been one of the main sources and inspiration of the reflections I have offered.

---

[14] J. Sweeney, 'To Emmaus or Jerusalem? Which journey for Today's Religious?', Religious Life Review, Sept/Oct. 1993, p.277

> *The parable of the sower going out to sow is the source of inspiration for evangelisation. The seed is the word of God. The sower is Jesus Christ. Two thousand years ago he proclaimed the Gospel in Palestine and sent disciples to sow the Gospel in the world. Today, Jesus Christ, present in the Church through his Spirit, continues to scatter the word of the Father ever more widely in the field of the world. The conditions of the soil into which it falls vary greatly.[15]*

This is the field – the people of God today – that we as Church in our time and place are called to cultivate - not with condemnation but in hope. Let us 'keep in mind the field in which the seed is sown' and 'do so with the perspective of faith and mercy'.[16]

---

[15] GDC n.15
[16] ibid. nn.14, 169.

Acknowledgements

Short extracts are acknowledged in the footnotes

Burns & Oates, c/o Continuum International Publishing Group Ltd: Aubert, R. 'Modernism', *Encyclopaedia of Theology*, K Rahner (ed.) (1975); Schmid, J. 'Biblical Exegesis', *Encyclopaedia of Theology*, K Rahner (ed.) (1975); Babin, A. *Options* (1967); Drinkwater, F.H. *Telling the Good News* (1960); Duckworth, F.H. *Educational Essays* (1951); Jungmann, J.A. *Handing on the Faith* (1959); Kasper, W. *An Introduction to the Christian Faith* (1980); Moran, G. *God Still Speaks* (1967); Moran, G. *Vision and Tactics* (1968)

The Catholic Education Service: *Spiritual and Moral Development Across the Curriculum*, published by the CES (1995); *Religious Education: Curriculum Directory for Catholic Schools*, published by the CES (1996)

Catholic Media Office: extracts from various issues of *Briefing*, including: Sacred Congregation for Catholic Education, *The Catholic School on the Threshold of the Third Millennium* (1999); *Bishops' Statement on Religious Education in Catholic Schools*; *Bishops' Statement on Religious Education in the Classroom*.

The Catholic Times: leader article, January 30th 2000

Used by kind permission of The Catholic Truth Society, Publishers to the Holy See: Paul VI, *Evangelisation in the Modern World* (1975); John Paul II, *Catechesis in our Time* (1979); The General Directory for Catechesis (1997); Sacred Congregation for Catholic Education, *The Catholic School* (1977); Sacred Congregation for Catholic Education, *Lay Catholics in Schools: Witnesses to Faith* (1982); Sacred Congregation for Catholic Education, *Religious Dimension of Education in a Catholic School* (1988). Used by permission.

Geoffrey Chapman/Libreria Editrice Vaticana: *The Catechism of the Catholic Church*, English translation for the United Kingdom (1994); Abbot (ed.) *The Documents of Vatican II* (1966)

Colliers/Macmillan, c/o International Thomson Publishing Services Ltd: Janelle, P. *The Catholic Reformation* (1977); Sloyan, G.S. 'The Relation of the Catechism to the Work of Religious Formation', in *Modern Catechetics*, Sloyan, G.S. (ed.), (1964)

Collins, c/o Harper Collins: *Code of Canon Law* (1983); Saris, W. *Living the Faith Together* (1985). Used by permission.

The Columba Press: Gallagher, M.P. 'The New Agenda of Unbelief & Faith' in Religion and Culture in Dialogue, Lane, D.A. (ed.) (1993); Gallagher, M.P. *Struggles of Faith* (1990); Lane, D.A. *Religious Education & the Future* (1986) re:

> Lane D.A. 'The Challenge Facing Religious Education Today'; Marthaler, B.L. 'Catechetical Directory or Catechism? Une Question malpose'; Murray, D. 'The Language of Catechesis';

Concilium Foundation: Alberich, E. 'Is the Universal Catechism an Obstacle or a Catalyst in the Process of Inculturation?' *Concilium* 204, 4, (1998). Used by permission.

Darton Longman & Todd: Gallagher, M.P. *Clashing Symbols* (1997); Lance, D. in the introduction to J. R. Rymer, *11-16 Old Testament* (1969); Lance, D. *Eleven to Sixteen* (1960); and for the verses taken from the Jerusalem Bible, published and copyright 1966, 1967 and 1968 by Darton Longman and Todd Ltd and Doubleday & Co Inc, and used by permission of the publishers.

Dominican Publications: McBride, D. *The Gospel of Luke* (1991); Sweeney, J. 'To Emmaus or Jerusalem?' in *Religious Life Review* (Sept/Oct 1993); *Doctrine & Life*; *Religious Life Review*; and *Vatican Council II, The Conciliar & Post Conciliar Documents* (General Editor, Flannery, A.) re:

> *Constitution on the Church in the Modern World; Decree on the Pastoral Office of Bishops; Decree on the Church's Missionary Activity; Decree on Christian Education; Decree on the Ministry & Life of Priests; Dogmatic Constitution on Divine Revelation*

Doubleday UK: Dulles, A. *Models of Revelation* (1983)

E.J. Dwyer: Rummery, R.M. *Catechesis and Religious Education in a Pluralist Society* (1975)

Evans-Methuen: Schools Council, *Religious Education in Secondary Schools* (1971)

Falmer Press: Groome, T. *What Makes a School Catholic?* in McLaughlin T.H., O'Keefe J. & O'Keeffe, B. (eds) *Contemporary Catholic School* (1996)

The Furrow: Groome, T. 'Hope for Dirty Hands' *The Furrow* (April 1998); Looney, A. 'On Being Faithful' (Dec 1999); Conway, E. 'Midwives to the Mystery' (July/Aug 1994); Murray, D. 'A Great Pilgrimage' (Dec 1998)

Handsel Press, Millfield, Boat of Garten PH24 3BY: Rodger, A.R. *Education & Faith in an Open Society* (1982). Used by permission.

Harper & Row, c/o Harper Collins: Groome, T. *Christian Religious Education* (1980)

Herder & Herder: Moran, G. *Theology of Revelation* (1966); McHugh, J.A. & Callon, C.J. *Catechism of the Council of Trent for Parish Priests* (1994); Van Caster, M. *The Structure of Catechetics* (1965); Denziger & Schonmetzer, *Enchiridion Symbolorum*, 32nd Edition (1963)

International Commission on English in the Liturgy Inc: *Rite of Baptism* (1969); *Rite of Initiation of Adults* (1985)

Ignatius Press: Ratzinger & Schonborn, *Introduction to the Catechism of the Catholic Church* (1994); Wrenn, M.J. *Catechisms and Controversies* (1991)

Liturgy Training Publications, Chicago: Connell, M. (ed.) *The Catechetical Documents: A Parish Resource* (1996)

Lumen Vitae: Jungmann, J.A. 'Theology and Kerygmatic Teaching,' *Lumen Vitae*, 5, 2-3, 1950

University of Manchester: Lundy, Dr Michael Anthony (Damian), *Doctoral Thesis* (1990)

The Month: Nichols, K. 'Continuity and Change in Catechetics', *The Month* 11, 3, 1978

Morehouse-Barlow: Westerhof, J.H. & Edwards, O.C. (ed.) *A Faithful Church* (1981) re:

> McGratch, M. 'Basic Christian Education from the Decline of the Catechumenate to the Rise of Catechisms'; Edwards, O.C. 'From Jesus to the Apologists'; Bryce, M.C. 'Evaluation of Catechesis from the Catholic Reformation to the Present'; Haugaard, W.H. 'The Continental Reformation of the Sixteenth Century'

The Murphy Center for Liturgical Research, Notre Dame University: Grant, R.M. 'Development of the Christian Catechumenate', *Made Not Born* (1976)

Catholic News Service: Final Report of the 1985 Extraordinary Synod Of Bishops; O'Hare, P. 'Neo-Orthodox Influence and Empirical Corrective'; Synod 1977: The Thirty-four Points, *Living Light*, 15, 1, 1978

Our Sunday Visitor Inc: Marthaler, B. *Catechesis in Context* (1973)

Pastoral Educational Services, New Jersey: Padovano, A. *Free to be Faithful* (1972)

Penguin Books: Chadwick, O. *The Reformation* (1964)

Religious Education Press: Barker, K. *Religious Education and Freedom* (1981)

Sadlier, New York: Dujarier, M. A History of the Catechumenate, the First Six Centuries (1979); Guzie, T. 'Theological Challenge', *Becoming a Catholic Christian*, WJ Reedy (ed.) (1981)

St Mary's Press: Warren, M. (ed.) *Sourcebook for Modern Catechetics* Volumes 1 & 2 (Christian Brothers Publication) (1962, 1983 & 1997) re:

> Amalorpavadass, D.S. 'Catechesis as a Pastoral Task'; Donnellan, M. 'Bishops and Uniformity in Religious Education: Vatican I to Vatican II'; Erdozain, L. 'The Evolution of Catechetics: A survey of Six International Study Weeks in Catechetics'; 'Final and Approved Report'; 'General Conclusions of the Study Week'; Liege, P.A. 'The Ministry of the Word'; Lombaerts, H. 'Religious Education Today and the Catechism'; Marthaler, B. 'The Modern Catechetical Movement in Roman Catholicism: Issues and Personalities'; Nebreda, A. 'East Asian Study Week on Mission Catechetics'; Warren, M. 'Evangelisation: a Catechetical Concern'

St Pauls Publishing: *A Report to the Bishops of England & Wales, Signposts and Homecomings* (1981); Bishops of England and Wales, *Teaching the Faith the New Way* (1973); Bishops of England and Wales, *The Easter People* (1980); Bourgeois, H. *On Becoming a Christian* (1984); International Council for Catechesis, *Adult Catechesis in the Christian Community* (1990); Martini, C.M. *Ministers of the Gospel*, (1981); Nichols, K. *Cornerstone* (1978); Nichols, K. (ed.) *The Voice of the Hidden Waterfall* (1980) re:

> Nichols, K; Exeler, A. 'Faith in Education'; Rummery, G. '1970-80: The Decade of Directories'

SCM - Canterbury Press Ltd: Schillebeeck, E. *Interim Report on the Books Jesus the Christ* (1980)

Scholars Press, Atlanta: excerpts from *Religious Education*, including Scott, K. 'The Local Church as an Ecology', *Religious Education* 76, 2, 1981;

Seabury Press, New York: Tracy, D. *Blessed Rage for Order* (1975)

SPCK: Marthaler, B. (ed.) *Introducing the Catechism of the Catholic Church* (1994)

The Tablet Publishing Co Ltd: extracts from various issues of *The Tablet*

Thomas More Press: Shea, J. *Stories of the Faith* (1978)

Veritas: Gallagher, M.P. *Help my Unbelief* (1983); Looney, A. *Teaching Religion to Young People Today* in Feheney, J.M. *From Ideal to Action* (1998)

Wrexham People: February 2000